Praise for *The Smart Woman's Guide to Plastic Surgery*

"For those wishing to be well-informed consumers of plastic surgery, this book will provide an outstanding learning resource. It is full of thorough, honest, understandable, and accurate information about cosmetic surgery."

—*Carolyn L. Kerrigan, M.D.*
President, Plastic Surgery Educational Foundation, 2007
Professor of Surgery, Dartmouth Medical School

"Updated and expanded, this well-written book remains preeminent in providing accurate and practical information to any woman contemplating cosmetic surgery."

—*Robert M. Goldwyn, M.D.*
Professor of Surgery, Harvard Medical School
Editor Emeritus, Plastic and Reconstructive Surgery

"The second edition is up-to-date and includes assessments of new technologies, including radio frequency, lasers, and ultrasonic devices. The writing is clear, concise, and objective. This information will help all potential cosmetic surgery patients."

—*Luis O. Vasconez, M.D.*
Professor and Chief, Division of Plastic Surgery,
University of Alabama at Birmingham

"At a time when many people turn to reality television shows for information about cosmetic surgery, it is a relief that an excellent resource such as this exists. Unlike reality TV, it provides detailed, objective information without pitching or promoting."

—*Peter Fodor, M.D., FACS*
Past President, American Society for Aesthetic Plastic Surgery
Associate Clinical Professor of Plastic Surgery,
UCLA Medical Center

"This is a clear, concise, well-organized book that provides a great deal of essential information for women seeking plastic surgery. It is highly organized and makes for easy reading. I suspect that many people, both male and female, will want to learn from the wide array of useful data that this book provides."

—*Ronald P. Gruber, M.D.*
Plastic Surgeon, Oakland, California

"This detailed and helpful book will be an asset to any patient considering plastic surgery."

—*Richard A. D'Amico, M.D., FACS*
President, American Society of Plastic Surgeons, 2008
Chief of Plastic Surgery, Englewood Hospital and Medical Center
Assistant Clinical Professor of Plastic Surgery,
Mt. Sinai School of Medicine, New York

"Dr. Loftus is uniquely suited to author this book. As a woman, she has insight into the minds of other women. As a plastic surgeon, she understands the procedures, their benefits, and their risks as only a plastic surgeon can. As a writer, she can communicate each concept with unmatched clarity. . . . Opening this book is the smartest thing you can do."

—*Henry W. Neale, M.D.*
Professor and Chairman, Division of Plastic, Reconstructive, and
Hand Surgery, University of Cincinnati
Chairman, American Board of Plastic Surgery, 1995–1996

"A valuable and long-needed book—not only for the lay public but also the plastic surgeon, young and old."

—*David G. Dibbell Sr., M.D.*
Professor of Plastic Surgery, University of Wisconsin

THE SMART WOMAN'S GUIDE TO PLASTIC SURGERY

- -

UPDATED SECOND EDITION

JEAN M. LOFTUS, M.D.

New York Chicago San Francisco Lisbon London Madrid Mexico City
Milan New Delhi San Juan Seoul Singapore Sydney Toronto

Library of Congress Cataloging-in-Publication Data

Loftus, Jean M.
    The smart woman's guide to plastic surgery / Jean M. Loftus. — Updated 2nd ed.
       p.   cm.
    Includes bibliographical references and index.
    ISBN 978-0-07-149419-9 (alk. paper)
    1. Surgery, Plastic.   2. Face—Surgery.   3. Women—Surgery.   I. Title.

RD119.L64   2008
617.9'5—dc22   2007023778

1 2 3 4 5 6 7 8 9 10 11 12 13 14 15 16 17 18 19 DOC/DOC 0 9 8 7

ISBN 978-0-07-149419-9
MHID   0-07-149419-7

Interior illustrations by Donna A. Talerico
Interior photographs by Jean M. Loftus, M.D.

McGraw-Hill books are available at special quantity discounts to use as premiums
and sales promotions, or for use in corporate training programs. For more information,
please write to the Director of Special Sales, Professional Publishing, McGraw-Hill, Two
Penn Plaza, New York, NY 10121-2298. Or contact your local bookstore.

This book is printed on acid-free paper.

For Jim, Jack, Jay, and Maddie

Contents

Acknowledgments

As with the first edition, I had assumed that writing a book about something I knew so well would be a simple task. I apparently had forgotten just how much work was involved, because when Doug Corcoran at McGraw-Hill invited me to write an updated second edition, I jumped at the chance, thinking, "How hard can it be?" Once again, I found that the work involved was an order of magnitude beyond what I had expected. Although I greatly enjoy writing, I am somewhat compulsive in my need to be complete and accurate, so I spent much time away from my family to revise and copyedit the manuscript. Hence, my greatest amount of thanks goes to my husband, James Giffin, M.D., for encouraging me to make this book the best it could possibly be and for being patient and understanding while I worked on it. As for Jack, Jay, and Maddie, I'm not sure if thanks or apologies are in order, as they are too young to understand why I spent so many Saturdays and Sundays in the office to work on this project.

Many other thanks are due as well, as writing a book is truly a committee project. All have contributed significantly, and they are listed in chronological order of their involvement with the book:

Doug Corcoran, for recognizing the importance of this work and for inviting me to write an updated second edition

Rick Balkin, the most gentlemanly agent an author could ever hope to have, for always representing me in the most professional and attentive manner

Beverly Letsinger Fight Scherpenberg, my extraordinary office manager, who cannot decide upon a last name, but who very ably kept my life in order while I was revising the manuscript and who painstakingly deciphered and transcribed my scribblings

Kathy Jones, B.S.N., RN, CPSN, the most knowledgeable and skilled plastic surgery nurse anywhere, for reviewing Chapters 11 through 13 and providing important editorial comment

Cathy Miller, RN; Emily Jones; and Libby Stocks for filling in details on skin care and permanent makeup

Donna Talerico, a freelance artist in Cincinnati, who set aside her work in impressionistic painting long enough to create a few more sketches for the second edition

My patients, who shall remain unnamed, for selflessly allowing me to use their stories and photographs for this book

Sarah Pelz, my editor at McGraw-Hill, for improving the manuscript through her insightful contributions and for providing important editorial comments in a gracious style that made refining the manuscript a pleasure

Julia Anderson Bauer, my project editor at McGraw-Hill, for once again attentively and patiently overseeing the production of this book

Heidi Murley, M.D., an emeritus member of the punctuation police, for helping put an end to comma abuse

Dr. David G. Dibbell Sr. and Dr. Henry Neale for lessons in surgery and lessons in life

My father, Joseph P. Loftus, P.E., the memory of whom continues to be a great inspiration

Your Responsibility in Reading this Book

This book does its best to provide you with the most useful, accurate, and complete information available about plastic surgery. But techniques and technologies are constantly changing, patients vary in their response to treatments, and the practice of plastic surgery is far more complicated than can be captured in one book.

Realize that this book is intended to facilitate the communication between you and your surgeon—not replace it. If you want advice about cosmetic surgery, you must see a trained medical professional. Do not adopt any of the advice contained in this book without first consulting your physician.

Do not use this book to self-diagnose your problem, prescribe your own treatment, or identify complications. All matters pertaining to your health require medical supervision. Regarding any and all issues related to your preoperative, intraoperative, and postoperative care, you must consult your doctor without hesitation. The author and publisher disclaim any liability arising directly or indirectly from the use of this book.

This Book Is for Women

Men are encouraged to read this book to gain a better understanding of what their female companions are undertaking, but the information contained herein pertains primarily to women. Although some specifics apply to men, many do not. Men have different skin texture, hair patterns, facial features, fat distribution, and body features, all of which merit separate consideration and changes in technique.

Introduction

Since the first edition of this book was published, many exciting changes have evolved in plastic surgery: new fillers, lasers, implants, techniques, ways to prevent pain and nausea after surgery, and ways to speed recovery and lessen bruising. All of these changes have enabled even better results—in many cases, with less risk and faster recovery.

Yet in spite of the progress we have made, one thing remains unchanged: before considering plastic surgery, women still want (and need) all the facts so they can decide whether it is right for them.

As a plastic surgeon, I spend much time helping women understand exactly what they can and cannot expect from cosmetic surgery procedures. Most of my patients are intelligent women who simply wish to fight the forces of gravity, change an inherited feature, or look as young as they feel. I am impressed with the insightful and pointed questions they ask.

Like my patients, you may be eager to have cosmetic surgery. You know it can be safe, and you have seen many good results. But you also know there can be disappointment, frustration, and complications. You seek to educate yourself so you can decide whether cosmetic surgery is for you. If you do choose to have it, you want to understand exactly what cosmetic surgery can and cannot achieve. And you understandably want to avoid pitfalls.

Many of you have turned to the first edition of this book for answers. I have received an enormous amount of positive feedback on the first edition, with many women stating that nowhere else could they find such complete and objective information. Plastic surgeons across the country have told me that they refer their patients to this book for reference. It was even printed in Hungarian.

I wrote the first edition of this book with the goal of teaching the reader about every aspect of cosmetic surgery. Although one book cannot relate every nuance in a field that surgeons spend a lifetime mastering, I included much of the information that you, as a consumer, must know. Because of the success of the first edition, I have been asked to write this updated second edition. Although a daunting task, I have enjoyed it immensely, as it has once again afforded me the opportunity to arm women with powerful knowledge. This knowledge will help you understand your options and provide you with the balanced view you need to make the right decisions.

The fact that you have in your hands a book on cosmetic surgery is evidence that you do not take this decision lightly. Nor should you. You have chosen to wage war against gravity, age, or genetics so that you may look and feel your best. As with any battle, you may emerge as a winner or a loser, but the more prepared you are, the better you will fare. I wish you the best as you set out on your quest to achieve safe and successful cosmetic surgery, and I believe that you will find this book to be a loyal and expert guide for every step of the way.

Succeeding with Plastic Surgery

Ten Steps for the Best Outcome

More than ever, plastic surgery permeates Western culture. The recent advent of reality television shows and dramas centering around plastic surgery further propagates it. It continues to be a favorite topic for talk shows, news segments, and magazine articles. Hollywood loves it. Famous actors often show telltale signs of plastic surgery. Advertisers promote it. Even you may discuss your aesthetic flaws with your friends or colleagues. Plastic surgery is everywhere. Yet in spite of this onslaught of information, it continues to be shrouded in misconception and misinformation.

Mary, a twenty-two-year-old college student majoring in engineering, was insecure and withdrawn. Even though she had excellent qualifications, her interviews failed to yield job offers. Following surgery to reduce her large nose, her job interviews were more positive, and she soon secured a competitive offer—not because of her appearance, but because of her newfound confidence.

You might have heard that there has been no better time to consider cosmetic surgery. Recent technological developments and new procedures have saturated the market; but how much is hype and how much is real?

Cosmetic surgery continues to see an unprecedented explosion in popularity. Between 1996 and 2000, the number of cosmetic procedures more than doubled, growing from one to three million per year in this country alone. From 2000 to 2008, it has doubled again. This tremendous growth is expected to continue as people of all ages, occupations, and social classes seek cosmetic surgery. But despite its popularity, such surgery is not for everyone.

Only you can decide whether cosmetic surgery is for you. This decision will be a complex one. One of your first steps will be to consult with a plastic surgeon, but as you will see, finding a qualified surgeon can be difficult.

The cosmetic surgery boom has confounded the ability of prospective patients to identify qualified plastic surgeons. Whereas cosmetic surgery once was performed primarily by plastic surgeons, many other physicians now offer cosmetic procedures. These physicians who are not plastic surgeons have entered the arena of cosmetic surgery intent on profiting from the popularity of this cash-up-front, fee-for-service specialty.

No federal or state law prevents these physicians from advertising as plastic surgeons, even though they may have had no formal training in plastic surgery. Even the most sophisticated patients can be fooled. As U.S. Senator Ron Wyden concluded at a congressional hearing when he was still a U.S. representative, "too many cosmetic surgeons have no formal surgical training. . . . In every state, any medical school graduate with a state license can perform cosmetic surgery. There are no barriers to entry, public or professional."

The search for a qualified plastic surgeon is just one of the obstacles you will face. A carefully planned and organized approach is essential as you pursue a safe and aesthetic result. Ten steps will provide you with what you need to temper your expectations and secure the best outcome.

The Difference Between Plastic Surgery and Cosmetic Surgery

Plastic surgery encompasses both reconstructive surgery and cosmetic surgery. The purpose of reconstructive surgery is to restore body form and function for patients who have suffered from accidents, cancer, burns, birth defects, hand deformities, or other problems. Cosmetic surgery aims solely to improve the appearance of healthy people. It is a subspecialty of plastic surgery. Thus all cosmetic surgery is plastic surgery, but not all plastic surgery is cosmetic surgery. In casual conversation, the more general term plastic surgery *is used when referring to cosmetic surgery. The public simply is more familiar with this term. For this reason,* plastic surgery *is used in the title of this book; however, this book focuses solely on cosmetic surgery.*

Step 1: Decide if Plastic Surgery Is Right for You

There are many reasons to consider cosmetic surgery. Many women seek to recapture their youthful appearance. Others desire to improve an inherited trait or to repair sun-damaged skin. Some hope to reverse the effects of pregnancy or weight gain. All have the same final goal: to look and feel their best.

Tina, a twenty-nine-year-old manicurist, wanted her breast implants removed. She explained that she had been encouraged by her boyfriend nine years ago to have breast implants placed. Because he paid for the surgery, she had thought there was no reason not to have it. Their relationship dissolved a few years later, but she was left with implants that she never really wanted. She felt self-conscious about her breasts, which seemed to draw a moderate amount of unwanted attention. Had she the option to turn back the clock, she would not have had the implants placed.

Ten Steps for the Best Outcome

1. *Decide if plastic surgery is right for you.*
2. *Find a qualified plastic surgeon.*
3. *Evaluate the surgeon during your consultation.*
4. *Understand the risks.*
5. *Know the deleterious effects of smoking and common medications.*
6. *Don't be the first to have a new procedure.*
7. *Plan your surgery.*
8. *Pay for it.*
9. *Have your surgery.*
10. *Recover and resume your regular routine.*

If the decision were easy, this book would not be necessary. The difficulty lies in balancing the potential drawbacks with the anticipated benefits. Cosmetic surgery imposes time away from work and play, financial cost, medical risk, and the possibility of disappointment, real or imagined. How can you predict whether your end result will justify braving these obstacles? This book highlights important issues that will play a role in your decision. But in the end, you alone must decide.

Consult Your Mirror

Physical appearance, inherited and acquired, affects self-image and interactions with others. As long as we have mirrors, our reflections will influence self-esteem. To obtain the best results from cosmetic surgery, you must first consult your mirror and determine what troubles you. Never consider a procedure solely to please another, nor be dissuaded from pursuing a change that you desire unless your surgeon thinks it is surgically infeasible or medically unsafe. After all, you are the one holding the mirror.

Set Realistic Expectations

The number one cause of disappointment following cosmetic surgery is failure of the procedure to meet the patient's expectations. Although this is sometimes due to a suboptimal surgical result, it is more often due to unrealistic expectations. Patients may recognize intellectually that there are limits to what they can expect, yet some deny this fact emotionally. Their emotions drive their expectations beyond reality, and they are destined for disappointment.

Do not seek plastic surgery with the notion that it will change your life. It will not. Plastic surgery will change your appearance, which may have a powerful impact on your self-perception, but it will not improve relationships, help you gain new friends, or win back an unfaithful husband. If you have such thoughts, either consciously or subconsciously, cosmetic surgery is almost guaranteed to result in dissatisfaction. Instead of having surgery, try to openly recognize your expectations and deal with the real problems at hand.

Recognize Asymmetry

You may have noticed that your own photograph does not look exactly like you. This is because you are accustomed to seeing yourself in a mirror, not in a photograph. A photograph represents your true image, which is the opposite of your mirror image. The images are different because we are all asymmetric.

As with the face, the entire human body is asymmetric. Because asymmetries can influence your perception of the final result, your surgeon might point them out to you in advance.

Accept the Drawbacks

Anyone who is seriously considering cosmetic surgery must fully appreciate the drawbacks: financial cost, social inconvenience, physical discomfort, and medical risk. Hopefully, you are not one of those people who say things like, "I'm not worried about discomfort," or, "That complication won't happen to me." An unwillingness to accept potential complications (however rare) is a sign that one is not ready for cosmetic surgery.

Resolve Conflict

A major source of inner conflict for some women is guilt. These women have focused their lives on their families, putting their own interests last. This pattern of placing others first becomes ingrained over a lifetime. They are predictably uneasy about cosmetic surgery, which they perceive as a selfish pursuit. They might feel guilty about spending money on themselves and requiring the attention and patience of family members as they recover. This can be true even when family members are supportive. Guilt can also

Computer Imaging

Computer technology enables plastic surgeons to manipulate patient photographs to demonstrate the effect of a proposed procedure. This may at first seem beneficial because it will help you decide if that procedure is right for you. Yet, computer imaging can be misleading and offer false promises. It might show ideal rather than typical results. Further, even though you will be told that your result is not guaranteed to match the computer-generated photograph, you will believe your eyes rather than your ears and are likely to be swayed by emotion rather than judgment. Protect yourself by declining computer imaging until after you have made your decision.

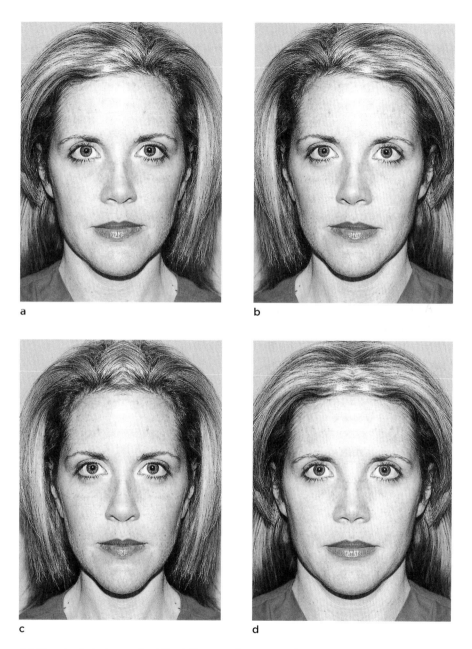

(a) Standard photograph of Danielle, one of my operating room nurses. (b) Mirror image of the photo. (c) The left side is matched with the mirror image of the left side. (d) The right side is matched with the mirror image of the right side. All images appear different because Danielle, like all of us, is asymmetric.

be a cause of temporary depression following cosmetic surgery. If you have a sense of guilt about cosmetic surgery, it is best to address and resolve it before proceeding.

Another potential source of conflict stems from others who might assert that you are vain or foolish for considering plastic surgery. Although these people clearly would not consider plastic surgery for themselves, it is unfortunate that they feel the need to impose their own negative opinions on you. The best advice here is to refrain from discussing your plans with those who might take this stance.

A final source of conflict is the well-meaning spouse or significant other. Some partners think they are being supportive by making comments such as, "You look great to me the way you are." These people are unaware that such comments are falsely supportive and only compound inner conflict. The message that the woman hears is, "Your concerns about yourself are silly or invalid." In contrast, a truly supportive comment sounds more like this, "I love you the way you are now, and I will love you however you will look after surgery. Do what is right for you."

If any one ingredient is lacking in your responses to the Formula for Success, then disappointment is likely. But if you can answer yes confidently to all the questions listed, then you are likely to be satisfied after cosmetic surgery.

Elmira, a retired seventy-three-year-old schoolteacher, knew that her ninety-seven-year-old live-in mother would disapprove of Elmira's plans for a facelift. So concerned was Elmira that she did not give us her home phone number for fear that her mother would answer the phone and discover that Elmira had seen a plastic surgeon. Elmira proceeded with surgery and managed to keep it a secret from her mother. In the end, both probably were happier this way. Yet had her mother discovered the clandestine surgery, Elmira was prepared to confess. She said, "It is easier to ask for forgiveness than permission."

Step 2: Find a Qualified Plastic Surgeon

Finding a qualified plastic surgeon can be challenging. Do not underestimate the complexity of this important task.

One valid way to find a qualified plastic surgeon is by personal recommendation. If a friend was satisfied with the care provided by a surgeon, then chances are that you will be similarly pleased. Or ask someone in the medical profession, such as your family doctor or a nurse. Keep in mind, however, that doctors and nurses often are more familiar with plastic surgeons' personalities rather than their skill, and they might refer based on friendship rather than ability.

Many cosmetic surgery patients prefer not to ask others for recommendations, to preserve the secrecy of their plans. If privacy is important to you,

| Formula for Success

- *Are you seeking cosmetic surgery for yourself rather than to please another?*
- *Do you have realistic expectations of what the procedure can accomplish?*
- *Do you fully appreciate the drawbacks, such as medical risk, physical discomfort, recovery, and expense?*
- *Have you addressed and resolved inner conflicts?*
- *Does your plastic surgeon understand your goals and agree they are realistic?*

then your task is more difficult. You may look for a board-certified plastic surgeon in the telephone directories or on the Internet, but as you will see, deceptive advertising tactics pervade cosmetic surgery. And the problem only starts there.

Board Certification

The American Board of Medical Specialties (ABMS) serves the public interest by overseeing the twenty-four legitimate medical boards in the United States. Examples of medical boards include the American Board of Plastic Surgery, the American Board of Anesthesiology, the American Board of Pediatrics, and twenty-one others. Each board is responsible for certifying only those physicians with the training, judgment, and skill necessary for safe, independent practice within that specialty.

The educated public thinks that it is shrewd to look for the term *board certified* as an assurance that a physician is capable and credible. But surprisingly, in the realm of plastic surgery, the term *board certified* means little, unless it is used with the phrase *by the American Board of Plastic Surgery*.

Certification by the American Board of Plastic Surgery (ABPS)

Plastic surgeons who are certified by the ABPS must complete all of the following requirements:

- Graduate from an accredited medical school
- Complete prerequisite training (typically three to five years) in an approved surgical residency program
- Complete two to three years of training in an approved plastic surgery training program
- Be recommended by their training program chairperson for ABPS eligibility
- Pass a comprehensive written examination
- Submit a detailed list of all operations performed, which is closely scrutinized by the ABPS

- Pass a three-day oral examination
- Meet moral and ethical standards set forth by the ABPS

Thus the phrase "certified by the American Board of Plastic Surgery" has significant meaning; the term *board certified* means little.

The American Society of Plastic Surgeons (ASPS) inducts only plastic surgeons who are certified by the ABPS. To obtain the names of these plastic surgeons in your area, call the ASPS in Chicago at 800-635-0635 or visit their website at plasticsurgery.org.

Telephone Directories

In most metropolitan telephone directories, only about two-thirds of the physicians listed under "Plastic and Reconstructive Surgeons" are certified by ABPS. The same is true for physicians listed under "Cosmetic Surgeons."

Some physicians listed may have no formal training in cosmetic surgery. Telephone directories in most states do not require physicians to state the board from which they received certification. Therefore, physicians may advertise under "Plastic and Reconstructive Surgeons" without being certified by the ABPS.

Sheila, a freelance artist and mother of three, decided to give herself a tummy tuck for her forty-fifth birthday. She called a doctor who was listed under "Plastic Surgeons" in the phone book. When she arrived for her appointment, she learned that the doctor was a general practitioner who was not trained to perform a tummy tuck. The office staff assured her that the doctor performed "beautiful" liposuction, as they pointed to a handsome wall certificate attesting to attendance at a weekend minicourse on liposuction. Sheila left the office in frustration and disgust. Determined that this would not happen again, she researched the issue. She obtained the names of several plastic surgeons certified by the ABPS. Following a tummy tuck and liposuction of her hips, she was satisfied with her result. Looking back, however, she cannot help but think that she dodged a bullet.

Self-Designated Boards

Any physician may seek certification from self-designated boards. A self-designated board is not recognized by ABMS. Requirements for certification from some of these "boards" are meager. Some self-designated boards have been accused of existing solely to promote their members.

Examples of self-designated boards according to the ABMS:

The American Board of Aesthetic Plastic Surgeons
The American Board of Cosmetic Plastic Surgery
The American Board of Cosmetic Breast Surgery
The American Board of International Cosmetic and Plastic Facial
    Reconstructive Standards

The American Board of Laser Surgery
The American Board of Plastic Esthetic Surgeons

These boards may sound impressive, but according to Joyce D. Nash, author of *What Your Doctor Can't Tell You About Cosmetic Surgery*, "Certification of competency from such organizations is probably meaningless."

Back in 1989, the U.S. House Subcommittee on Regulation held hearings on cosmetic surgery. The congressional staff report concluded, "Anyone and any group can create a board, call itself anything, and issue certificates suitable for framing. So far, 102 of these self-designated boards have sprung up." Since then, little has changed. Most states have no laws restricting the formation of boards.

Legal but Unqualified Surgeons

The public assumes that if physicians perform a surgical procedure, they are appropriately qualified. This might be true in the hospital setting, but it is not necessarily true in the doctor's office.

Hospitals hope to ensure quality of care through two mechanisms: privileges and peer review. Physicians must have privileges for each procedure they perform. The hospital credentials committee, composed of physicians, attempts to limit permission to only those physicians who are qualified to perform a given procedure. Then physicians' performances are subjected to peer review. If the quality of care they deliver is deemed substandard, then they might lose their privileges to perform that procedure in the future.

But in the doctor's office, uniform regulations do not exist. In many states, physicians may perform any procedures they choose, whether qualified or not. This unregulated setting has made it possible for untrained physicians to perform cosmetic surgery. If your doctor suggests office surgery, be certain he or she has privileges to perform the same procedure in the hospital, as evidence that peers have deemed the doctor qualified. Also, understand that hospital privileges are neither foolproof nor consistent throughout the country.

To confirm that hospital privileges exist, ask your surgeon the name of the hospital at which he or she can perform your procedure. Then call the hospital and ask to speak with someone in the medical staff office. That person should be able to tell you whether your surgeon has privileges for your operation.

Accreditation of Office Surgery Facilities

In an effort to regulate office and freestanding surgical facilities, more states now mandate that they be accredited.

If your surgeon suggests that your surgery be performed in the office, ask if the office is accredited for surgery and by which organization. The three main organizations for accreditation are:

- The American Association for Accreditation of Ambulatory Surgery Facilities (AAAASF)
- The Accreditation Association for Ambulatory Health Care (AAAHC)
- The Joint Commission

In order to be accredited, an office surgical facility must meet stringent safety requirements for the layout, equipment, staff, and physicians. Physicians operating at an accredited facility must have privileges to perform the same procedures at an accredited hospital, where peer review applies.

Does ABPS Certification Guarantee That I Will Be Pleased?

No. Many factors determine whether you will be pleased with your result, as explained in Step 1. Further, not every ABPS-certified surgeon is experienced in the procedure you seek. The information and questions provided in each chapter of this book may help you distinguish between those physicians who are experienced and those who hope to gain experience while operating on you.

Scheduling an Appointment

When calling to schedule your appointment, ask questions freely. Expect the staff to be courteous, informative, and accommodating. If they are not pleasant before surgery, they certainly will not be afterward.

Is the Doctor Certified by the American Board of Plastic Surgery (ABPS)?

If the receptionist hesitates, does not know, or states the doctor is certified by a similarly named board, this should raise serious concern.

What Is the Surgery Fee?

Although many fees figure into the total price of cosmetic surgery, a telephone quote might only include the surgeon's fee, in order to sound more affordable. As the cost of the operating room, anesthesiologist, and implants can add thousands to the total price, you must ask if these are included in the estimate. Many offices will give a range of fees, but do not accept the response, "We cannot give you an estimate until we see you." This might be a ploy to lure you into the office.

Scheduling an Appointment: A Checklist

☐ *Is the doctor certified by the ABPS? (Beware of any other board certification even if it sounds similar or better.)*

☐ *What is the surgery fee? (Does the cost include the anesthesiologist, the facility, and the implant?)*

☐ *What is the consultation fee? (Is it deducted from the cost of surgery?)*

☐ *Is the doctor punctual? (If so, then expect to be seen promptly.)*

What Is the Consultation Fee?

The cost for consultation can range from no fee to more than $150. Some plastic surgeons provide free consultations to avoid deterring potential patients. Others charge a fee because they incur an overhead cost with each patient seen in the office. If no consultation fee is charged, then surgical fees might be higher. If you are charged a consultation fee, ask if it will be deducted from your surgical fee.

Is the Doctor Punctual?

If the receptionist's answer is an unequivocal yes, then expect to be seen promptly, but be understanding if your surgeon was detained by an operation or an emergency. If you wait more than thirty minutes, it is reasonable to ask the doctor to waive your consultation fee.

Summary Advice

Finding a qualified plastic surgeon might seem like a daunting task. It can be. It's easy to mistakenly conclude that an unqualified physician is a qualified plastic surgeon. Unqualified physicians make great efforts to create the impression that they are plastic surgeons. In many states, unqualified physicians may legally perform procedures in which they have not been trained. If you understand these issues, then you are well ahead of the general public.

To begin your search, call the ASPS, ask for the names of surgeons in your area, and carefully evaluate the surgeon during your consultation.

Step 3: Evaluate the Surgeon During Your Consultation

During your consultation, the plastic surgeon should do the following:

- Explain each procedure thoroughly, including alternatives, risks, and limitations
- Describe recovery in detail
- Clearly explain what the proposed procedure will and will not achieve

- Use understandable terms and answer your questions fully
- Put you at ease so that you are comfortable discussing all of your concerns

If you achieve this rapport with the first plastic surgeon you see, there is no need to seek another opinion. If not, this does not necessarily mean that the surgeon is a poor one—but only that you did not establish rapport. Nevertheless, the surgeon you choose will eventually be operating on you, so if you are less than completely comfortable, consider seeing another plastic surgeon.

When you consult with a surgeon, listen for exaggerated claims regarding outcome. If the surgeon promises or guarantees results, be wary. Advertisements may allege that liposuction will result in a fifty-pound weight loss or that a facelift will help you look twenty years younger. Do not be seduced by these extravagant claims, but recognize them as lures to bring you to a particular office and as a reflection of a potentially unethical surgeon.

Questions to Ask During Your Consultation

The following are some important questions to ask your surgeon during your consultation. Each chapter of this book also outlines additional questions to ask that are specific to each procedure.

Will I Be Awake or Asleep During Surgery?

Your surgeon will make a recommendation regarding which type of anesthesia is most appropriate in your case. (The different types of anesthesia are explained in Step 9.) Do not hesitate to express concerns about anesthesia, discomfort, or awareness during surgery. These are common concerns, and they should be discussed with your surgeon openly.

About How Many of These Procedures Have You Performed in the Past Year?

Depending on the surgeon and the operation, the learning curve varies dramatically. Some surgeons can execute some operations expertly after having performed only a few. Other surgeons continue to improve and refine their techniques after performing them hundreds of times.

Evaluating a Plastic Surgeon: A Checklist

- ☐ *Certified by the ABPS?*
- ☐ *Explained procedures, risks, and alternatives in detail and with clarity?*
- ☐ *Described recovery time and postoperative care?*
- ☐ *Conveyed realistic expectations?*
- ☐ *Answered questions thoroughly?*
- ☐ *Listened to your concerns?*
- ☐ *Made you feel comfortable?*

The answer will also vary depending on the popularity of the procedure. For common procedures, expect the answer to be high. If you seek a new procedure, do not expect your surgeon to have extensive experience.

How Do You Avoid the Telltale Signs of Surgery?

A telltale sign is evidence to others that you have had cosmetic surgery. It is an unnatural physical characteristic that can be attributed to nothing else. Telltale signs are different for each procedure. Examples of telltale signs are a tight face following a facelift, an unnaturally pale complexion after a phenol chemical peel, and a surprised look after a forehead lift. Some are preventable, whereas others are not. Plastic surgeons should aim to avoid telltale signs when possible. Bring the appropriate list of telltale signs in this book to your consultation and ask how your surgeon plans to prevent them.

Do You Show Pictures of Others Who Have Had the Same Procedure?

The usefulness of viewing before-and-after photos of others who have had the same procedure is overblown, as the results of others do not predict or guarantee your results. Furthermore, most plastic surgeons show photos of only their best results, which is why many refer to it as their "brag book." If you suspect this is the case, ask to see photos of patients who were unhappy with their results.

Before-and-After Photographs

It is standard practice for plastic surgeons to obtain before-and-after photographs. This documents your preoperative appearance and facilitates evaluation of your results.

Your surgeon may show you before-and-after photographs of other patients who have allowed their photos to be viewed. Your surgeon should not allow others to see your photographs without your signed permission.

May I Speak with One of Your Patients Who Has Had the Same Procedure?

In general, this is not always a helpful exercise. No matter what, your experience will be different. For example, you may ask another patient about recovery, but each person's recovery has unique aspects. Also, as with childbirth, she might have forgotten or suppressed the unpleasant aspects of the experience.

If you do speak with another patient, avoid asking her about the risks and benefits of the procedure, as laypeople are not qualified to discuss this and might unknowingly give you false information. Perhaps the most important question is whether the surgeon was available and sensitive to her needs following surgery.

In Which Hospitals Do You Have Privileges to Perform This Procedure?

Qualified physicians apply for hospital privileges to perform procedures for which they have been properly trained. They welcome the scrutiny of hospital credentials committees and peer review because they are confident of their training and the quality of their care. Physicians with inadequate training will not seek hospital privileges, because they will be denied. If your surgeon explains that hospital privileges are unnecessary because the procedure can be performed in the office, be wary.

Will Surgery Be Performed in the Office or the Hospital?

If you are given the choice, consider the following. Facility charges might not vary much between office and hospital. Office surgery provides privacy, confidentiality, and convenience. Hospital surgery offers a full complement of medical specialists available if you have problems. It also ensures that your surgeon is approved through peer review to perform your procedure. If a lengthy operation such as large-volume liposuction or body lift is planned, you should strongly favor having surgery in the hospital and be concerned if your doctor suggests the office. For most other procedures, you may follow the recommendations of your doctor.

If Surgery Takes Longer than Expected, Who Will Pay the Extra Cost?

If your procedure is performed in a hospital, then the operating room and anesthesiologist might charge on an hourly basis. Your surgeon must predict the length of your operation to estimate your total fee. If your operation takes longer than expected, then the hospital and anesthesiologist may bill you afterward. Because most cosmetic surgery is paid in advance, an additional bill might be an unpleasant surprise.

How Do You Charge for Revision Surgery?

All surgeons have patients who require revision surgery. The likelihood of needing revision varies with the procedure. The national revision rate following breast augmentation is 25 percent within five years. Following facelift or eyelid surgery, revision is sought by fewer than 5 percent.

Revision surgery is only appropriate when:

- The original surgery has left you with asymmetry, deformity, or other problems that both you and your surgeon recognize.
- The deformity either resulted from or was not corrected by the original surgery.
- The deformity can be improved through further surgery.

Otherwise, surgical revision will not improve your problem.

Surgical revision usually is delayed for six to twelve months because changes will continue to occur during this time. Operating too soon can result in overcorrection of the problem. Additionally, many deformities self-correct as they mature, rendering revision unnecessary.

Some surgeons charge a fee for revision that may be as high as the cost of the original operation. Some waive all fees. Others waive only the surgeon's fee, leaving you responsible for the operating room and anesthesia fees. You should understand your surgeon's policy on revision surgery before your original surgery. Most surgeons honor their revision policies for six to twelve months, after which time you are responsible for the full cost of revision.

During Your Consultation: A Checklist

☐ *Will I be awake or asleep for surgery? (Consider general, sedation, and local anesthesia. Note that you may sleep during either general or sedation anesthesia, although the depth of sleep varies.)*

☐ *About how many of these procedures have you performed in the past year? (The answer may or may not be useful to you.)*

☐ *How do you avoid the telltale signs of surgery? (Bring a list of telltale signs to the doctor's office.)*

☐ *Do you show pictures of others who have had the same procedure? (Remember that most will show you their best pictures.)*

☐ *May I speak with one of your patients who has had the same procedure? (Remember that most will refer you only to their satisfied patients.)*

☐ *In which hospital do you have privileges to perform this procedure? (Even if the procedure is performed in the office, your surgeon should have hospital privileges to perform this procedure as evidence of his or her qualifications.)*

☐ *Will surgery be performed in the office or hospital? (Consider the advantages of each.)*

☐ *If surgery takes longer than expected, who will pay the extra cost? (When surgery is performed in the hospital, operating room and anesthesia fees may accrue hourly.)*

☐ *How do you charge for revision surgery? (Who pays for the operating room and anesthesia fees? How long does the revision policy apply?)*

☐ *Will I be charged for follow-up appointments? (Expect at least one year of follow-up appointments at no charge.)*

Will I Be Charged for Follow-Up Appointments?

Following cosmetic surgery, you will require follow-up for suture removal and to ensure you are healing properly without complications. You should not have to pay for these visits, as they are a necessary part of your post-operative care. Some surgeons might begin charging you after a year. Others never charge for follow-up appointments. Be sure you understand your surgeon's policy.

Step 4: Understand the Risks

Complications may follow any operation but are most poorly accepted when they occur after cosmetic surgery. With medically necessary procedures, most complications are outweighed by the necessity to have surgery to solve an existing or potential problem. With cosmetic surgery, no existing or potential medical problems have been remedied. Thus when a complication occurs, a patient is likely to think, "I wish I had never had this procedure."

But for the best outcome, you must fully acknowledge the risk of complications and be willing to accept any that occur. In addition, if your surgeon is well qualified and experienced, you will have the best chance of having a reasonable outcome following any complication.

The following are general risks inherent in all procedures. Specific risks for each procedure are addressed in subsequent chapters.

Less Improvement than Expected

One of the most common problems is getting less improvement than you expected. All patients should think of this as a potential risk. Although it might be due to inadequate surgery, it is more often due to unrealistic expectations. (Refer to "Set Realistic Expectations" in Step 1 for a full explanation.)

Infection

Infection can occur following any operation and is often treated with antibiotics alone. Occasionally, it is necessary to remove stitches to allow the infection to drain. Sometimes the wound is left open, which can result in a more visible scar that can often be revised at a later date. For severe infections, additional surgery and admission to the hospital for intravenous antibiotics might be necessary.

Hematoma

A hematoma is the accumulation of blood within the surgical site after the skin incision has been closed. A small hematoma usually causes minor bruising and swelling, which often resolves on its own. A large hematoma is more serious. It can threaten the overlying skin, lead to infection, and compromise the final cosmetic result. Surgical exploration and removal of the hematoma is usually required if it is large.

Seroma

A seroma is a collection of clear fluid that weeps into the wound several days following surgery. Your surgeon can remove most seromas in the office with a needle. Surgeons may prevent some seromas by placing plastic drainage tubes at the time of surgery and removing them during a postoperative office visit.

Skin Death or Skin Breakdown

Skin death may occur where skin is under tension or where circulation has been compromised. This is often seen following infection or hematoma and is most common in smokers. Treatment involves waiting for the dying skin to separate from the surviving skin. The dead skin is then surgically removed, and the remaining tissue is allowed to heal or is closed surgically. As you might imagine, this can potentially alter the cosmetic outcome.

Asymmetry

A natural and symmetric appearance is the universal goal of both patient and surgeon. Surgery might, however, fail to correct preexisting asymmetry or might create new asymmetry. Mild degrees of asymmetry are normal. Moderate or severe asymmetries might require surgical revision.

Numbness or Tingling

Sensory changes may occur following many operations. Sometimes these changes are expected, such as temporary cheek numbness after a facelift, persistent abdominal numbness after a tummy tuck, or temporary tingling after liposuction. Other times they are unexpected, such as permanent nipple numbness after breast augmentation. In the majority of instances, sensory changes eventually return to normal. Until that time, they can cause significant distress. Sensory problems are detailed in each chapter.

General Anesthesia

Because general anesthesia involves greater stress to the body than sedation or local anesthesia does, it carries greater risk. Patients who have a history of cardiovascular disease, lung disease, or obesity are at higher risk for complications. Problems can include pneumonia, stroke, heart attack, and blood clots in the legs or lungs. Fortunately these complications are less likely in healthy individuals.

Insurance Coverage for Complications

If you experience a complication from cosmetic surgery, such as infection, pneumonia, or blood clots, you might require hospitalization and further surgery. Most plastic surgeons will not charge you directly, but some may bill your insurance company if you need further surgery. Be certain to clarify this with your surgeon as soon as possible if complications arise. Other doctors, the hospital, and the operating room will definitely charge you.

Your insurance company might not pay for treatment of these medical problems if sustained following cosmetic surgery. One could argue that this is equivalent to your insurance company denying coverage for treatment of lung cancer because you chose to smoke or for treatment of injuries sustained in an automobile accident because you chose to travel by car. In each scenario, a serious medical problem results from a personal choice. As hospital-based management of complications can cost tens of thousands of dollars, you should know your company's policy in advance. When you contact your insurance company, ask for a response in writing.

Step 5: Know the Deleterious Effects of Smoking and Common Medications

Smoking and some common medications—both prescription and over-the-counter—may prevent you from achieving optimal results from your surgery. It's important to give your surgeon a full history, including your current smoking habit and medication list, before undergoing any operation. Being up-front and following your doctor's advice will help ensure that you get the best results possible.

Smoking

Smoking hinders the body's ability to recover from surgery, due to the effect of nicotine. Smokers have a higher rate of infection, skin separation, skin death, and anesthesia complications following certain operations. The difference is so striking that most plastic surgeons insist that patients stop smoking for at least two to four weeks prior to a facelift, tummy tuck, or breast lift. Some surgeons may perform surgery despite a patient's continued tobacco use. However, the risks are greater, and the final result may be unsatisfactory. Nicotine patches and gum must also be discontinued prior to surgery, as it is the nicotine, not the tar, that causes healing problems.

Rebecca, a thirty-nine-year-old convenience store clerk who had successfully lost eighty pounds, thought she was doomed to spend the rest of her life with droopy breasts and a flabby abdomen. When her grandfather left her a small inheritance, she decided to have a breast lift. Although she vowed to quit for one full month prior to surgery, she continued to smoke. But she kept it a secret because she did not want to postpone surgery. Following surgery she had healing problems, and she finally admitted that she had never quit smoking. Her scars were unusually visible. One year later, she desired a tummy tuck. Because complications following a tummy tuck in a smoker can be disastrous, she was told she would have to consent to blood testing for nicotine prior to surgery. So far, she has not consented.

Prescription Medications

If you take prescription medications, advise your surgeon. Some medications might interfere with cosmetic surgery.

Nonprescription Medications and Alcohol

Aspirin, ibuprofen, and other anti-inflammatories increase the risk of bleeding during surgery and of hematoma following surgery. Many cold and sinus remedies contain hidden anti-inflammatories. Even though a medication may be available without prescription, never assume it is safe. Check with your plastic surgeon.

Avoidance of all nonprescription medications for two weeks prior to surgery should prevent problems. The main exception is plain acetaminophen (Tylenol). It is safe in recommended doses.

Vitamin E

Vitamin E supplements may contribute to bleeding during and after surgery when taken in doses greater than 100 international units (IU) per day. They should be discontinued two weeks prior to surgery and may be restarted two to four weeks following surgery.

Vitamin E cream does not contribute to bleeding. It is used by many with the false notion that it facilitates healing and minimizes scarring. It does neither.

Herbal Medications

Some plastic surgeons suspect that herbal medications, such as Saint-John's-wort and ginkgo biloba, may promote bleeding or other intraoperative problems. Your plastic surgeon might ask you to discontinue all herbal medications prior to surgery and may postpone or cancel your procedure if you do not comply. If you take herbal medications and your doctor does not ask you about them, raise the question yourself.

Diet Pills

Fully discuss any past or present diet medications with your plastic surgeon before surgery, as some have been tied to serious postoperative complications.

Alcohol

Alcohol is a drug that might affect the outcome of your surgery. It might reduce your ability to form clots, increase your bleeding, and heighten your risk of developing a hematoma. To minimize these problems, abstain for at least three days prior to surgery.

Step 6: Don't Be the First to Have a New Procedure

No laws govern the procedures that can be performed or by whom they may be performed. Procedures and devices are developed regularly with promise of great results, only to cause disappointment or deformity at a later date.

The FDA regulates implantable materials, granting approval for those that have demonstrated reasonable safety and efficacy. Yet, plastic surgeons often use materials that have not been approved by the FDA for the settings in which they are used. This is called "off-label use." One example is Botox, which was used for scowl lines long before it received FDA approval for this purpose. So, just because your plastic surgeon offers a procedure or implantable material does not mean that it has received FDA approval.

Liquid Silicone Injection

From the 1950s through the early 1980s, liquid silicone was injected into breasts and lips for augmentation. Initially, results were fabulous, natural, and sustained. Many women who received those injections later developed pain and deformity as the silicone caused local inflammation. Because it infiltrated the tissue, it was difficult or impossible to remove. Many of the women remain deformed. (Injected liquid silicone differs from silicone gel breast implants. See Chapter 7 for details.)

Radio-Frequency Facelift

Around the year 2000, some companies developed a device that applied radio-frequency energy to the skin to stimulate skin tightening. Whereas it did (and does) accomplish this to varying extents, a number of women who were treated during the early years developed fat shrinkage of their face, leaving them looking hollow, ill, irregular, and deformed. The company that manufactures the device has since changed the settings, thereby reducing the likelihood of this complication, but those who already sustained it cannot turn back the clock. See Chapter 2 for more details on this procedure.

Carbon Dioxide Laser (CO₂ Laser)

This laser became popular around 1995. It was effective in tightening skin, reducing wrinkles, and improving skin discolorations. Unfortunately, those who gained the most benefit from it also suffered the consequences of permanently pale, waxy skin. Since this has been identified as a sequela of aggressive CO_2 laser treatments, most plastic surgeons have become more conservative when using this modality. Yet many of the women who underwent this procedure in the mid- and late 1990s cannot reclaim a natural skin color and texture.

Step 7: Plan Your Surgery

Planning your operation is similar to planning a trip. You must address many details, and this list will help you get started.

Media Coverage of Cosmetic Surgery

Use caution when considering information on cosmetic surgery provided through television and radio news segments, talk shows, and magazines. The mass media often deliver information in two waves, an initial wave of excitement and inflated expectation, followed by a second wave of disappointment and disaster stories. In the 1980s, the media touted Retin-A as a cure for wrinkles, even though most plastic surgeons noted that its effect was minimal. The subsequent wave exposed Retin-A as ineffective for patients but lucrative for doctors and manufacturers, which is equally untrue. Similarly, liposuction has been portrayed as a simple, painless procedure that can be performed while the patient is chatting on the telephone with friends. It has also been portrayed as dangerous and ineffective. Neither portrayal is accurate.

• Consider the time of year. Some procedures are best performed in the cool months. After liposuction, you must wear a compression garment, similar to a girdle, continuously for several weeks. This can be cumbersome and uncomfortable in the warm months. After laser resurfacing, you must avoid direct sun exposure for several months, which can be impractical in the summertime.

• If you work weekdays, schedule your operation on a Friday to give you an extra weekend of recovery before returning to your job.

• A mammogram is usually obtained before breast surgery. If you are older than forty or have medical problems, you might also need an electrocardiogram (EKG) or chest x-ray. Preoperative testing usually requires a separate visit.

• Purchase two weeks of groceries and household supplies. Prepare single-serving meals and freeze them.

Ellen, a thirty-one-year-old advertising assistant, was encouraged by a network news story on stretch marks to seek laser treatment for hers. The story touted laser removal of stretch marks and explained how simple and effective it was. Ellen was surprised when she learned the truth: lasers do nothing to improve stretch marks. Ellen found it ironic that with her experience in advertising she was easily fooled by these false claims. She had assumed that because the information was presented on a reputable program, it must be true. In the end, she admitted that newspeople must sell, too.

• Anticipate the need following facial surgery to apply cold compresses and elevate your head to reduce swelling. Crushed ice can be placed in a plastic bag, wrapped in a small towel, and freshened regularly. Alternatively, a bag of frozen peas or corn is tidy, reusable, and maintains its cold temperature. For elevation of your head, stacked pillows are prone to failure, but you can purchase a dependable backrest in department stores for less than twenty-five dollars. A recliner is a reliable way to elevate your head but might be uncomfortable for sleeping. If you are industrious, you may incline your entire bed by placing cinder blocks under the head posts.

• If you are uncomfortable telling your friends and coworkers you are having cosmetic surgery, then you might wish to tell them:
   1. You are taking vacation at home.
   2. You are having reconstructive surgery, which explains why your excuse note is written by a plastic surgeon.
   3. You are having "female surgery." Few will ask details, especially if you indicate that it is personal.

Planning Your Surgery: A Checklist

☐ *Consider the time of year.*

☐ *Schedule your surgery on a Friday if you work weekdays.*

☐ *Expect to have routine preoperative testing.*

☐ *Purchase two weeks of groceries and household supplies.*

☐ *Anticipate the need to reduce swelling following surgery.*

☐ *Decide what to tell your friends and coworkers.*

☐ *Arrange for transportation.*

☐ *Ask someone to stay with you your first night at home.*

☐ *Fill your prescriptions prior to surgery.*

• Arrange transportation for the day of surgery and for your follow-up appointments. Anticipate that you will not be able to drive on the day of surgery or while you are taking pain medication.

• Ask a friend or family member to stay with you during your first night at home. This person should be willing and able to refresh your ice packs, prepare your food, check on you through the night, and call your doctor if you or she has concerns or questions. If no one is available, consider hiring a private duty nurse. Your plastic surgeon can direct you to a reputable nursing agency. Anticipate paying $300 to $500 per day for this service.

• Fill prescriptions for antibiotics and pain medication prior to the day of surgery. You may pick up the prescriptions from your doctor's office when you pay for your surgery and have them filled when you stock up on groceries. Alternatively, you may have a friend fill them during your operation. You may fill the prescriptions on your way home from surgery, but you will likely prefer to avoid this extra stop.

Step 8: Pay for It

Whether or not you can afford the procedure you are contemplating is just one of many issues pertinent to paying for plastic surgery. Other issues include shopping around, additional costs, financing, and possible insurance coverage. Each of these topics is addressed in this section.

Cosmetic Surgery Is a Luxury Item

The cost of the cosmetic procedures discussed in this book ranges from $60 to $25,000. At least some procedures are within reach of many people. Yet, high or low, the cost of cosmetic surgery should be considered in the same light as other luxuries—items you do not need to survive. A trip to the Bahamas, a television set, jewelry, and a candy bar are all examples of luxury items. Although most people can afford inexpensive luxury items, most financial advisers recommend against buying high-end luxury items unless you have sufficient funds available to pay for them. It simply does not make sense to get a facelift when you are struggling to pay for housing or health insurance.

Justifying the Cost

Some people justify cosmetic surgery by figuring the monthly cost over the time they will have the improvement. For example, the average fee for a facelift is $8,000. As a facelift will last seven to ten years, the cost can be broken down accordingly: $8,000 divided by 120 months (assuming ten years) equals $67 per month. The same amount can be spent on monthly facials, which do nothing for loose skin. Similarly, liposuction of the abdomen and hips will cost $4,000 to $6,000 and permanently removes fat cells. The average liposuction patient is thirty-five years old and can expect to live another forty years. The cost of liposuction over a lifetime therefore is about $10 per month ($5,000 divided by 480 months). Some people spend more money on their appearance through health club memberships, diet books, medications, and home exercise equipment, yet they remain unable to lose diet-resistant fat. This is not to suggest that liposuction should be performed in lieu of diet and exercise, because the latter clearly offer benefits that liposuction does not. It simply compares the monthly costs of cosmetic surgery and of other things that improve how you look and feel.

For most people, justifying the cost of cosmetic surgery in this way is not necessarily helpful. The best approach is to decide if you have the funds available and whether you want to spend them on cosmetic surgery or another luxury item.

Quality and Price

In the arena of cosmetic surgery, quality and price may correlate but often do not. The best surgeons may perform quality surgery, develop favorable reputations, and become busy. They then raise prices in response to greater demand. A higher fee, however, does not guarantee a good result. Neither does a lower fee necessarily indicate lesser quality or experience in the realm of cosmetic surgery.

Shopping Around

Shopping around for the best price makes sense when you are purchasing a particular model of a new car, because the car will be the same at every dealership. Such is not the case with plastic surgery. Avoid the mistake of choosing your surgeon based on cost. Rather, find a plastic surgeon who is well trained, who puts you at ease, and who has earned your trust. If you are satisfied with the first plastic surgeon you see, then there is no need to see a second. If you see more than one surgeon, base your decision on quality and rapport, not price.

Fees

Several fees contribute to the overall cost of cosmetic surgery. Be certain you understand which fees are included in your quote for the procedure. An office employee might quote only the surgeon's fee when giving you an estimate. This may not include the anesthesiologist's fee or the operating room fees. If this is the case, you may believe that the cost of your procedure is much lower than it actually is.

The average fees across the United States for each procedure are itemized in the following chapters. They are based on a survey of plastic surgeons in 2007. Cosmetic surgery fees typically rise an average of 2 percent per year. Hence, if you are reading this book after the year 2007, factor an additional 2 percent increase in price per year. Fees are generally similar across the United States, with the exception of New York City, where fees are consistently 50 percent higher than the rest of the country.

Surgeon's Fee

The average surgeon's fee listed in each chapter derives from a poll of plastic surgeons across the country. You may encounter a surgeon whose fees are outside of the stated range. If your surgeon charges a lot more, you might question whether you will be getting your money's worth. You should also be suspicious if your surgeon charges significantly less.

Anesthesia Fee

The anesthesia fee usually depends on the length of the procedure. If your surgeon administers your sedation or if only local anesthesia is used, there should be no anesthesia fee.

Facility (Operating Room) Fee

If surgery is performed in the hospital, there will be a separate operating room fee. If it is performed in the office, there may be a facility fee.

Implant Fee

This fee applies to the cost of medical materials such as breast implants, facial implants, and injectable fillers. The price of your implants may be marked up as little as 10 percent or more than 100 percent. For example, saline breast implants cost about $900 to $1,100 per pair from the manufacturer, but you may be charged up to $2,000 for a pair. Your surgeon or the surgery center may profit from the sale of implants.

Financing Your Cosmetic Surgery

Cosmetic surgery, with rare exceptions, is paid in full before surgery. If you lack the liquid assets, you might be able to obtain financing through credit cards or bank cards, payment plans, bank loans, and mortgage plans (which offer the advantage of tax-deductible interest).

But as already stated, plastic surgery is a luxury item. Few people would borrow money or mortgage their homes to pay for a vacation. So why consider this for plastic surgery? Think about it.

Insurance Coverage

Cosmetic surgery is not covered by health care plans. Exceptions to this rule exist when the proposed procedure corrects a functional problem or deformity. One example is excess upper eyelid skin, which can interfere with eye opening and can be corrected through eyelid surgery. Paralysis of one side of the face can be improved by a one-sided facelift or forehead lift. A severe hollow of the chin or cheek resulting from trauma or cancer surgery can be restored by placement of an implant or bone graft.

A surgeon who agrees that your anticipated procedure is aimed at improving a deformity or solving a problem may write a letter to your insurance company on your behalf explaining that the surgery should be covered. However, health care plans often will not cover treatment for these medical conditions. So do not rely on coverage from your insurance company, even if you have a legitimate medical need.

Combining Plastic Surgery with Medically Necessary Operations

If you are in need of a medically indicated procedure and would also like to have a cosmetic procedure, then you might be able to combine them. A common example is combining a tummy tuck with a hysterectomy. If you would like to pursue this option, discuss it with the surgeon who will perform the medically necessary procedure first. If the surgeon agrees that combining operations is appropriate, then the surgeon will refer you to a plastic surgeon with whom he or she has worked. Insurance companies might cover the cost of medically necessary operations, but you will be financially responsible for the portion of fees related to cosmetic surgery. By combining procedures, you may save on the hospital and anesthesia fees, as the time required to perform one combined procedure is less than that of performing two separate procedures.

Step 9: Have Your Surgery

You probably will question your decision to have cosmetic surgery countless times before actually proceeding. This is natural. Proceeding with cosmetic surgery takes courage.

Many doubts will race through your mind before surgery. You will be concerned about rational issues such as risk of infection or whether you will be satisfied with your result. You might also be concerned about less rational issues such as whether you will wake up afterward. Central to these concerns is the same basic question: is it worth it? Only you can answer this question. If you feel it is, proceed. If you are uncertain, you should cancel. Because many surgeons charge a fee for canceling within a few days of surgery, ask about this before you cancel. If you are considering cancellation, let your surgeon know as soon as possible.

While battling your last-minute doubts, bear in mind that remaining calm on the day of surgery offers significant rewards. Those who are nervous or anxious prior to surgery naturally release adrenaline, causing the heart rate and blood pressure to increase. Adrenaline also fuels anxiety, which releases even more adrenaline. Patients with higher amounts of circulating adrenaline usually require higher doses of anesthetic agents and narcotics to obtain and maintain an appropriate level of anesthesia. The body takes longer to metabolize these higher doses, which also are associated with slower recovery from anesthesia, higher incidence of nausea after surgery, and greater postoperative discomfort. So whereas being nervous prior to surgery will not affect your aesthetic result, it will likely make your recovery more unpleasant. If possible, try to figure out a way to stay calm the morning of surgery.

The Morning of Surgery

Do not eat or drink anything unless otherwise instructed by your surgeon. This might seem like a punitive way to start an already anxious day, but there is a reason. Your stomach must be empty during surgery to minimize the risk of vomiting during surgery. If you take prescription medications, ask your plastic surgeon whether or not you should take them on the morning of surgery with a sip of water. Leave your jewelry at home. Do not drive in yourself, unless your doctor told you that you would be able to drive home.

When you arrive, you will change into a gown. The nurse will start an IV and check your temperature, blood pressure, heart rate, and respiratory rate. Your surgeon will usually mark your skin before surgery. You may be given a sedative before being brought to the operating room.

Maria and Angela were twenty-eight-year-old identical twins who underwent breast augmentation on the same day. Maria was calm and confident the morning of surgery. Following her procedure, she reported little pain, had no nausea, and was able to return to work in five days. Angela was "stressed out," as she put it. Her procedure went well, but she was slow to wake up afterward. She remained nauseated for a day, required more pain medication, and was unable to return to work for ten days.

Anesthesia Basics

Three anesthetic techniques are used in cosmetic surgery: general, sedation, and local anesthesia.

General Anesthesia

General anesthesia induces a deep sleep and temporarily paralyzes your body. You will no longer breathe on your own, so the anesthesiologist or anesthetist will place a breathing tube into your windpipe after you are asleep. After surgery, you will be awakened, and the tube will be removed prior to regaining consciousness. Some people experience nausea following general anesthetic, but with recent improvements in antinausea medications, this is becoming less common.

General anesthesia is needed for large operations such as a thigh lift, a body lift, a tummy tuck, and large-volume liposuction. Many plastic surgeons also prefer it for other operations such as breast surgery and facelifts, especially when performed in combination with other procedures.

Some patients wonder what would happen if they do not "wake up" following general anesthesia. This is not a rational concern. Once the anesthetic agents wear off, you will wake up. General anesthesia is safe, provided that you are healthy and a qualified anesthesiologist or anesthetist is present to administer it and supervise your care.

The same patients also wonder what will happen if they wake up during surgery. To prevent this, agent monitors should be used to confirm the amount of anesthetic gas you are receiving and how rapidly you are metabolizing it. Another safety measure is to ask the surgeon if paralyzing medications can be avoided during surgery. If so, then you will begin moving long before you develop consciousness, thereby indicating to the operating team that more anesthetic agent is required.

Sedation Anesthesia

Sedation anesthesia, also called twilight anesthesia or monitored anesthesia care (MAC), uses intravenous medication to induce drowsiness and relaxation. Many procedures, such as a facelift, eyelid surgery, nose surgery, and small-volume liposuction, can be performed comfortably and safely under sedation anesthesia.

Because you continue to breathe on your own, a breathing tube is not necessary. After you are sedated, your surgeon will inject the appropriate area of your body with lidocaine, which is similar to Novocaine. Most likely, you will not feel the injections. Depending on how deeply you are sedated, you might sleep through the entire procedure and remember nothing, or you might wake periodically. If you awaken, you may be aware that you are in the operating room, but most likely you will not care. You will feel at ease, even if you are prone to anxiety. If you are squeamish about being awake during surgery, make this known to your surgeon or anesthesiologist before your procedure. Thorough discussion with them will likely allay your fears.

Local Anesthesia

Local anesthesia involves numbing an area of your body without using sedation. Injection of local anesthesia, which is similar to Novocaine, causes initial burning. Burning is soon replaced by numbness. Local anesthesia is appropriate for lip augmentation, removal of moles, and other small procedures.

During Surgery

If you are having general anesthesia, you will remember nothing from the time you are brought to the operating room to the time you wake up in the recovery room. If you are having sedation anesthesia, you will experience deep relaxation or light sleep during surgery, and you likely will not remember the details. If you are having local anesthesia, you will be awake throughout the procedure, including the time your plastic surgeon injects numbing medication. Numbness will last from two to twenty-four hours depending on the agent used.

Length of Surgery

The length of your procedure may vary greatly depending on your surgeon. Surgeons work at their own pace. A faster surgeon is not necessarily more skilled, nor is a slower surgeon necessarily doing better work by taking plenty of time. One plastic surgeon I know takes two hours to perform a facelift, forehead lift, and eyelid surgery. Another surgeon using the same technique takes seven hours. Both surgeons charge the same fee, work in the same setting, and achieve excellent results. Each, however, works at his own pace.

After Surgery

Following most operations, you will be allowed to go home when you are awake and alert. Extensive or uncomfortable procedures, such as a tummy tuck or large-volume liposuction, usually merit an overnight stay.

Step 10: Recover and Resume Your Regular Routine

This section contains advice for the recovering cosmetic surgery patient. Regardless of which procedure you have, revisit this section as the date of your surgery approaches.

The First Few Days

Following are some tips to help you know what to expect during the early stages of recovery.

• Expect to look worse before you look better. Nearly all cosmetic surgery procedures involve swelling and bruising, which typically peak three to five days after surgery. The amount varies greatly from individual to individual.

• If you had surgery on your face or neck, keep your head elevated and apply ice packs for two to three days to minimize swelling and speed recovery. Do not underestimate the importance of elevation and ice: it will reduce your recovery time, whereas failure to do so might prolong it.

• Your doctor will likely remove your bandages during your first office visit. Stitches will be removed in three to ten days, depending on the location. Absorbable sutures do not require removal.

• Your surgeon might place a drain under the skin, near the site of incision. It is a small, pliable plastic tube connected to a suction reservoir. It evacuates fluid and can reduce the incidence of fluid collections called seromas. Drain removal is performed in the office after surgery and causes brief discomfort.

• Ask your doctor when you may shower, bathe, and wash your hair. Often this is allowed within a day or two of surgery.

• Makeup may be worn five to ten days after facial surgery. Exceptions are carbon dioxide laser resurfacing, phenol peel, and dermabrasion, which require about two weeks without makeup.

• You will be able to return to work between three days and two weeks following most cosmetic operations, depending on the procedure and your occupation.

Out-of-Town Surgery

Some choose to have cosmetic surgery away from where they live because:

• *They perceive that results will be better if they travel farther and pay more.*

• *They have heard that the reputation of a particular surgeon is good.*

• *They seek anonymity.*

Among the problems with seeking surgery away from home, aside from the obvious nuisance and expense of travel, are the very real issues of postoperative care. If you wish to return home immediately after surgery, who will remove your stitches? If you have a complication that becomes evident after you get home, how will your plastic surgeon be able to help you? If your result merits a minor touch-up procedure, will you bother to pursue it if doing so means another trip out of town? These are important drawbacks to consider, especially because with a little effort you most likely can find an excellent plastic surgeon close to home.

That having been said, some plastic surgeons draw patients from all over the country. Those willing to stay for a few days and willing to return in the event of a problem tend to do very well.

• Discomfort ranges from minimal following lip augmentation to significant following a tummy tuck or a body lift. It is also highly variable from person to person. For example, most women find that a facelift involves minimal discomfort. However, others find it very uncomfortable.

• Do not drive while you are taking pain medication, because it will alter your judgment and delay your responses. Following most operations, you will be able to drive once you stop taking pain medication. Exceptions to this rule exist for a tummy tuck, a thigh lift, and a body lift, which might impose a longer period of not driving.

Tips for a Faster Recovery

You may encounter advice from well-meaning friends regarding medications to expedite your recovery. Some remedies have merit, some do not, and some are disputed among plastic surgeons. Always discuss them with your surgeon before taking them.

Nausea

If you are prone to nausea after surgery, this might be averted by taking preventive measures prior to surgery. Ask your plastic surgeon whether he or she plans to give you any or all of the following: intravenous steroids, promethazine, and scopolamine. Each targets a different cause of nausea, so you might need more than one of them. They work best if administered before or during surgery. Additional medications that prevent nausea include ondansetron and metoclopramide.

Pain

Whereas surgery can be associated with significant discomfort, it does not have to be. Ask your surgeon about using long-lasting anesthetic (bupivacaine) at the time of your procedure. Although this will wear off within twelve to twenty-four hours, it can have a significant effect on your overall recovery. If your surgeon does use bupivacaine (either as an injection at the time of surgery or by way of a postoperative continuous infusion), you should still be prepared for discomfort, as bupivacaine does not eliminate pain. I

How Long Will I Be Bruised?

Following most surgical procedures, bruising lasts five to ten days, but may vary depending on the person, the procedure, and factors that cannot be controlled. In my practice, I do not take the credit for those who look great within a week, and I do not take the blame for those who are still bruised after two to three weeks.

tell my patients to hope for the best but be prepared for the worst. Most have a substantial benefit from its use.

Constipation

Because narcotics are constipating, begin taking a stool softener the day prior to surgery and throughout the time you are taking narcotics.

Swelling and Bruising

Some herbal medications such as arnica and bromelain may reduce swelling and bruising following surgery. An excellent herbal remedy for swelling and bruising, if allowed by your plastic surgeon, is Pro-Trauma. Cost is $17 for a full course, which begins following surgery.

Because they are derived from plants, herbal medications draw many laypeople, who assume that herbal medications improve health "naturally" without risk. But some plastic surgeons think herbal medications promote, rather than reduce, bleeding. These surgeons may prohibit herbal medications around the time of surgery. So if you wish to take herbal medications, be certain to have assent from your surgeon.

Supplemental Vitamins

Without question, vitamin E in oral doses greater than 100 IU per day can promote bleeding. Other vitamin supplements, however, are considered more controversial. Although some surgeons have observed speedier recovery for their patients on vitamin supplements, solid proof is lacking. Some surgeons have found no evidence of speedier recovery and suspect that many supplemental vitamins may even promote bleeding or other problems.

Glycerine

After finishing liposuction of the face on a twenty-two-year-old woman (not a common procedure), I told her parents that the procedure had gone well but that their daughter was already markedly bruised and swollen, which is common after liposuction of the face. They hardly seemed concerned and assured me that she would be fine. Four days later, when the young woman returned for suture removal, she was fully recovered with no swelling or bruising. I was astounded, as I had expected her to be bruised and swollen for weeks. Her parents, who were farmers, told me that they administered topical glycerine every hour and that this is "an old farming remedy that always works." I now advocate this for all of my patients, although I hear that it is becoming hard to find. Apparently glycerine can be used to make explosive devices, so it has become limited in availability.

They staunchly oppose use of any vitamins around the time of surgery. If you take vitamins, be certain to ask your doctor about them. Do not assume they are harmless. Additional remedies for swelling and bruising include topical glycerine (applied hourly), whole food supplements, and eating five to seven kiwis per day. These measures seem to help some people more than others and sometimes have a profound impact.

Steroids

Systemic steroids may reduce swelling and provide a psychological lift following surgery. Many doctors give a onetime dose intravenously during surgery; others may have you take oral steroids for a few days. If taken incorrectly, steroids can be dangerous, so they are available through prescription only. If you are a healthy individual with no history of stomach ulcers, it is unlikely that you will have problems. You should discuss steroids with your doctor. (Medical steroids differ from the anabolic steroids taken by athletes to promote muscle growth.)

Exercise

Exercise, if performed too soon after surgery, will worsen swelling and potentially trigger bleeding. Avoid exercise for two weeks following facial surgery and two to four weeks following body surgery. Those who have liposuction or submuscular implant placement are particularly prone to swelling with exercise. When you do resume exercise, start with half of your normal routine. Soreness or swelling the following day indicates overexertion. Lack of soreness or swelling indicates that you may gradually increase your workouts.

Although not considered true exercise, housework is a form of exertion that must be limited all the same, especially vacuuming and laundry.

Sexual Relations

Many doctors are uncomfortable discussing sex, and many patients are uncomfortable asking about it. If so, just ask your doctor when you may exercise. In general, as soon as you are allowed to exercise, you may have sex.

Back to the Sun

During the first year following surgery, healing scars may become permanently darkened if exposed to direct sunlight. The same is true for areas of liposuction. Therefore, use caution: protect all surgical sites with potent sun block (SPF 15–40), and completely avoid tanning beds for one year.

Scars

Scars are a reality of surgery, and they are permanent. The body heals through scar formation, and the final appearance of your scar depends on several factors. Thin skin, such as eyelid skin, leaves a barely noticeable scar. In contrast, areas such as the cheek, chest, shoulders, back, elbows, knees, and buttocks are prone to poor healing and may yield unsightly scars. Skin closed without tension leaves less noticeable scars than skin closed under tension. Most important, everyone heals differently. Because of these variables, no one can predict the final appearance of your scar.

In adults, scars are most visible two to four months after surgery. They can become thick, red, and raised, especially in fair-skinned women. Over time, they will fade, but some scars take months or years to fade. Plastic surgeons sometimes recommend topical steroids (cordran tape, fluocinonide cream) during the early phase of scar formation. As steroids reduce inflammation, they can sometimes prevent the scar from becoming as thick or red as it might otherwise. By reducing the inflammatory phase of the scar, steroids help the scar achieve its mature (flat, soft, faded) appearance sooner. In some cases, steroid injections are recommended. In all cases, scar massage with moisturizing cream (after the scar is well healed) is beneficial. Silicone sheeting, available through your plastic surgeon or online, also helps scars mature. Vitamin E is falsely perceived to minimize scar visibility. Whether taken in pill form or as a topical cream, there is no evidence that it improves scar appearance. Some plastic surgeons think it may worsen scars.

Remember, you will have scars, but they will fade with time. Hopefully, they will become difficult to see, but no one—not even your plastic surgeon—can guarantee or predict your final scar appearance.

Emotional Recovery

The feelings you might experience following surgery are wide-ranging. Shortly afterward, you might be elated that you had the confidence and courage to undergo surgery. Alternatively, you might become sad or depressed, especially if you develop second thoughts during your recovery period. You might become disappointed or angry if you perceive your result will not be as you expected, even though it is too early to tell. You might feel guilty that your friends or family members must be called upon to care for you. You might be frustrated and disappointed that others do not notice a change. Sometimes, well-meaning friends will make statements that they consider to be innocuous, such as, "You don't look any different," or "You really did not need the procedure." These statements might aggravate or embarrass you, even though that was not their intent.

Your emotional response in part depends on your psychological preparedness for surgery, your understanding of recovery, and the appropriateness of your expectations. Be aware that despite well-laid plans, your emotions may surprise both you and your family. Interestingly, those who openly share their plans for cosmetic surgery with friends tend to have a smoother emotional recovery than those who try to keep it a secret. Regardless of your initial response, your emotions will stabilize as your recovery progresses. Most women adjust within days or weeks, although some require months.

Your family's emotional response to your decision to have surgery is another issue. You may have stable emotions but find that your family does not. This seems particularly problematic among teenage daughters who do not get along with their mothers. They disapprove of the mother having plastic surgery. Afterward, they express disgust over postoperative swelling and bruising and are critical of the cosmetic result. You will find that no amount of explaining will help. So deal with them as you would in any matter that primarily concerns you: do what you know to be right, and be patient. With time, they will accept your decision and your new appearance.

Barbara, a forty-two-year-old soccer mom, expressed disappointment six months following liposuction and a tummy tuck. She felt that surgery did not have much impact on her appearance. In truth, she had a dramatic result, but had forgotten how she looked prior to surgery. When she saw her before-and-after photos compared side by side, she exclaimed, "I didn't look that bad before surgery. Did you switch my pictures with someone else's?" Fortunately, she recognized the underclothing on the before photo, which confirmed that the photos were of her. Some people simply forget—or choose not to remember—their original appearance.

Joan, a sixty-six-year-old widow, planned to have a facelift, eyelid surgery, and a forehead lift, but she wanted to keep it a secret. She told her bridge club that she was going to visit relatives for two weeks. Prior to surgery, she bought a new line of makeup with brighter shades and color tones than she previously used. Upon her return, they all commented on how well rested and vibrant she looked and attributed it to her trip and new cosmetics.

To Tell or Not to Tell?

As the popularity of cosmetic surgery has soared, many people have chosen to be open about their plans for surgery. They have found that their friends and relatives are excited and enthusiastic for them. Some derive confidence from the admiration they receive from others for having the courage to proceed. Yet not everyone is prepared to be open about their plans for cosmetic surgery, and some prefer to keep it a secret. They want others to notice that they look better, but they do not want them to know why.

We instinctively attribute changes in others' appearance to alteration in hairstyle, clothing, makeup, or weight, but not to surgery. For example, if you had a tummy tuck, your friends might assume you lost weight. So you can simply acknowledge whatever change your friends perceive and thank them for noticing. Furthermore, you can change your hairstyle or color and buy a few new outfits. This will provide others with a concrete reason for your new look.

2

Trading Faces

Facelift

Every time you turn on the television, you see an ad or news segment promoting a new procedure for facial rejuvenation. They catch your attention because each time you look in the mirror, you catch glimpses of your mother. Perhaps the skin of your cheeks has fallen, or you have developed heavy skin folds around your nose and mouth. Maybe your neck has lost distinction from your jawline. You may be ready for a facelift, but how can you be sure? With everyone touting a new and different procedure, how can you know which is right for you?

Facelifts Are Poorly Named

One might imagine that an operation called a facelift would result in improvement from the top of one's forehead to the jawline, as that constitutes the face. Not so. A facelift tightens the tissues of the lower half of your face and neck. It really should be called a lower-face-and-neck lift. Unfortunately, we are stuck with the term facelift.

The Good News: Things a Facelift Can Improve

Your cheeks and neck descend due to aging and gravity. A facelift counters this by removing excess skin and tightening the remaining tissues. A facelift tightens the skin of your cheeks, resulting in some improvement in the nasolabial fold, a crease that runs from your nose to your chin, curving around your mouth. This crease may improve following a facelift but does not disappear, as it is present each time you smile. Even children have this crease.

39

If you place your fingers on the center of your cheek and press the skin up and back, you will see the effects of a facelift (Figure 2-1 and Figure 2-2). Your heavy skin folds are lifted and improved, but they do not disappear. Your jowls may be eliminated. Do the same thing with your neck skin. If these maneuvers improve the appearance of your cheeks, jawline, and neck to your satisfaction, then you may be ready for a facelift.

The Bad News: Things a Facelift Cannot Improve

A facelift can have a dramatic impact on your lower face and neck, but it will not affect your forehead or eyelids (see Chapters 3 and 4). It also will not affect the quality of your skin. Therefore, wrinkles, texture problems, and color irregularities will not be improved. See Chapters 11, 12, and 13 for solutions to these problems.

Barbara, a fifty-one-year-old empty nester, wanted to rejoin the workforce at the managerial level. Despite her enthusiasm and previous experience, she had difficulty finding the right opportunity. The reason, she suspected, was her mature appearance. A facelift subtracted several years from her apparent age and bolstered her self-confidence. She received three attractive job offers. She later appropriately concluded that the offers came because of her improved self-esteem, not because of her actual appearance.

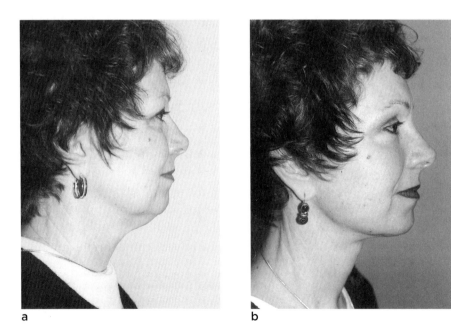

a   b

Facelift. (a) A forty-nine-year-old woman before a facelift. (b) Thirteen months after the facelift. This woman also had an upper blepharoplasty (Chapter 4).

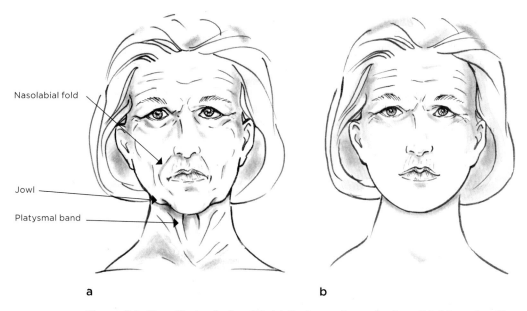

Nasolabial fold

Jowl

Platysmal band

a   b

Figure 2-1: *The effects of a facelift. (a) Features of an aging face. (b) After a facelift, the jowls are improved or resolved and the neck appears tighter and smoother. The nasolabial folds have variable improvement depending on the patient and technique. The forehead, eyes, and lips are unchanged.*

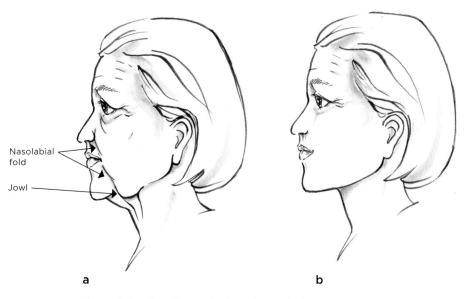

Nasolabial fold

Jowl

a   b

Figure 2-2: *The effects of a facelift. (a) Profile of an aging face. (b) After a facelift, the jowls are gone and the "turkey-gobbler" neck has been refined, but the forehead and eyes are unchanged.*

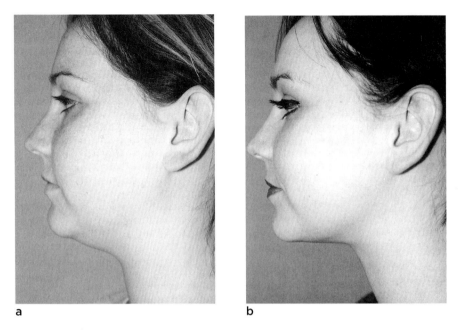

a   b

Neck liposuction in a young woman. (a) A twenty-two-year-old woman with fatty neck and good skin tone. (b) Five months after neck liposuction. Note that skin tightens and becomes smooth in young women with good skin tone.

Lift Versus Lipo

Neck liposuction is sometimes a better option than a facelift. Women who are troubled by a fatty neck but do not have loose skin are the best candidates for this. Most often, these are young women with good skin tone. Women who have both loose neck skin and fat are better suited to a facelift, as liposuction alone poses a higher risk of skin irregularities in women with loose neck skin.

Forehead and Eyelids

Because a facelift only lifts your lower face and neck, it does not change the appearance of your forehead or eyelids. Therefore, a facelift alone may create facial disharmony, as your rejuvenated cheeks and neck may cause your forehead and eyes to appear older by comparison. To obtain a uniformly youthful appearance, many women opt for facelift, forehead lift, and eyelid surgery at the same time. In contrast, some women age faster in their neck and jawline than in their eyes and forehead. It is as though the lower half of their face looks ten years older than the upper half. These women are more likely to choose a facelift alone to bring their neck and jawline into harmony with the upper half of their face.

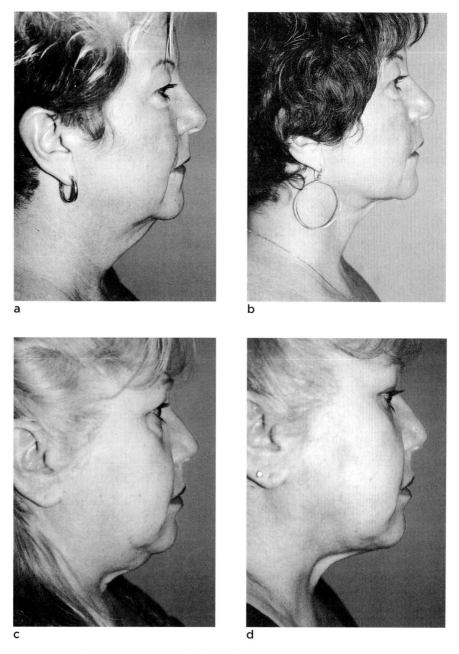

Neck liposuction in older women. Both are fifty-seven years old and are shown (a and c) before neck liposuction and (b and d) three months after neck liposuction. Note that the reduction of fat gives an overall better appearance, but the skin is still loose, as expected. These photos show that variable results can be achieved. In both cases, further improvement can be obtained through a facelift, as a facelift will tighten the neck skin. Risk of irregularities is higher in women with loose neck skin following liposuction.

When to Start Thinking About a Facelift

Women as young as thirty or as old as eighty-five seek this procedure. The most common age for a first facelift is between forty-five and sixty years, but appearance, not age, is the main factor. The aging process does not take place at a fixed rate. Accelerated aging may occur in response to illness, emotional stress, depression, tobacco use, and, of course, heavy sun exposure. When considering the timing for a facelift for yourself, perform the maneuvers described previously. If you are satisfied with the improvement you see, then it is time to start thinking about a facelift.

Facelift Techniques

As with many procedures in plastic surgery, there is more than one way to accomplish a good facelift. Years of spirited debate and volumes of published material have not led plastic surgeons to a consensus regarding which facelift technique is the best.

A facelift is the result of the artistry, judgment, and skill of your surgeon. A surgeon selects the technique that produces the best and most reliable results in his or her own hands. Perhaps here, more than anywhere else in plastic surgery, knowing someone who has had successful results can be essential in helping you choose a surgeon.

If you are uncomfortable with the recommended technique, with the explanation of its rationale, or with the answers to your questions, then seek a second opinion.

Components of a Facelift

Most facelift techniques have five basic parts.

Face
- Removing excess facial skin
- Tightening tissue under the skin

Neck
- Removing excess neck skin
- Tightening the neck muscle
- Removing neck fat

Betty, a fifty-three-year-old intensive care nurse, survived a stormy divorce only to discover a new set of problems. Although she was eager to meet men, she had not been on a date in almost thirty years and found that she was surprisingly self-conscious about her appearance. Following a facelift, eyelid surgery, and a forehead lift, she felt better about herself and dating. Her most satisfying moment came when she saw her ex-husband at a social gathering. Although they did not speak, she caught his glimpse from across the room. The expression on his face clearly said, "Wow, I can't believe how good you look!" She defiantly returned the unspoken message, "Yes, I do . . . and I've gotten over you."

Each part can be modified and combined with other parts in a variety of ways to achieve your goals. Not all parts are necessary in every case.

Of the five parts listed previously, three are aimed at improving the neck. So when you seek a facelift, expect your neck to be included. Be certain you understand exactly how your surgeon defines a facelift before you proceed. Some surgeons divide a facelift into two procedures, each with separate charges: lower facelift and neck lift. Whereas some women are indeed candidates for these separate procedures, most benefit from combining them.

Skin-Only Facelift

The skin-only facelift, also known as a one-layer facelift, involves removal of excess face and neck skin, with no surgery on the deeper tissues. This technique may be appropriate in some instances; however, some plastic surgeons hold that it is less effective than the two-layer technique, and it may not last as long. Also, because it relies upon skin tension, it might increase the risk of unnatural appearance in women with very loose skin.

The Two-Layer (SMAS) Facelift

The two-layer technique is one of the most common. The first layer is facial and neck skin, the excess of which is removed. The second layer is tissue under the skin, which is lifted or tightened. The layer under the facial skin is a fibrous tissue. It is called the subcutaneous musculoaponeurotic substance or superficial musculoaponeurotic system (SMAS) and is located only on the face. In the neck, the second layer is a thin, broad muscle called the platysma. With the two-layer technique, both the SMAS and platysma are tightened. Multiple techniques are available for tightening the SMAS, and plastic surgeons vigorously debate over which one is best.

The two-layer approach allows surgeons to tighten and lift each layer independently. The SMAS and platysma are tightened snugly to improve jowls, heavy folds around the mouth, and "turkey-gobbler" neck. Then the face and neck skin is draped over this layer to achieve a natural appearance without tension. This combination provides a significant lift, but without

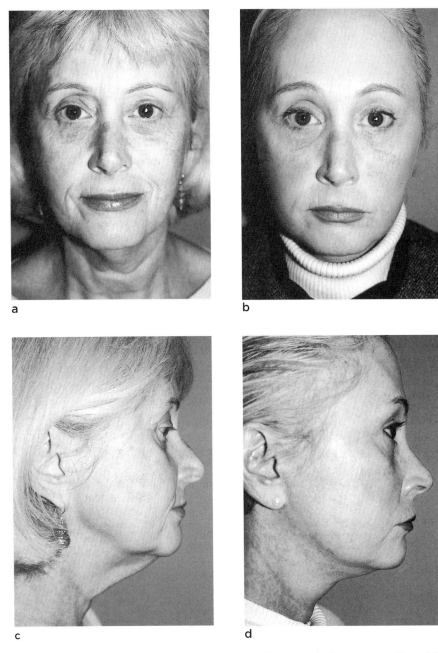

Combined procedures. (a and c) A fifty-six-year-old woman before surgery. (b and d) Four months after a facelift, a subcutaneous brow lift, and upper and lower blepharoplasty with canthopexy.

the associated tight or windblown look that can develop when the skin alone is overly tightened.

A final benefit of the two-layer technique is potential cheek augmentation. Some women with flat cheekbones seek more cheek projection. Cheek augmentation typically involves placement of implants on top of your cheekbones (see Chapter 6). However, if you are having a two-layer facelift, your surgeon may instead use your extra SMAS to build up your cheeks.

Subperiosteal (Deep) Facelift

Although the title of this chapter is "Trading Faces," the last thing you want from a facelift is to look like a different person. The deep facelift, also called subperiosteal facelift, may do just that. With this technique, all tissues, including the SMAS and deeper facial muscles, are separated from the underlying bone and lifted higher. The technique can cause persistent swelling, result in droopy lower eyelids, and alter basic facial characteristics.

A facelift that turns back the clock to a younger you is enthusiastically received, but one that alters facial characteristics poses problems. By the age of forty or fifty, your perception of yourself is so entrenched that any change in basic facial structure, no matter how good, makes for a difficult adjustment. The older you are, the harder it will be for you to adapt to a new look after a subperiosteal lift.

In spite of this, many plastic surgeons report a favorable experience with subperiosteal facelifts. They report better improvement in nasolabial folds and creases. If your surgeon recommends this technique, it is appropriate to ask to speak with a previous patient. You may also ask to look at before-and-after photos and inspect them for any alterations in basic appearance.

Cheek Lift

The cheek lift, also called a mid-facelift, evolved in the mid-1990s. Many surgeons have adapted this procedure because of its effectiveness in rejuvenating the cheek area. It is a limited version of the subperiosteal lift, and, not surprisingly, it poses some of the same potential problems. It may alter your basic appearance, cause droopy lower eyelids, and leave you swollen for weeks or months. If your surgeon proposes this procedure, ask about risks, alternatives, how many she or he has performed, and the reasons for recommending it to you.

Mini Facelift

The mini facelift has been around for a very long time and has changed little. Yet, that has not stopped some profiteers from trying to promote it under a different name. You might have heard of the short-lift, quick lift, S-lift, smart lift, lifestyle lift, swift lift, or weekend lift. All are similar versions of the same operation: mini facelift. A mini facelift usually employs standard facelift incisions but involves limited surgery under the skin. When you hear "mini facelift," you should think of the word *minimal*. Most mini facelifts involve minimal surgery, remove minimal skin, and provide minimal improvement. Yet if your degree of excess skin is mild, then this might be a reasonable option for you, regardless of what it is called.

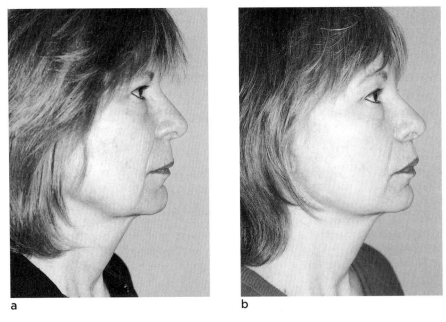

a   b

Mini facelift. (a) A sixty-year-old woman with mild skin excess and no neck fat before surgery. (b) Two months after a mini facelift. Note that jowling is improved but not resolved, and the jawline is smoother.

Platysmaplasty

A platysmaplasty, also called submentoplasty, is for those who have a sagging platysma muscle without a sagging face and without excess neck skin—an uncommon combination. The surgeon makes a small incision under the chin, tightens the platysma muscle, and removes neck fat.

If you pursue this procedure, you must limit your expectations. This procedure is performed through a single incision under the chin. Because it does not remove excess skin, it will not provide the same degree of improvement as a full face and neck lift, in which neck skin is tightened. Women who are candidates for this procedure are usually also good candidates for neck liposuction, which may give a smoother final result in some women, although it does not tighten the platysma muscle.

Thread Lift

The newest option in the facelift arena is the thread lift. It involves placing permanent sutures under the skin without extensive scars around the ears. The threads are then tightened during the procedure to provide an upward pull on the sagging tissues, especially the jowls, cheeks, and neck. The benefits of this procedure include minimal incisions and a faster recovery. The disadvantages are that it involves no removal of excess skin, so it is best offered to patients who have minimal excess skin. If performed on someone with moderate or severe excess skin, then there is a good chance it might result in bunching and puckering of skin around the ears (if the suture is tightened to the point of resolving jowls). Alternatively, if the suture tension is compromised in an effort to avoid the bunching of skin, then improvement in jowling and loose neck skin may be negligible. This procedure is best for women with minimal excess skin or those who expect modest improvement.

Nonsurgical Facelifts with Radio-Frequency Treatments

As alluring as this concept is, like most things, if it sounds too good to be true, it probably is. The so-called nonsurgical facelift involves application of radio-frequency energy to the skin, thereby stimulating the skin to thicken and tighten on its own. This modality offers anywhere from 0 to 50 percent of the improvement of a facelift. It reduces wrinkles and fine lines but does not eliminate them. The treatment involves discomfort, but recovery is typically one day. Thereafter, skin contraction is gradual and takes up to six months to complete. Because improvement is slow, some have a hard time seeing it. Cost is about $1,500–$2,000 for part of the face and about $3,000–$4,000 for the full face and neck. Some seek a second treatment after six months to gain further improvement. Results last three to five years. This procedure can provide modest rejuvenation to women with mild skin laxity, but it has been disappointing for most women with moderate to severe facial aging. It is produced and marketed by several companies, including Thermage and Titan. It offers definite advantages in wrinkle reduction and active acne. Yet it is not a replacement for the facelift.

Incisions and Scars

Most facelift techniques involve an incision that extends from above the ear, down the front of the ear, around the earlobe, up the back of the ear, and into the hairline behind the ear. There is another incision beneath the chin (Figure 2-3). Two weeks after surgery, the incisions may be concealed with makeup.

Most scars from a facelift are hard to see once they heal. Scars usually fade in four to twelve weeks, except for the scar behind your ear, which takes longer and sometimes becomes wide and thick before fading.

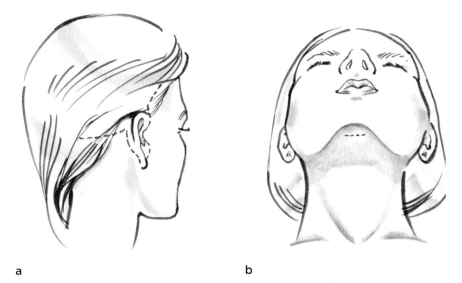

a   b

Figure 2-3: *Facelift incisions. The incisions for a facelift are well hidden (a) behind the hairline, around the ear, and (b) under the chin. There are several variations of these incisions, but those shown are among the most common.*

What to Expect

- **Anesthesia:** *Sedation or general.*

- **Location of operation:** *Office or hospital.*

- **Length of surgery:** *One to four hours. If you are also having eyelid surgery and a forehead lift, the total time may be three to six hours.*

- **Length of stay:** *An overnight stay may be recommended to monitor for hematoma (blood collection under your skin) and to ensure that you sleep with your head elevated. If you have reliable help at home, this may be performed as an outpatient procedure.*

- **Discomfort:** *Mild. Anticipate up to three days of pain medication; Tylenol alone may be adequate. Many women report no discomfort afterward. If you have severe pain, contact your surgeon immediately to be certain you do not have a hematoma.*

- **Swelling and bruising:** *Improve in two weeks, but will last longer after a deep (subperiosteal) facelift. Your face will feel tight for the first few weeks due to swelling. You can reduce swelling through constant head elevation and frequent application of cold compresses.*

- **Numbness:** *Cheek numbness lasts several weeks.*

- **Bandages:** *Changed in one to two days.*

- **Stitches:** *Removed in four to ten days (four to six days for ears and chin, seven to ten days for hairline). Staples may be used behind your hairline. Usually, neither stitch nor staple removal is painful.*

- **Drain:** *If your surgeon places a drain at the time of surgery, it will be removed in one to three days.*

- **Makeup:** *May be worn in one to two weeks.*

- **Presentable in public:** *Most will be presentable in one to two weeks with the help of makeup. To be certain, allow three weeks before an important event. If a deep (subperiosteal) lift is planned, allow one to two months because swelling will be greater.*

- **Work:** *You may feel capable of returning within five days, but your appearance will be the limiting factor.*

- **Exercise:** *May be resumed in two to three weeks.*

- **Sun protection:** *Six months with SPF 15 or higher.*

- **Final result:** *Seen in four to eight weeks following most facelifts, but two to four months following a deep (subperiosteal) facelift.*

- **Duration of results:** *A facelift may reduce your apparent age by a decade, but the aging process does not stop. Your more youthful face will continue to age, and in seven to ten years, you may be ready for a second facelift.*

Complications

When your operation is performed by a qualified plastic surgeon, both your procedure and recovery will likely be uneventful. Even in ideal circumstances, however, complications may occur. In addition to the specific complications mentioned here, refer to Chapter 1 for general complications with any procedure.

Hematoma

A hematoma is a collection of blood that may form under the skin, usually within a day of surgery. Hematomas are suspected when patients develop one-sided facial pain following a facelift. If you have such pain, notify your doctor immediately. A small hematoma may be removed without reopening the incision. If you have a medium or a large hematoma, your surgeon will probably choose to open your incisions for removal. If treated soon enough, even large hematomas will not affect your final results. The risk of hematoma is about 4 percent, but is higher in redheads, hypertensive patients, and those taking anti-inflammatory medication such as aspirin or ibuprofen.

Skin Death

If and when skin loses circulation, it dies. Skin death occurs most often when the patient has an untreated hematoma or smokes, but it can occur in anyone. If it occurs, it most often does so around the ear. If large, it might lead to an open wound and eventually leave a thick, irregular, and highly visible scar. Fortunately, this is not common.

Facial Weakness or Paralysis

Facial weakness or paralysis may be caused by injury to the facial nerve or one of its branches. Injury may occur to this nerve if it is cut, stretched, or cauterized* during surgery. This may lead to temporary or permanent loss

---

*Surgical disruption of small blood vessels can cause bleeding. To stop the bleeding, your surgeon may cauterize the bleeding vessel, using an instrument that delivers a low-level electrical current. Nearby nerves may be temporarily or permanently injured, resulting in weakness or paralysis.

of one or more facial expressions: raising the eyebrows, scowling, closing the eyes, squinting, smiling, frowning, and pursing the lips. Fortunately, the risk of permanent facial weakness or paralysis is less than 1 percent, but if it happens to you, you would most likely wish you had never had this procedure.

Ear Numbness

Whereas transient cheek numbness following a facelift is expected, numbness of the ear is not. Temporary or permanent numbness of the skin surrounding the ear may be caused by surgical injury or cautery near the great auricular nerve. Subsequent recovery of sensation may be partial, complete, or confounded by sharp pains in the neck or ear.

Parotid Injury

The parotid gland is a salivary gland located in front of each ear. Although it is not usually exposed during a facelift, women who have a very thin layer of tissue covering their parotid glands are at higher risk for injury to the parotid gland during a facelift. Symptoms of parotid injury include persistent fluid accumulation under the skin, especially after eating. This can cause persistent drainage, known as a parotid fistula. Most parotid fistulae heal on their own while the patient avoids sour foods and takes medication that temporarily suppresses secretions.

Early Relapse

Early relapse is the premature return of sagging skin and jowls, well before the seven to ten years that a facelift is expected to last. Relapse may occur within six months. The cause of relapse is not clear, but it seems to be more common in women with fair complexions and sun-damaged skin. Early relapse occurs in 1 percent and can be treated by another facelift.

Telltale Signs

Prior to surgery, ask how your surgeon plans to prevent each of the following telltale signs of cosmetic surgery (see "Questions to Ask Your Plastic Surgeon" at the end of this chapter).

Attached Earlobe

An attached earlobe, "pixie ear," occurs when too much skin has been removed nearby. The remaining, stretched skin pulls the earlobe down and into the neck (Figure 2-4).

The "Joker Look"

This is an unnatural appearance of the cheeks upon smiling. I don't know how the term evolved, but I assume it came from the Joker on the original Batman television series, whose face was painted to accent the nasolabial creases in an unnatural way. His appearance is similar to the joker look that sometimes occurs after a facelift. Interestingly, this appearance may occur after a well-executed facelift, often developing years later. Plastic surgeons debate over the cause, as well as over how to prevent and correct it. Many believe it is due to the natural aging process. As a person ages, subcutaneous fat shrinks and descends. In some cases, this exposes a previous facelift. This may not necessarily be avoidable in some women. If fat shrinkage is the problem, then fat injections may help restore a more natural appearance.

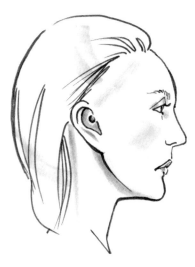

Figure 2-4: *Telltale signs of a facelift. Possible telltale signs following a facelift include an attached earlobe, a wide-open ear canal, a tight face, and absent sideburns. (Your surgeon will try to avoid telltale signs.)*

Open Ear Canal

Look at the side of your head by using two mirrors. To do this, stand with your shoulder to a wall mirror. Hold a hand mirror in front of you and tilt it toward the wall mirror. As you look straight ahead into the hand mirror, you should see the reflection of your profile. Notice that the cartilage in front of your ear canal partially hides your canal from view. If a facelift places tension on the skin of this cartilage, it will be pulled forward and widen your ear canal (Figure 2-4). A wide-open ear canal appears unnatural.

Most people do not notice a wide-open ear canal and are not bothered by it. At any rate, it is difficult to fix until your facial skin is once again loose. So, if you wish to have it fixed, you may need to wait for your next facelift.

Tight Face

A tightly pulled face, also called the "wind-tunnel look," appears unnatural and can result from removing too much skin. It can also develop following multiple facelifts. Once skin has been removed, it cannot be easily replaced. Thus a tight face is difficult to correct.

Loss of Sideburns

Your sideburns can migrate upward with each facelift depending on the technique used. After two facelifts, your sideburns can be lost entirely. Many women do not consider sideburns a vital facial feature but soon realize their importance if they are lost (Figure 2-4). As high or absent sideburns are difficult to correct, you may wish to request that your plastic surgeon employs a modification in surgical technique to preserve your sideburns. This can be accomplished if your plastic surgeon designs the incision to stay below your sideburn in front of each ear.

Margaret, the owner of a small shop, had her first facelift at fifty-three. She noticed afterward that her sideburns had migrated upward. When she sought her second facelift, at sixty-one, she did not want to risk further distortion of this feature. She interviewed three plastic surgeons before finding one whose technique would not result in further upward migration of her sideburns. After surgery, she was pleased with her result and glad she still had sideburns.

Skin Irregularities and Cobblestone Appearance

Fat is a natural buffer between skin and muscle. An unnatural cobblestone appearance can result if fat shrinks or if too much is removed. If this occurs, the condition can be improved through fat injections.

Cost

In the United States, the range of total fees for a facelift extends from $6,000 to $12,000. The average cost is:

Surgeon's fee	$5,500
Anesthesiologist's fee	$1,200
Operating room (facility) fee	$1,700
Hospital fee for overnight stay	$600
Total	$9,000

See "Fees" in Chapter 1 for various factors that might affect your own actual cost.

Multiple Facelifts

There is no limit to the number of facelifts you may have. Multiple facelifts, however, may cause loss of sideburns or a tight face (see the previous section, "Telltale Signs"). If you are seeking a second or third facelift, ask how your surgeon preserves sideburns and avoids an unnaturally tight appearance.

Satisfaction

Most women who undergo a facelift have a reasonable result without complications, and they are typically satisfied. As with many things in life, the greater the degree of improvement, the happier one is for having sought the change. Such is the case with facelifts. The greater your facial sagging, jowls, and neck laxity beforehand, the more dramatic your improvement and likely the more satisfied you will be with the procedure.

Questions to Ask Your Plastic Surgeon

Where will the scars be?
Will your technique make me look like a different person?
How do you prevent high or absent sideburns?
How do you avoid the wind-tunnel look?
How do you avoid attached earlobes?

Eileen, a seventy-three-year-old grandmother, and Debbie, her forty-eight-year-old daughter, both wanted to look younger. They had facelifts performed on the same day so that they could recover side by side. They had similar facial features, and both were pleased with their results. Although Debbie continued to look much younger than Eileen, Debbie's change was not as dramatic. She was almost envious of her mother's impressive change compared to her own modest change.

Tips and Traps

- *Because a facelift will only rejuvenate the lower two-thirds of your face, consider eyelid surgery and a forehead lift at the same time to restore youth and maintain harmony, if those areas lend themselves to rejuvenation.*

- *Quit smoking two weeks to two months prior to surgery.*

- *Quit taking aspirin and other anti-inflammatory medications at least two weeks before surgery.*

- *If you are considering a deep facelift (subperiosteal or cheek lift), anticipate prolonged swelling (one week to six months) and an alteration of your basic facial appearance.*

- *Ask your surgeon to use bupivacaine, a long-lasting local anesthetic, to reduce your postoperative discomfort.*

- *Sleep in a recliner or with your head elevated on pillows for the first several days to minimize swelling. Apply ice frequently.*

- *Expect that your facelift will turn back the clock by about seven to ten years. Your face will continue to age, and you may be ready for another lift within a decade.*

- *Know that repeat facelifts might confer a higher risk of leaving you with telltale signs.*

Concluding Thoughts

Facelift surgery is the cornerstone of facial rejuvenation. It can tighten lax skin, eliminate jowls, reduce double chins, soften the skin fold of your cheeks, and sharpen the angle between your neck and jawline. Because it does not rejuvenate the eyes, the forehead, or facial wrinkles, many women consider other procedures as well—peels, laser resurfacing, eyelid surgery, and a forehead lift. As long as you understand what can be reasonably accomplished by a facelift, you will likely be satisfied with your results.

3

Raising Your Eyebrows

Forehead Lift

The forehead and eyebrows remain the most influential area of the face with regard to facial expression. The eyes and forehead alone can reveal if a person is happy, curious, uncertain, anxious, angry, or contemplative. No other part of the face can achieve this degree of silent communication.

As such, an aging forehead with low brows and deep creases can make a person appear tired or angry. Fortunately, a forehead lift, also called a brow lift, can have a dramatic effect and is among the most powerful options in facial rejuvenation.

Donna, a pleasant sixty-one-year-old, was told by others that she looked angry even though she was a cheerful woman who seldom was irritated. One day, her seven-year-old granddaughter said, "Nanny, why are you always so mad at me?" Not surprisingly, she sought a plastic surgery consultation within a week. Following a forehead lift, her scowl lines softened and her unintended frown faded.

The Good News: Things a Forehead Lift Can Improve

A forehead lift will improve brow position, lateral hoods, horizontal forehead wrinkles, and scowl lines (Figure 3-1).

Brow Position

Put your finger on your eyebrow and press inward toward the bone. Feel for the position of the bony rim above your eye. If your eyebrow position is ideal, it will be above the bony rim of your eye socket. If it has descended, it will be at or below the rim. While looking in the mirror, place your thumb and index finger on your forehead and lift your forehead skin up against the bone. You will see the effect a forehead lift can achieve. A forehead lift will raise your brow to the level of your bony rim or above.

There are two reasons for low brow position: age and genetics. As we age, our skin and soft tissues lose elasticity. This makes them more susceptible to the pull of gravity. Yet aging is not the only reason the brows may be low. Some women inherit low eyebrows. These women often seek a forehead lift in their thirties.

Lateral Hoods and Pseudo Excess Upper Eyelid Skin

Lateral hoods are folds of skin between the eyebrow and the eyelid near the outside corner of the eye. They are named for the hooded appearance they give the

Alex, a thirty-three-year-old police detective, felt she had two strikes against her when it came to meeting new people: her serious job and her serious appearance. This combination made her seem intense and unapproachable. Her serious air stemmed from her low eyebrows—a family curse. Following a forehead lift, her appearance softened, and she felt as though her appearance more closely reflected her lighthearted personality. "It was a good thing the forehead lift helped me," she said laughingly, "because I really didn't want to change careers."

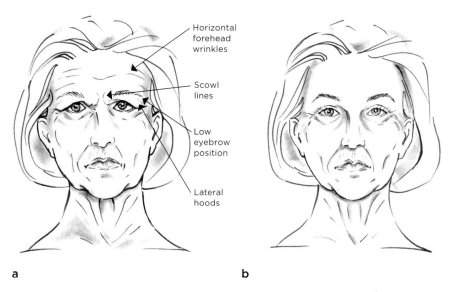

Horizontal forehead wrinkles

Scowl lines

Low eyebrow position

Lateral hoods

a   b

Figure 3-1: *The effects of a forehead lift. (a) Features of an aging face. (b) After a forehead lift, the furrows are improved, the horizontal forehead lines are softened, the eyebrows are higher, and the hoods have been minimized. The crow's feet, excess eyelid skin, puffy eyelids, and the rest of the face are unchanged.*

Arlene, a fifty-eight-year-old concert violinist, had eyelid surgery and was disappointed because she felt her upper eyelids were still baggy. She complained to her surgeon about this, but he refused to remove any more skin. Instead, he recommended a forehead lift. Frustrated, Arlene sought a second opinion from me. After examining her, I told her that her first surgeon was correct. She had had an excellent result and would need a forehead lift for further improvement. Had additional eyelid skin been removed, she would have been unable to close her eyes.

The Good News About Forehead Lifts

- *Brow position can be elevated.*
- *Lateral hoods can be reduced.*
- *Pseudo excess upper eyelid skin can be improved.*
- *Horizontal forehead wrinkles can be softened.*
- *Scowl lines between the eyebrows can be improved.*

eyes. Study your face in the mirror. If you have lateral hoods, you will notice improvement in them when you use your finger to lift your forehead.

When you use your fingers to raise your brow, you will notice an apparent improvement in the excess skin of your entire upper eyelid. The portion of the upper lid that improves is termed *pseudo excess* because it is not truly excess skin—it only appears excess when the brows are descended. When your plastic surgeon evaluates your upper eyelids and forehead, he or she should tell you how much of your upper eyelid problem is due to pseudo excess skin (remedied by a forehead lift) and how much is true excess skin (remedied by eyelid surgery). This will help you decide whether you should have a forehead lift, eyelid surgery, or both.

Horizontal Forehead Wrinkles

Looking in the mirror, raise your eyebrows and note the creases across your forehead. The creases are a direct result of your repeated efforts to raise your eyebrows. As your eyebrows descend with age, you use your forehead muscle progressively more, and the problem worsens over time. A forehead lift elevates your brows, allows your forehead muscle to relax, and reduces your horizontal wrinkles. If you have low eyebrows and deep horizontal forehead creases, you probably look tired and may improve your appearance through a forehead lift.

Scowl Lines

While looking in the mirror, try to frown or look angry. You will drive your eyebrows downward and inward toward your nose, creating furrows and vertical wrinkles between your brows. These are called scowl lines. If you have well-developed scowl lines, you can see them without frowning, because the corrugator muscles that cause them have been well conditioned through repetitive use. This is referred to as an unconscious frown because it lends an unintended angry expression. A forehead lift aims to diminish the muscles responsible for scowling, thereby diminishing the vertical wrinkles between the eyebrows and eliminating the angry look.

The Bad News: Things a Forehead Lift Cannot Improve

A forehead lift will not improve the portion of upper eyelid excess skin that is truly excess. For this, eyelid surgery (blepharoplasty) is needed. It will also not affect crow's feet or puffy eyelids.

Forehead Lift Techniques

Lifting the forehead skin and altering the forehead can be accomplished through three different surgical techniques: endoscopic, coronal, and subcutaneous. Each has advantages and disadvantages. You and your plastic surgeon will select the most appropriate one based on which advantages are most important to you and which disadvantages you can most easily accept.

Some surgeons modify one of these three techniques or combine two techniques. Often such approaches (like those described in this chapter) have more than one name, which confuses patients. If your plastic surgeon uses an unfamiliar term, ask him or her to explain it.

Endoscopic Lift

Endoscopic forehead lift is the most common technique for mild brow droop. Endoscopic surgery enables your surgeon to view the procedure with a tiny camera, the size of an eraser head, inserted under your skin. The surgeon makes four to six small incisions hidden behind the hairline (Figure 3-2, short solid lines). Muscles responsible for scowling are partially removed. Then skin is shifted backward on the head. To ensure temporary support for the skin until it has healed in its new location, some surgeons place

Edith, a sixty-six-year-old newspaper editor, was told by her reporters that she always had a disapproving look when she read their articles. Although the articles were not perfect, they did not deserve the scowls their authors thought they evoked. Edith did not intend her harsh facial expressions and sought to remedy her scowls and deep forehead creases. However, she did not want surgery. She tried Botox injections. Although the injections improved her wrinkles, they caused her forehead muscle to relax, thereby allowing her brows to droop farther. She finally had a forehead lift and was satisfied with the improvement in her wrinkles and brow position.

Kathy, a fifty-three-year-old nurse, sought rejuvenation of her upper eyelids. I estimate that in her case about 70 percent of her upper eyelid problem was due to her low brows and 30 percent was truly excess skin. She chose to have a forehead lift alone, which not surprisingly improved her upper lids by 70 percent. If she had undergone eyelid surgery alone, her improvement would have been about 30 percent. Had she undergone both, her improvement would have been close to 100 percent. All women are different, and the percent contribution due to a descended brow versus excess upper eyelid skin should be estimated by the plastic surgeon prior to surgery.

Betty, a thirty-eight-year-old paralegal, had mild aging. She did not want the numbness or the long scar associated with a coronal forehead lift. Because she wore her hair off her face, she did not want the hairline scar associated with a subcutaneous lift. She chose to have an endoscopic forehead lift and was pleased with her decision.

drill holes or small screws into the skull. Finally, they place sutures around the screws or through the drill holes to anchor the skin. If metal screws are used, they will be removed in the office two weeks later. If absorbable screws are used, they will dissolve within a few months.

Endoscopic lift has several distinct advantages. Large incisions are avoided. Temporary numbness on the top of the scalp (which always occurs following coronal lift) is not usually a problem. Typically, you can expect 50 to 75 percent improvement in wrinkles after an endoscopic lift. Most will still be present, but improved.

The endoscopic forehead lift also has disadvantages. It can raise your hairline by about one-half inch, which may be a problem for those with high foreheads. Although screw and drill hole placement is safe, some women are uncomfortable with this idea. Also, because the frontalis muscle is not altered, women who use their forehead expressively may find that horizontal lines are little improved and quick to return. And those with an overwhelm-

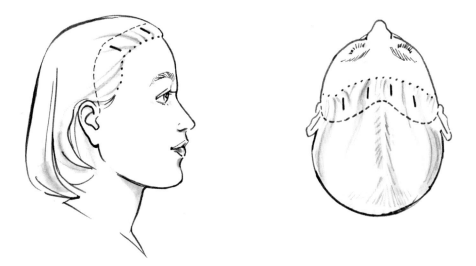

Figure 3-2: *Forehead lift incisions. The endoscopic forehead lift involves four to six small incisions, hidden behind the hairline (short solid lines). The coronal forehead lift involves a single long incision from one ear to the other, behind the hairline (dashed line). The subcutaneous forehead lift involves a single long incision on top of the forehead, at the hairline (dotted line).*

ing descent of the brow or deep creases will likely be disappointed with an endoscopic lift because they will find it less effective and shorter lasting than the other options.

Generally, women with minimal to moderate forehead aging and an average or low hairline height prefer this technique to the other two (see Table 3-1).

Coronal Lift

In a coronal forehead lift, the incision extends across the top of the head from ear to ear (Figure 3-2, dashed line). The forehead muscle (the frontalis muscle) and the corrugator muscles are surgically weakened. The surgeon then removes excess skin, up to an inch in width and sometimes more.

Scowl Lines Alone

If you are troubled by scowl lines but do not have droopy brows, your surgeon can alter the corrugator muscles, which are responsible for scowl lines, through upper eyelid incisions. This is especially useful if you are also interested in upper eyelid surgery (see Chapter 4).

Table 3-1 Comparison of Techniques

	Endoscopic	Coronal	Subcutaneous
Site of incision?	Multiple small incisions behind hairline	Incision from ear to ear across top of head	Incision across top of forehead
Scalp numbness?	Rarely	Yes, lasts about 6 months	Rarely
Raises hairline?	Yes	Yes	No
Requires attachment to skull?	Recommended	No	No
Risk of recurrent forehead droop?	Some	Rare	Rare
Effect on horizontal wrinkles?	Mild to moderate	Significant	Significant
Effect on vertical scowl lines?	Moderate	Moderate	Moderate
Safe to have forehead laser or peel at the same time?	Yes	Yes	No
Who should not have this operation?	Those with severe brow droop, deep horizontal creases, or a high hairline	Those with a high hairline	Those who wear their hair off their face, smokers, and those unwilling to accept scar
Ideal candidate for this procedure?	Those with mild to moderate aging of their forehead	Those with severe aging: major brow droop and deep horizontal wrinkles	Those with a high forehead who wear bangs

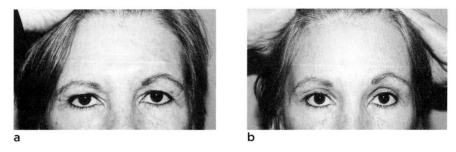

a   b

Coronal brow lift. (a) A sixty-year-old woman before surgery. (b) Six weeks after a coronal brow lift and upper blepharoplasty. Note that brow asymmetry is improved but is not resolved.

Coronal lifts offer several advantages. All muscles that contribute to wrinkles and scowling can be altered, including the frontalis muscle, which is responsible for deep horizontal creases. Screws are not necessary, and the lift may last longer than with the endoscopic technique because excess scalp is removed rather than shifted up and back. Typically the scar is not visible in those with thick hair. This technique can be used in anyone, but is particularly useful in women with severe descent of the brows, deep forehead creases, and a low hairline.

Coronal lifts impose several disadvantages. Numbness and itching behind the scar on top of the head can last for six months. The scar is long, which is a disadvantage for those with thin hair. As with the endoscopic lift, your hairline will be raised following surgery, which can be an advantage if you have a low hairline, but a problem if you have a high hairline. Generally, women with advanced forehead droop and an average or low hairline height prefer this procedure to the other two techniques.

Mary, a seventy-nine-year-old widow with advanced forehead aging, desired a forehead lift, eyelid surgery, and a facelift. Because of her advanced wrinkles, deep furrows, and very low brows, she had a coronal lift for the maximal effect. An endoscopic lift would not give her enough improvement, and she did not want a subcutaneous lift, because she wore her hair back.

Subcutaneous (Skin Only) Lift

The incision for a subcutaneous forehead lift is just below the hairline (Figure 3-2, dotted line). Subcutaneous lifts offer several advantages. Because the incision is in front of the hairline, the hairline is not shifted upward when skin is removed. In contrast to a coronal lift, the sensory nerves to the top of the head are not divided, and problems with numbness and itching are uncommon. Improvement in horizontal creases is dramatic, just as in a coronal lift.

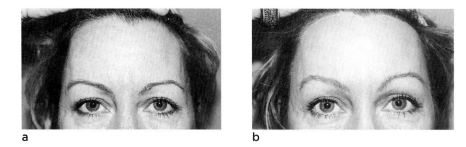

a   b

Subcutaneous brow lift. (a) A fifty-four-year-old woman before surgery. In her case, 70 percent of excess upper lid skin was due to droopy brows, and 30 percent was due to excess eyelid skin. (b) Five months after subcutaneous brow lift. Note the hairline scar. This woman would have had subtle additional improvement if a blepharoplasty had also been performed.

The main disadvantage is a visible scar along the hairline, a concern for women who wear their hair back. The scar may heal imperceptibly, but this can neither be predicted nor guaranteed. Skin circulation is compromised more with a subcutaneous lift than with an endoscopic or a coronal lift because of technical details pertaining to the procedure. Therefore, smokers will have more healing problems with this technique than with other techniques, and they must quit smoking prior to surgery.

Women who have a high forehead and are willing to accept a scar along the hairline may prefer this technique to the other two.

Complications

If a qualified plastic surgeon performs your operation, both your procedure and recovery are likely to be uneventful. Even in ideal circumstances, however, complications may occur. In addition to the specific complications mentioned here, refer to Chapter 1 for an explanation of general complications that may occur with any procedure.

Ann, a sixty-two-year-old nonsmoker with heavy brows and deep wrinkles, wore bangs over her face and had a high forehead. She chose the subcutaneous lift for a few reasons. An endoscopic lift would not have provided as much improvement, and a coronal lift would have shifted her hairline back farther. Because she wore her hair forward, her hairline scar was hidden.

Pam, a fifty-year-old fund-raiser, sought rejuvenation of her forehead. After discussing the options, she made it clear that she did not want a coronal lift or an endoscopic lift because her hairline was already high. She did not want a subcutaneous lift because she wore her hair pulled back, was unwilling to change her hairstyle, and was concerned about scar appearance. It became evident that accepting her current brow droop was better in Pam's case than imposing a higher forehead or visible scar. She rightly decided to forgo surgery.

What to Expect

- *Anesthesia:* Sedation or general.

- *Location of operation:* Office or hospital.

- *Length of surgery:* Thirty to ninety minutes.

- *Length of stay:* Outpatient (home same day).

- *Discomfort:* Mild; anticipate one to four days of prescription pain medication. Some take only Tylenol.

- *Swelling and bruising:* Improves in ten to fourteen days. You can reduce swelling through constant head elevation and frequent application of ice. You may develop black eyes temporarily.

- *Bandages:* Removed in one to three days.

- *Stitches:* Removed in seven to ten days. If your surgeon placed metal screws in your skull (for endoscopic lift), they will be removed in two to four weeks.

- *Contact lenses:* May be worn in one week.

- *Makeup:* May be worn in three to five days.

- *Presentable in public:* Seven to fourteen days, with the help of makeup.

- *Work:* You may feel capable of returning within three days, but your appearance will be the limiting factor.

- *Exercise:* May be resumed in two weeks.

- *Final result:* Seen in two to four weeks.

- *Duration of results:* Depending on your age, degree of brow droop, depth of forehead creases, and technique chosen, your forehead lift may last five to twenty years, with most lasting ten to fifteen years.

Forehead Paralysis

Paralysis of one side of the forehead occurs in fewer than 1 percent of patients. It is usually temporary, and full motion generally returns within a few months.

Brow Asymmetry

After a forehead lift, your new brow position may appear higher on one side than on the other. In most cases, the asymmetry was present before surgery. Therefore, it is important for you and your surgeon to recognize any asymmetry and discuss it prior to surgery. Asymmetry can be managed in two ways. The first option is for your surgeon to lift both brows to the same level. This may seem ideal, but if you have become accustomed to looking at your asymmetric brows for decades, as most have, then you may have difficulty adjusting to your new symmetric look. As noted in Chapter 1, everyone is asymmetric. Maintaining your asymmetry, therefore, is a reasonable option.

Permanent Loss of Hair

Following a coronal or an endoscopic lift, small bald spots may occur along the scar line. If your hair fails to grow back, you may comb your hair over the bald spot or have hair transplanted to fill the bald spot. Depending on its size, you may also ask your plastic surgeon to surgically remove the bald spot.

Numbness

As previously mentioned, temporary numbness on the top of the head is expected following a coronal lift. Numbness of the entire forehead, however, can occur with any technique when there has been damage to the sensory nerves. These nerves emerge through the forehead bone directly above the eye and run through the scowl muscles. Because the scowl muscles are removed or modified during surgery, these nerves are at risk for being stretched, cut, or burned, even when your surgeon is cautious and experienced. Numbness may be temporary or permanent.

Early Relapse

Early relapse means that your brow descends again within a few months. This may occur in anyone, but it is more common after an endoscopic lift if your forehead was inadequately suspended at the time of surgery. Because screws and drill holes are now usually employed, this problem has become less common. Early relapse does not usually occur after a coronal or subcutaneous forehead lift.

Telltale Signs

As with any procedure, you should be aware of the possible telltale signs before you proceed.

Unnatural Facial Expression

If your eyebrows are not raised in harmony to a natural level, unnatural facial expressions can result. The brows may be raised to an artificially high position, leaving you with a surprised look (Figure 3-3). If the inner half of your eyebrow is raised more than the outer half, a sad appearance may occur (Figure 3-4a). If the outer half is raised more than the inner half, a strange or sinister look may result (Figure 3-4b). The brows may spread

Figure 3-3: *The surprised look is a telltale sign that results after the eyebrows have been excessively raised. This problem is difficult to correct.*

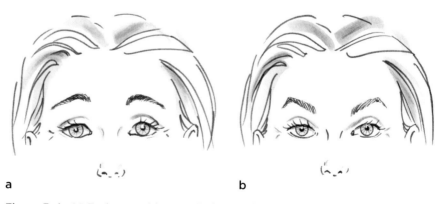

a   b

Figure 3-4: *(a) Eyebrows with excessively raised inner portions result in a telltale sad appearance. (b) Eyebrows with excessively raised outer portions result in a sinister appearance.*

apart, creating an unnaturally wide gap between them. Some of these problems can be corrected through further surgery, others cannot be corrected. The best way to prevent these problems is through selection of a qualified and experienced plastic surgeon. Even so, these expressions might occur.

Visible Scar

When a subcutaneous lift is performed, the scar may be visible if you wear your hair pulled back off your face. Avoid this technique if you are unwilling to wear bangs.

High Hairline (High Forehead)

If you have a high hairline and choose a technique other than the subcutaneous one, your hairline will be shifted farther upward, creating an unnatural appearance (Figure 3-5). This can be avoided by choosing a subcutaneous lift.

Muscle Bulges

Small, soft bulges may occur above your nose between your eyebrows following surgery. These can be corrected through revision brow surgery or Botox injections.

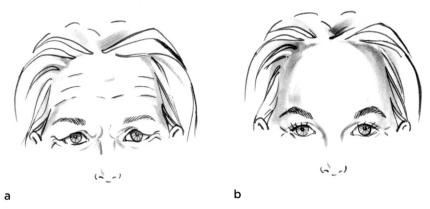

a   b

Figure 3-5: *(a) A high hairline before forehead lift. (b) Following either endoscopic or coronal lift, an already high hairline can appear unnaturally high.*

Questions to Ask Your Plastic Surgeon

Do I need eyelid surgery too?

Which technique do you recommend in my case?

If endoscopic surgery is planned, how will you secure my new brow position?

Can you correct my brow asymmetry?

Where will the incisions be?

Maureen, a forty-nine-year-old cellular phone salesperson, returned to work two weeks following a secret forehead lift and was inundated with comments about how well rested she looked. They all wanted to know where she had vacationed. She simply smiled and said, "Jamaica." Then she quickly added, "I wore a lot of sunscreen."

Cost

In the United States, the range of total fees for a forehead lift extends from $3,500 to $5,500. The average cost is:

Surgeon's fee	$ 2,800
Anesthesiologist's fee	$ 700
Operating room (facility) fee	$ 900
Total	$ 4,400

See "Fees" in Chapter 1 for various factors that might affect your own actual cost.

Satisfaction

As with many plastic surgery procedures, satisfaction following a forehead lift is tied to expectations and the degree of improvement. Those persons with advanced droop of their brows and deep creases are likely to see greater change than those with more subtle signs of aging. Regardless of the starting point, all will see some improvement in brow position, horizontal forehead wrinkles, and scowl lines. Because a forehead lift improves lateral hoods, it can also enhance the appearance of the upper eyelids. However, some women are disappointed due to inflated expectations, complications, telltale signs, or recurrence of forehead droop. Most are reasonably satisfied with their results, provided their expectations were realistic.

Concluding Thoughts

An aging upper face can cause you to unintentionally appear tired or angry. A forehead lift involves raising your brows and altering the underlying muscles to soften your appearance. Depending on the severity of your problem, the height of your forehead, and your hairstyle, one of several techniques may be chosen and tailored to your needs.

Among all facial rejuvenation procedures, a forehead lift can have the most dramatic effect on a person's overall appearance.

Tips and Traps

- *Quit taking aspirin and other anti-inflammatory medication for two weeks prior to surgery. Discuss all of your nonprescription medications with your doctor.*

- *If you have mild to moderate brow droop and horizontal wrinkles, an endoscopic lift may be the most appropriate.*

- *If you have advanced brow droop with deep wrinkles, a coronal forehead lift may be the most appropriate.*

- *If you have a high forehead and wear your hair forward, a subcutaneous forehead lift may be the most appropriate.*

- *If you have a high forehead and are unwilling to wear bangs or accept a hairline scar, you probably should not have a brow lift.*

- *Anticipate that your forehead will look higher after an endoscopic or coronal lift than it did before surgery.*

- *A forehead lift will not improve your baggy eyelids or crow's feet.*

- *To minimize swelling, sleep in a recliner or with your head elevated on pillows for the first several days after surgery. Apply ice compresses frequently!*

4

Rejuvenating Your Eyes

Eyelid Surgery

yelid surgery, or blepharoplasty, remains the third most commonly performed cosmetic procedure in the United States. This is not surprising, as our eyes are central to communication. When we speak, we look each other in the eye. When we wish to better understand one another, when we ask questions, and when we search for answers, we look into the eyes of the other person. Much emphasis is therefore placed on the appearance of the eyes. But before exploring the changes that eyelid surgery can accomplish, it is helpful to understand the aesthetic goal of eyelid surgery.

Joyce, a sixty-three-year-old widow, was alone for several years before meeting and falling in love with a man eight years her junior. He did not mind, but she was self-conscious about their age difference, and she wanted to close the apparent gap. She underwent eyelid surgery, which restored a more energetic and youthful appearance.

The Ideal Eyelid

In the aesthetically ideal eyelid (Figure 4-1), the upper lid rests just below the top of the iris, which is the colored ring around the pupil. The lower lid rests just above the lower border of the iris. Hence, the white of the eye should not be seen either above or below the iris when you are looking straight ahead.

Figure 4-1: *Aesthetically ideal eyes. Note the position of the eyelids as they relate to the iris. (The iris is the colored ring around the pupil.)*

The Good News: Things Eyelid Surgery Will Improve

Most cosmetic eyelid surgery is performed to correct bagginess and puffiness of the eyelids, sometimes altering the lid position as well (Figure 4-2).

Excess Skin of the Eyelids (Baggy Eyelids)

Excess skin of the eyelids creates a heavy and tired appearance. Look in the mirror and close one eye while leaving the other eye open. Using your thumb and index finger, pinch the extra skin of your closed upper eyelid. The amount of skin that you can easily pinch between your thumb and finger with your eye closed is roughly the amount of skin that can be removed from the upper eyelids during eyelid surgery. Excess skin of the lower eyelid, if it exists, can be seen without special maneuvers.

Protruding Fat of the Eyelids (Puffy Eyelids)

It is normal to have fat surrounding your eyeball. But over time this fat may protrude into the eyelids, creating puffiness and casting a shadow or dark circle under your eyes. Surprisingly, this is not related to weight gain, and weight loss will not improve it. It is simply related to genetics and aging. Removing fat through eyelid surgery will reduce puffiness and improve dark shadows, if the shadows are due to bulging fat.

Look in the mirror and close one eye. While gently pressing on your eye through the closed upper lid, watch the skin above and below that eye. If the skin above and below your closed eye bulges while you are pressing, then protruding fat is likely causing your puffy eyelids, and you would benefit from the removal of fat during eyelid surgery.

> **The Good News About Eyelid Surgery**
>
> - *Excess skin of the upper and lower eyelids is removed.*
> - *Puffiness of the eyelids due to fat improves.*
> - *Droopy upper eyelids improve.*
> - *Lax lower eyelids improve.*

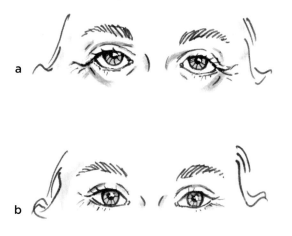

Figure 4-2: *The effects of eyelid surgery. (a) Eyelid bagginess, puffiness, upper lid droopiness, and lower lid laxity. (b) Eyelid surgery can correct these problems, but it will not affect crow's feet, furrows, brow position, or lateral hoods.*

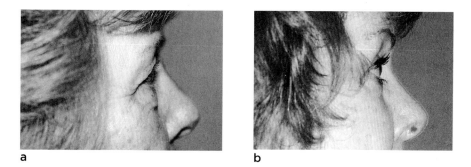

Upper and lower blepharoplasty with canthopexy. (a) A fifty-nine-year-old woman before surgery. (b) Two years after surgery.

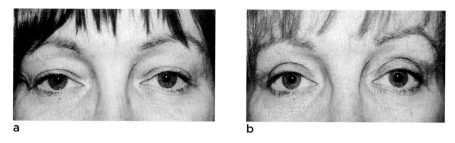

Upper blepharoplasty. (a) Before upper blepharoplasty in a fifty-two-year-old woman. (b) Eleven months after surgery. A brow lift would have given additional subtle improvement, as brow droop was and continues to be a minor contributor to apparent excess skin in the upper eyelid.

Droopy Upper Eyelids

Look in the mirror. Pay careful attention to the lower edge of your upper eyelid. As previously mentioned, it should fall just below the top of your iris. You should be able to see most of the iris above the pupil, but not the very top of it (Figure 4-1). If the lower edge of your upper eyelid blocks more than the very top of your iris, then your upper eyelid is droopy (Figure 4-3). Plastic surgeons call this condition *eyelid ptosis* (the *p* is silent).

In some cases, droopiness is so severe that the edge of the upper eyelid encroaches upon the pupil and interferes with vision. Those with droopiness of the upper eyelid are often told that they look tired or

Melissa, a thirty-two-year-old stay-at-home mom, was frustrated that her eyes appeared puffy. Her friends of similar age did not have this problem. Following eyelid surgery during which only fat was removed, her puffiness was gone. Not surprisingly, her sister had the same eyelid problem and requested the same procedure. When young women have the problem of protruding fat, it is almost always an inherited trait.

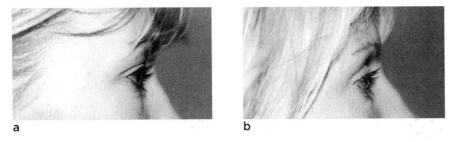

a   b

Blepharoplasty in a young woman. (a) A thirty-four-year-old woman before upper and lower blepharoplasty. Note the puffiness. (b) Three months after surgery.

Figure 4-3: *Droopy upper eyelids. The upper eyelid covers some of the pupil and more of the iris than normal.*

that their eyes appear small. The most common cause of eyelid droop is weakness or detachment of the levator muscle, which is responsible for holding the eyelid open.

Lax (Loose) Lower Eyelids and Canthopexy

Looking in the mirror, pay careful attention to the position of the upper edge of your lower eyelid. As previously mentioned, it should rest just above the lower border of your iris so that you can see no white below your iris. If it doesn't, you have loose lower eyelids, or what plastic surgeons call lax lower eyelids. If laxity is mild, it may cause dry eye symptoms but the lids will look normal. If laxity is severe, dry eye symptoms may be debilitating, and the lids may look droopy. Severely lax lower lids droop below the iris, allowing the white of the eye to be seen between the pupil and the lid (Figure 4-4).

Even if your lower lid position appears normal, you may still have mild or moderate laxity. If your lid is slow in returning to your eyeball when you pull your lower lid down with your finger, then mild or moderate laxity is present. Your lid should snap back instantly; if there is a delay, you have at least mild laxity. If you must blink to get your lower lid to return to your eyeball, then laxity is at least moderate.

Figure 4-4: *Droopy lower eyelids. Severe lower lid laxity appears as droopy lower eyelids. The white of the eye can be seen below the iris.*

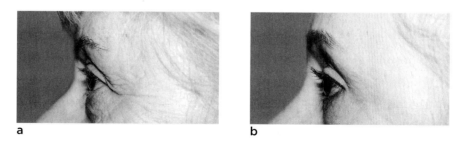

a   b

Blepharoplasty in a middle-aged women. (a) A fifty-six-year-old woman before surgery. (b) Four months after upper and lower blepharoplasty with canthopexy.

Laxity is important because it is associated with postoperative dry eye syndrome. Any degree of laxity must be recognized prior to surgery so that it can be addressed. Untreated laxity will worsen as a result of lower eyelid surgery. To correct laxity, a procedure called canthopexy may be performed with your eyelid surgery. It involves placement of a stitch to tighten your lower eyelids—preventing droopiness and hopefully averting dry eye symptoms. Your surgeon should assess eyelid position and tone to determine your need for this procedure. If canthopexy is recommended, you should agree to it, but anticipate a lengthier recovery during which time your eyes will appear temporarily slanted.

Scowl Lines

The scowl lines between your brows can be improved during upper eyelid surgery. If this is a concern to you, ask your surgeon about altering your corrugator muscles, which cause scowl lines, during your upper eyelid procedure.

The Bad News: Things Eyelid Surgery May Not Improve

As with any operation, there are limitations to what eyelid surgery will be able to improve. To better ensure satisfaction with your eyelid surgery, it is just as important to be aware of the problems that it will not correct as those it does.

Dark Circles

Dark circles under your eyes may be caused by shadows or skin discoloration. If your dark circles are due to shadows caused by bulging fat, eyelid surgery will help. If they are due to discoloration, eyelid surgery alone will not help.

To determine if your dark circles are due to discoloration or shadows, study your eyelids in the mirror. Using your index and long fingers, stretch the skin of your lower eyelid upward and outward. If the dark circles disappear, then they were due to the shadow cast by fat bulges of your lower eyelids and may improve following lower eyelid surgery. If the dark circles remain, they are due to skin discoloration and will not improve following eyelid surgery. Chemical peels or laser resurfacing can sometimes improve discoloration.

Malar Bags

Malar bags are areas of puffiness on the cheeks, just below the eyelids. They are often confused with puffy eyelids because the two are so close. To determine whether your puffiness is due to eyelid fat or malar bags, close one eye. Gently press on your eyeball through your closed lid. Eyelid fat will bulge in response to pressure, but malar bags will not change.

Although close in proximity, they are worlds apart with regard to treatment. Eyelid fat is improved through eyelid surgery. Malar bags are not. Many treatments have been used for malar bags, but none have achieved consistent or reliable results. Malar bags are due to swelling, and swelling is something that surgery (with few exceptions) does not generally improve.

Tear Troughs

Tear troughs are the creases that some women have from the inner corner of the eye to the cheek. Eyelid surgery does not directly affect tear troughs, although removing protrusive eyelid fat above them often makes the tear troughs less obvious by comparison: if one lowers a hill, the valley does not appear as deep. Tear troughs can be addressed through fillers (see Chapter 11).

Crow's Feet

Crow's feet, the tiny wrinkles that appear at the outer corner of eyes, will not be improved through eyelid surgery. These wrinkles can be treated with nonsurgical options.

Pseudo Excess Skin

Things would be simple if all of the excess skin you see in your upper eyelids were just that: excess skin. Too often, it is not. In most cases, the eyebrows have dropped, contributing to the problem of excess skin of the upper lids.

To determine how much of your upper lid problem is due to your descended brows, use your fingers to pull your brow up to the bone above your eyeball (Figure 4-5). When you do, you will note a definite improvement in your upper lids. The amount of improvement you see with this maneuver is termed *pseudo excess*, as it is due to low brows, not excess skin of the upper lids.

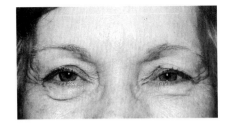

a

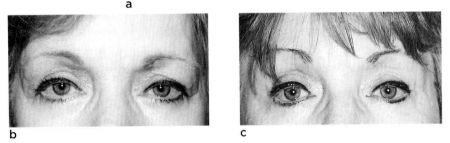

b   c

Blepharoplasty alone. (a) A fifty-nine-year-old woman before upper and lower bleph-aroplasty. Fifty percent of her excess eyelid skin was true excess, and 50 percent was due to droopy brows. (b) Twelve months after upper and lower blepharoplasty with canthopexy. Although she has substantial improvement, additional brow lift would have given her more. (c) The same woman is shown raising her eyebrows. This mimics the effect of a brow lift with respect to brow position and apparent reduction of upper eyelid skin.

Figure 4-5: *The effect of a droopy forehead on baggy eyes. This woman is raising her left eyebrow to demonstrate that a significant portion of her apparent excess eyelid skin is actually due to a droopy forehead.*

As you lift your forehead skin, you will continue to note some excess eyelid skin, although it will appear less abundant than it did when you were not supporting your forehead. The excess skin you see is from your eyelid and will be improved through eyelid surgery.

This exercise is worth repeating because it demonstrates that the excess upper eyelid skin that you perceive is not truly all excess. Anywhere from

Potential Components of Eyelid Surgery

- *Upper eyelid skin removal (for baggy upper eyelids)*

- *Upper eyelid fat removal (for puffy upper eyelids)*

- *Upper eyelid lift (for droopy upper eyelids)*

- *Lower eyelid skin removal (for baggy lower eyelids)*

- *Lower eyelid fat removal (for puffy lower eyelids)*

- *Lower eyelid tightening (for lax lower eyelids)*

10 to 90 percent is due to excess eyelid skin and the rest is due to droopy eyebrows. This percentage differs for everyone. Your surgeon should determine your ratio of excess to pseudo excess skin prior to surgery to help you understand the variable improvement you can expect from eyelid surgery, forehead lift, or both. In short, if you have both a droopy forehead and excess eyelid skin, eyelid surgery alone will improve only the portion that is due to true excess, and brow lift surgery will only improve the portion that is due to droopy brows (see Chapter 3).

The Operation

Eyelid surgery is highly individualized. Some women seek surgery of the upper lids, some seek surgery of the lower lids, and some seek both. Some need skin removal, some need fat removal, and some need both. Some need their lower lids tightened, some need their upper lids raised, and some need both. Your plastic surgeon makes these determinations with the maneuvers described earlier. Your operation should be tailored to your needs.

Upper Eyelid Surgery

Upper eyelid surgery is performed through an incision that is designed to remove excess skin. The resultant scar falls along the natural crease of your upper eyelid and will be nearly invisible once it heals (Figure 4-6). Through this incision, upper eyelid fat can be removed, if necessary.

a

b

Figure 4-6: *Incisions and scars. (a) The standard incisions for both upper and lower eyelid surgeries (dashed lines). (b) The resultant scar positions (solid lines). Due to the position of the scars and the nature of skin in this area, these scars usually are not visible to others.*

Lower Eyelid Surgery

Lower eyelid surgery can be performed through one of two incisions. The traditional incision is just below your lower eyelashes and extends out along one of your crow's feet (Figure 4-6). Through this incision, excess skin and fat can be removed if necessary. Lower eyelid tone can be also be improved through a canthopexy, which is performed on the outer corners of the eyes. The traditional incision heals well and often becomes imperceptible within two to four weeks.

The other option is for those who have excess fat of the lower eyelids but no excess skin, such as young women with puffy lower eyelids. The surgeon makes an incision on the inside of the lower eyelid called a transconjunctival incision (Figure 4-7). Through this incision, fat but not skin can be removed from the lower eyelid. This incision is not visible, even immediately following surgery. Stitches are unnecessary.

Complications

When your operation is performed by a qualified plastic surgeon, both your procedure and recovery will likely be uneventful. Even in ideal circumstances, however, complications may occur. In addition to the specific complications mentioned here, refer to Chapter 1 for an explanation of general complications that may occur with any procedure.

Blindness

Blindness occurs in about 1 in 10,000 who undergo eyelid surgery and is usually related to bleeding following removal of eyelid fat. Bleeding behind an eyeball pushes it outward and exerts pressure on the retina, causing blindness in that eye. This is rare, but almost always permanent.

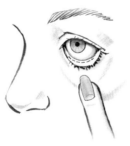

Figure 4-7: *Incision on the inside of the lower eyelid. This incision (dashed line) may be used when removing only fat.*

Visual Disturbance

Double vision or blurred vision can occur due to damaged or swollen eye muscles. It occurs in less than 1 percent of women, is most often temporary, and usually improves within a few days or weeks.

What to Expect

- **Anesthesia:** *General, sedation, or local.*
- **Location of operation:** *Office or hospital.*
- **Length of surgery:** *Thirty to ninety minutes.*
- **Length of stay:** *Outpatient (home same day).*
- **Discomfort:** *Mild. Anticipate one to five days of prescription pain medication or Tylenol. Some require no pain medication.*
- **Swelling and bruising:** *Improve within three to fourteen days, depending on the extent of surgery. Following skin removal only, expect three to five days. Following skin and fat removal with canthopexy, expect seven to fourteen days. You can reduce swelling through constant head elevation and frequent application of ice.*
- **Bandages:** *None. You will be instructed to place ice compresses on your eyes for one to three days.*
- **Stitches:** *Will be removed in two to five days. If surgery of the lower lids is performed through the inside of the lids, suture removal is unnecessary.*
- **Watery eyes:** *Expect that your eyes will temporarily be prone to excess tearing, especially when you are outside on a windy day. This typically improves within several weeks.*
- **Slanted eyes:** *If you have canthopexy, anticipate that your eyes will appear slanted for about two weeks. There will also be greater discomfort.*
- **Contact lenses:** *May be worn in seven to fourteen days. Glasses may be worn immediately.*
- **Eye makeup:** *May be worn in seven to ten days.*
- **Presentable in public:** *Three to fourteen days with the help of makeup, depending on the extent of surgery.*
- **Work:** *You may feel capable of returning within one to five days, but your appearance will be the limiting factor.*
- **Exercise:** *May be resumed in two weeks.*
- **Sun protection:** *Six months SPF 15 or higher.*
- **Final result:** *Seen in four to eight weeks.*
- **Duration of results:** *Expect your results to last ten to twenty years, although there is quite a bit of variation.*

Dry Eye Syndrome

Dry eye syndrome is a condition in which the eyes feel dry and gritty, as though there is sand in them. The eyes usually water in response to these sensations. Vision is blurred, eyes are often painful, and sensitivity to light may be markedly increased. Although many report these symptoms temporarily following eyelid surgery, the eyes should return to normal within a few days or weeks. If persistent, dry eye syndrome can markedly compromise your quality of life.

Persistent dry eye syndrome can result from lower eyelid surgery; upper eyelid surgery is less likely to cause it. A number of possible causes exist. Not all are predictable or preventable. Dry eye syndrome may sometimes be prevented in high-risk patients by limiting the amount of skin and fat removed from the lower lids and by tightening the lower lids through a canthopexy procedure.

Treatment for dry eye syndrome depends on the cause. If due to lower lid laxity, it may be improved through canthopexy. If due to the removal of too much eyelid skin, it may be improved through skin grafting to the eyelids. If due to insufficient tearing, then eye drops, lacrimal plugs, and your ophthalmologist may help.

Inability to Close Your Eyes

If you are unable to close your eyes the day of surgery, do not be alarmed. Most often, that ability will return shortly. If not, frequent use of eyedrops and lubricant will help until you are able to do so.

Corneal Abrasion

During surgery, you may sustain an inadvertent scratch to your cornea. A corneal abrasion is extremely painful and is treated by patching the eye closed for one to three days.

Chemosis

Chemosis is the swelling and irritation of the whites of the eyes, also called the sclera. It also involves swelling of the lining of the eyelids. This most often occurs in association

Risk Factors for Dry Eye Syndrome After Eyelid Surgery

1. *Lax lower lid before surgery: if canthopexy was not performed, your lower lid may be pulled down with resultant dry eye syndrome.*
2. *Dry eye tendencies before surgery: for example, those who use eye drops routinely before surgery are at higher risk for dry eye syndrome.*
3. *Preoperative features of flat cheeks and prominent eyes: for uncertain reasons, this particular anatomy may predispose a person to dry eye syndrome.*
4. *Bad luck: dry eye syndrome may occur for no known reason.*

with the transconjunctival incision, the canthopexy procedure, or both. In each case, symptoms are temporary and will improve faster with judicious use of steroid eyedrops.

Skin Cysts

Tiny skin cysts, called milia, may appear along the scar line. This is more common when stitches remain for five or more days. Milia go away on their own or may be removed in the office as a minor procedure.

Telltale Signs

Unlike the telltale signs of a facelift or a forehead lift, which cause only cosmetic problems, some telltale signs of eyelid surgery can alter eyelid function and seriously compromise your quality of life.

The Lower Eyelid Retraction Versus Droop

A retracted lower eyelid is pulled downward due to previous surgery or trauma. A droopy lower eyelid is pulled downward due to natural causes such as gravity and lid laxity. The appearance may be similar, but the cause is different.

Lower Lid Retraction

If the lower eyelid falls below the iris, then the white of the eye will be visible. This is called lower lid retraction, or ectropion, and is considered a cosmetic problem (Figure 4-8), but may also cause dry eye syndrome. This problem is most commonly due to a lax lower eyelid, but it may also be due to the removal of too much skin. This is a difficult problem to solve. Treatment involves canthopexy (tightening the lower lid), skin grafting to the lower lid, or both.

Figure 4-8: *Lower lid retraction is evident by the white of the eye below the iris. It may be caused by too much skin removal, lack of lower eyelid support, or both.*

Upper Lid Retraction

Upper lid retraction, also called lagophthalmos, is an inability to close the eye completely and can be due to overzealous skin removal. In order to correct this problem, a skin graft to the upper eyelid may be required. Skin grafts never look the same as natural skin, and the final cosmetic result may unfortunately be less than satisfactory.

Hollow (Sunken) Eyes

If too much fat is removed or if the remaining fat shrinks after surgery, your eyes will appear sunken. Hollowness conjures images of malnutrition. This is one of the most common telltale signs of eyelid surgery and may be improved through fat injection.

Cost

In the United States, the range of total fees for eyelid surgery extends from $3,000 to $7,000. The average cost is:

Surgeon's fee	$2,600
Anesthesiologist's fee	$700
Operating room (facility) fee	$800
Total	$4,100

See "Fees" in Chapter 1 for various factors that might affect your own actual cost.

These averages are for the removal of skin, fat, or both from the upper and lower eyelids. If you need repair of droopy upper or lower lids, expect to pay more. If you are interested in the removal of skin or fat from either the upper or the lower lids, but not both lids, then plan to pay an average total fee of $2,000 to $3,000.

Questions to Ask Your Plastic Surgeon

Are my upper eyelids droopy?

Do I have adequate tone of my lower eyelid?

Do I need lower eyelid support?

Will the lower eyelid incision be inside or outside of the eyelid?

How do you avoid removing too much skin or fat?

Am I at risk for dry eye syndrome?

Do I need a forehead lift, too?

Satisfaction

Eyelid surgery can rejuvenate old, droopy, tired eyes. Because the eyes are the focal point of the face, eyelid surgery can affect the whole appearance. The procedure and recovery are relatively brief. Satisfaction is generally high, and eyelid surgery is one of the three most commonly sought cosmetic operations.

Tips and Traps

- *If your surgeon tells you a forehead lift is also recommended, ask how much improvement you can expect from eyelid surgery alone, how much from forehead lift alone, and how much if combined. Then make your decision.*

- *Dark circles under your eyes will not disappear after eyelid surgery unless you can make them disappear before surgery by stretching your lower eyelid skin.*

- *Your crow's feet will not improve through eyelid surgery.*

- *Do not have a chemical peel or laser procedure within three months of lower eyelid surgery if the incisions are made on the outside of your eyelids.*

- *If you do not need skin removed from your lower lids, then request an incision on the inside of your eyelids.*

- *Eyelid surgery will not rejuvenate your skin. For that, pursue skin care or a resurfacing procedure described in Chapters 11 and 12.*

- *If you have dry eyes, get evaluated by an ophthalmologist before surgery to identify correctable causes. Surgery can usually be performed; however, your surgeon should consider canthopexy or remove less skin than initially planned. Otherwise, your dry eye symptoms may worsen.*

- *Beware any plastic surgeon who does not assess your lid tone or who does not recommend canthopexy if your lid tone is weak.*

- *Understand that canthopexy causes more swelling and may delay recovery by an additional week.*

- *Sleep in a recliner or with your head elevated on pillows for the first several days after surgery to minimize swelling.*

- *Ask your plastic surgeon to use a tiny (30-gauge) needle for injection of local anesthesia during the procedure, as this will reduce your bruising.*

Concluding Thoughts

Cosmetic eyelid problems may due to be a combination of excess skin, protruding fat, and unfavorable eyelid position. Surgery should be closely tailored to the needs of the individual. As with any procedure, there are risks; but here the stakes are high, as complications can result in disabling eye problems. Finding a well-qualified plastic surgeon, together with your understanding of the issues, will give you the best chance for a safe and successful outcome.

5

Refining Your Nose

Rhinoplasty

Betsy, a twenty-nine-year-old computer programmer, was shy. She had difficulty meeting people and was always the quiet one in the crowd. Whenever she met someone, she felt certain that the person was staring at her nose, even when the person wasn't. She knew that the problem was not in the way others saw her, but in how she saw herself. Her large nose distorted her self-image and made it difficult for her to be comfortable around others. After undergoing rhinoplasty, she immediately became confident, outgoing, and talkative. She felt better about herself and was therefore more comfortable around others. Within six months, she moved from the programming division to the sales division—something she had never imagined she would want to do.

Indisputably, the nose is a pivotal facial feature. A nose in harmony with the rest of the face blends and is unnoticed. A nose in disharmony draws attention. Because the nose is a focal point, any minor unattractive feature may seem magnified and can alter self-image, which is why many women choose to alter this feature.

Cosmetic nose surgery is known as rhinoplasty. The name derives from the Greek term *rhino* (meaning "nose") and *plasty* (meaning "to shape or reform"). Rhinoplasty can change noses in many ways. It is possible to enlarge a small nose, reduce a large nose, smooth a bumpy nose, lift a droopy nose, straighten a crooked nose, narrow a wide nose, lengthen a short nose, and so on. Yet limitations exist.

Is There a Perfect Nose?

Every face is different in size, shape, and contour, and thus the perfect nose for each face is different. Despite this, certain nasal characteristics are considered aesthetically pleasing for nearly everyone.

89

When evaluating your nose critically, you and your surgeon should consider the following characteristics but not be confined by them. Some features of a cosmetically appealing nose are a straight nasal dorsum, a narrow nasal tip, a small dip between the nasal dorsum and the tip, an appropriate angle between the nostrils and upper lip, an appropriate amount of nasal projection from the face, and an appropriate width. Some surgeons will measure the angles of your nose to help formulate a surgical plan (Figure 5-1).

Nancy, a thirty-one-year-old advertising executive, thought her nose was too big for her face. In reality, her problem was a weak chin. She accepted this when she saw her profile in a photograph. She underwent chin implant placement, which brought her whole profile into harmony.

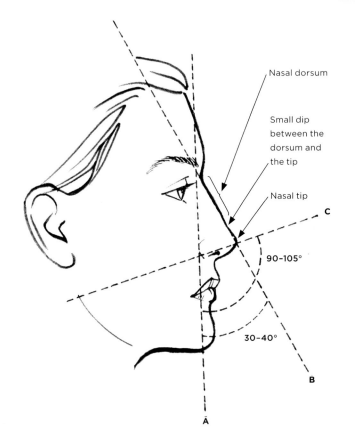

Figure 5-1: *Evaluation of your nose. Your surgeon may study your photographs to determine the angles between your nose and face. For women, the ideal angle between lines A and B is 30 to 40 degrees. If it is greater than 40 degrees, then your nose is too prominent. If it is less than 30 degrees, then your nose is too flat. Line C is through the base of the nose and reflects tip rotation. If it is greater than 105 degrees, then your tip may be upturned. If it is less than 90 degrees, then your tip may be too low for most women (although typical for a man).*

The Importance of Your Chin

Your chin plays a crucial role in the appearance of your nose (see Chapter 6). A weak chin can make an appropriately sized nose stand out. This problem should be addressed through chin augmentation, not nose surgery.

Is Rhinoplasty for You?

Not everyone is a good candidate for rhinoplasty. To have successful surgery, you must meet four criteria:

- You can describe specifically what bothers you.
- You are young enough to adjust to your new nose.
- You do not use nasal medications or drugs.
- You accept that revision surgery may be needed.

If you fail to meet any of these criteria, your chance for a satisfactory outcome will be much lower.

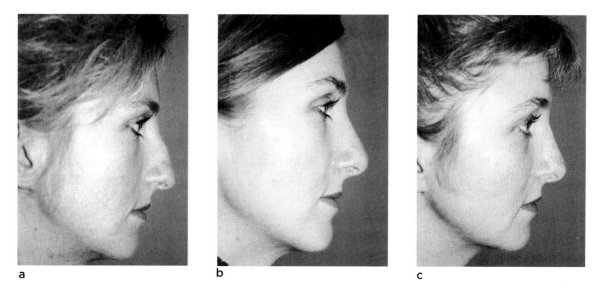

a   b   c

Rhinoplasty. (a) A thirty-two-year-old woman before surgery. (b) Five months after rhinoplasty. One might think that this is the final appearance of the nose, but it is not. (c) Two and a half years after rhinoplasty. Most noses reach their final appearance within two years of surgery.

Describe Specifically What Bothers You

It is difficult for a surgeon if you simply say, "I want my nose to look better." Be specific about the changes you seek, and do not assume that the changes you desire are necessarily the changes your plastic surgeon would make without your input.

Before you see your plastic surgeon, spend time with your mirror. Decide which nasal features specifically bother you. Write them down so you do not forget to mention each concern. Careful discussion is the only way to ensure that your goals are aligned.

Cosmetic nasal surgery results in specific structural changes in the nose. If you are unable to identify specific features of your nose that you dislike, it is unlikely that any change will result in satisfaction.

Be Young Enough to Adjust to Your New Nose

Every day of your life, you look at yourself in the mirror. The image you see is what you identify as yourself. The older you are, the more you have looked, and the more deeply you associate your mirror image with your identity.

By the time you reach your fifties, you will be so used to your facial structure that any change in appearance, no matter how positive, will make you look different and therefore not like yourself. You might look in the mirror and say, "I like what I see, but it just does not look like me." It might take years for you to incorporate your new image into your self-identity.

Younger women do not have this problem. In general, if you are younger than thirty, you will easily become accustomed to your new appearance. If you are thirty to forty years old, it may take one to two years for you to embrace your new look. If you are older than forty, it will take longer. Some may never adjust. This is why younger women are better candidates for rhinoplasty than older women.

This issue of adjustment applies to structural changes in bone, cartilage, and muscle that alter basic facial features. It usually does not apply

Janet, a thirty-four-year-old woman, disliked her nose but was unable to express exactly which features bothered her. She simply wanted to "make it better." Her nasal tip was somewhat bulbous, and her nose was slightly wide and prominent. Yet without her input, there was no way to know which specific features troubled her. I was unwilling to perform rhinoplasty without her guidance, so she found another surgeon. Several months later, she returned complaining that the other surgeon had ruined her nose, yet her nose appeared much improved. I pointed out that without her input, no surgeon could possibly know how to make her nose to her liking. She subsequently had at least one revision surgery by another surgeon and, not surprisingly, is still displeased.

Kay, a forty-six-year-old social worker, had always wanted rhinoplasty and was finally able to afford it. She knew exactly how she wanted her nose changed and was a good candidate for surgery. However, at her age, she was accustomed to her nose, despite her displeasure with its appearance. Because of this, she was at risk for dissatisfaction with her result. Knowing this, she still wished to proceed. Following rhinoplasty, her result closely matched her goal, but she was uncomfortable with her appearance. It took two years for her to finally accept her new nose, and she admitted that she had underestimated the difficulty of adjustment.

to rejuvenation procedures such as eyelid surgery or forehead lift, because they do not typically affect the underlying structure of the face.

Do Not Use Nasal Medications or Drugs

If you use nasal medications or drugs, you will be at increased risk for bleeding and healing problems. You should stop using nasal medications for at least three months before surgery to ensure the safest outcome. If you abuse cocaine, then it is probably safe to assume that you have more problems than potential healing difficulties. Regardless, do not seek any nasal surgery until you have refrained from cocaine use for one year and notified your surgeon of your previous abuse.

Accept That Revision Surgery May Be Needed

About 20 percent of all women who have rhinoplasty will seek a revision. The reasons are many. Perhaps the result appears unnatural. Perhaps the changes were inadequate. Perhaps the initial results were promising, but the nose changed unfavorably over subsequent months.

Operations on the nose are fraught with difficulty and unpredictability. Before you have your first rhinoplasty, you must accept the fact that at best there is a one in five chance that you will be dissatisfied.

Incisions and Scars

Your surgeon has two main options for rhinoplasty incisions: closed and open (see comparison Table 5-1).

Closed Rhinoplasty

In a closed rhinoplasty, all incisions are made inside the nose, so there are no visible scars. The surgeon has a limited view of the cartilage and bone. Yet many plastic surgeons are comfortable with this technique and achieve excellent results.

Table 5-1 Comparison of Closed and Open Rhinoplasty

Rhinoplasty Type	Advantages	Disadvantages
Closed	No scar outside the nose Less swelling	May be difficult to correct some complex nasal problems
Open	Excellent view for surgeon	Small scar under the nose More swelling

Open Rhinoplasty

In open rhinoplasty, the nose skin is lifted, allowing the surgeon a better view of the cartilage and bone. The surgeon makes a small incision on the underside of the nasal tip, between the two nostrils (Figure 5-2). Additional incisions are also made inside the nose. Some surgeons prefer this approach because it allows them greater visibility of some portions of the nose.

Two disadvantages of open rhinoplasty are (1) a scar between the nostrils and (2) significant postoperative swelling. Although scars are permanent, they are often imperceptible once they heal, but not always. Swelling following an open rhinoplasty lasts months or years longer than after a closed rhinoplasty. With diligent use of ice and elevation, some are able to minimize the duration and degree of swelling.

Figure 5-2: *Open rhinoplasty incision. An open rhinoplasty relies on a small incision between the nostrils. This incision usually heals imperceptibly. The bigger problem is swelling, which may take months to improve.*

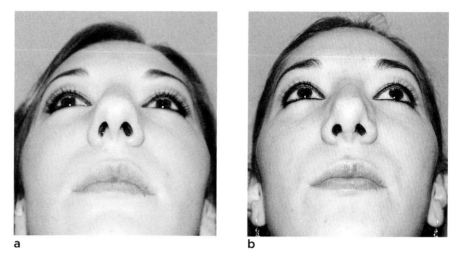

Rhinoplasty from a worm's eye view. (a) An eighteen-year-old before surgery has a wide, boxy tip. (b) Four months after open rhinoplasty, the tip is more narrow. The scar between the nostrils is still highly visible but will fade.

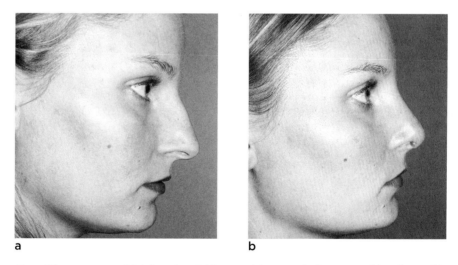

Expediting recovery. (a) A twenty-eight-year-old woman before open rhinoplasty. (b) Three weeks after surgery, she remains slightly swollen but can pass for normal due to vigilantly sleeping with her head elevated after surgery.

Closed Versus Open

Your plastic surgeon will likely recommend the technique he or she feels will yield the optimal results in your case.

Modifying Bone and Cartilage

The upper half of your nose is bone, and the lower half is cartilage. Rhinoplasty modifies both.

Bone

Modification of bone may involve making it smaller, augmenting it, or refining it. Often it must be fractured and repositioned if it is to be reduced. So, if you have a hump on your nose, expect that your doctor will fracture your nose after removing the hump.

Women who seek revision surgery because their nose was made too small often require bone augmentation. This can be achieved through use of your own bone. Your surgeon can harvest bone from your skull, rib, or hip bone, which leaves you with another area of pain, healing, and scarring. Despite this temporary disadvantage, using your own bone lowers the risk of infection and is more stable than the alternative, namely, prosthetic material such as plastic polymers or coral derivatives. If your surgeon sees a need for bone augmentation, be certain you understand the plan.

Cartilage

Cartilage can be modified by reducing it, refining it, or augmenting it. Initial rhinoplasties usually involve reducing and refining the cartilage; revision rhinoplasties are more likely to require rebuilding with grafts or prosthetic material. Cartilage grafts may be harvested from your nose, ear, or rib. As with bone grafts, this involves another incision. Synthetic material is not commonly used for cartilage replacement, due to its propensity to dislodge, extrude, warp, or cause infection.

Modifying Your Nasal Airway

In altering the appearance of your nose, rhinoplasty may or may not affect your nasal airway.

Improvement in Nasal Airway

Your nasal septum is on the inside of your nose and separates the left and right nasal passages. If your nasal septum is crooked, straightening it may improve your breathing. This surgical procedure is known as septoplasty

What to Expect

- **Anesthesia:** *Sedation or general. (Tip: request general anesthesia to reduce the incidence of nausea and vomiting after surgery.)*

- **Location of operation:** *Office or hospital.*

- **Length of surgery:** *One to three hours.*

- **Length of stay:** *Outpatient (home same day).*

- **Discomfort:** *Moderate. If your nasal bones are broken as part of the procedure, expect five to ten days of prescription pain medication. If not, expect two to seven days. Request a greater palatine block, which involves injecting local anesthesia in the roof of your mouth and markedly reduces postoperative discomfort. Use a humidifier and nasal saline spray to keep your nasal passages moist and comfortable.*

- **Bruising:** *Improves in three to five days if your nasal bones are not broken, and five to fourteen days if they are. Black eyes are not unusual during this time.*

- **Swelling:** *The majority of swelling subsides within two weeks after closed rhinoplasty and four weeks after open rhinoplasty. Minor swelling can persist much longer, but it is usually not bothersome. Sleeping in a recliner after surgery helps substantially. Applying ice for two to five days is also important.*

- **Numbness:** *Numbness of the tip of your nose is expected and will last for several weeks.*

- **Bandages:** *Your nose will be taped at the completion of surgery. If your nasal bones were broken, you will also receive a small cast. The cast and tape are removed in five to ten days.*

- **Stitches:** *You will have absorbable stitches on the inside of your nose. If your rhinoplasty was open, you will also have stitches under the tip of your nose. They will be removed in four to seven days.*

- **Packing:** *May be used to control bleeding. If so, it will be removed in one to seven days. While packing is in place, it is uncomfortable. Removal is also unpleasant. This is probably the worst part of rhinoplasty. Ask your surgeon if it can be avoided.*

- **Makeup:** *May be worn after the cast and tape have been removed.*

- **Presentable in public:** *You will be presentable in one to two weeks, but you may need makeup to conceal your bruises. Swelling will last longer than bruising and may make you self-conscious, but it will not be an automatic telltale sign of rhinoplasty.*

- **Work:** *You may feel capable of returning within a week, but your appearance will be the limiting factor.*

- **Exercise:** *May be resumed in two to four weeks. Avoid contact sports for six weeks.*

- **Final result:** *May be seen as soon as three months or as late as two years or longer. The majority see their final result within six months.*

- **Duration of results:** *If you are satisfied with the final results after the swelling has resolved, then you should never need further surgery.*

and is performed through incisions on the inside of your nose. It does not alter appearance. It may be performed with or without rhinoplasty. Your insurance company may pay for this portion of the procedure if your physician can prove that it is medically necessary. Neither septoplasty nor rhinoplasty will improve nasal obstruction due to other causes such as allergies, nasal swelling, polyps, or enlarged turbinates.

Worsening of Your Nasal Airway

One potential complication of rhinoplasty is nasal obstruction. If this occurs, it can sometimes be improved through further surgery.

Complications

When a qualified plastic surgeon performs your operation, both your procedure and recovery are likely to be uneventful. Even in ideal circumstances, however, complications may occur. In addition to the specific complications mentioned here, refer to Chapter 1 for general complications with any procedure.

Bleeding and Other Major Complications

Severe bleeding may occur during or after surgery, and nasal packing may be needed to control it. The risk of severe bleeding is less than 2 percent. Exceedingly rare but life-threatening problems associated with the brain can also occur, including leakage of cerebrospinal fluid (CSF), accumulation of air around the brain, meningitis, and even death. These complications may arise because the human brain and nose are separated by nothing more than a delicate bone, which may fracture from the forces delivered during rhinoplasty.

Bumpy Nose

If you have thin skin, you will easily feel any irregularities or see any asymmetries of your underlying cartilage or bone. These issues may or may not be improved through additional surgery.

Implant Extrusion

If synthetic material was used to augment your nasal bones or cartilage, it may (in rare cases) wear through the skin or through the lining of your nose. If the implanted material extrudes, it must be removed. Later, you will need another operation to reconstruct your nose. Synthetic material should not be used again. Your own cartilage or bone should be used because they will not extrude after healing. Use of synthetic materials is more common in cases of revision rhinoplasty than in primary rhinoplasty.

Telltale Signs

Because the nose can change in unpredictable ways following rhinoplasty, telltale signs may evolve in spite of the best efforts of your surgeon.

Scooped Out Nose

Also called ski slope nose, a scooped out nose can occur if too much bone and cartilage was removed during surgery (Figure 5-3a). This appears unnatural because the nose starts too low on the face. It can be corrected by placing a cartilage graft, bone graft, or synthetic implant into your nose to raise the nasal dorsum.

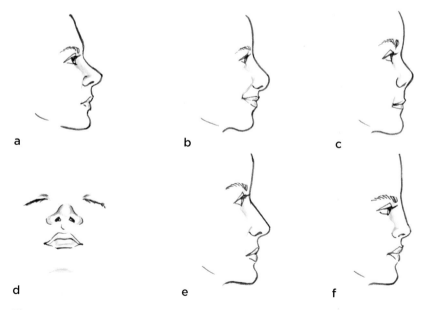

Figure 5-3: *Telltale signs. (a) Scooped out nose, (b) polly beak, (c) pug nose, (d) pinched tip, (e) straight nose, (f) nose that starts too high.*

Polly Beak

A polly beak, or parrot beak, characterized by fullness above the tip of the nose, is another telltale sign (Figure 5-3b). It may not be evident for a year or more after surgery, and correction requires revision rhinoplasty. Persistent swelling following rhinoplasty can sometimes mimic this condition.

Pug Nose

A pug nose is an upturned nose that is unattractive and unnatural (Figure 5-3c). This may be corrected through revision rhinoplasty with cartilage grafts.

Pinched Tip

The tip of your nose may appear pinched, notched, or collapsed (Figure 5-3d). This may be corrected by placing cartilage grafts during revision surgery.

Straight Nose

If your nose appears perfectly straight in profile, it might appear unnatural (Figure 5-3e). Natural noses may appear relatively straight, but they usually have a small dip just above the tip of the nose (Figure 5-1).

Nose Starts Too High

If you look at your own nose in profile, you will see that your nose begins at the level of your upper eyelashes. If your nasal dorsum has been built up with a graft or implant, it can appear that your nose starts too high on your face (Figure 5-3f). This can be corrected through revision rhinoplasty. Interestingly, in some parts of the world, a high nose is considered attractive.

Cost

In the United States, the range of total fees for rhinoplasty extends from $3,500 to $12,000. The average cost is:

Surgeon's fee	$3,800
Anesthesiologist's fee	$700
Operating room (facility) fee	$900
Total	$5,400

See "Fees" in Chapter 1 for various factors that might affect your own actual cost.

The Final Result

Because natural forces continue to act on your nose after surgery, your final result may not be evident for one to two years. You may be pleased with your early result once the swelling has improved, but this is not a guarantee that you will be ultimately satisfied. If you are pleased with your results after two years, then you can rest assured.

Satisfaction

Rhinoplasty is a powerful operation. When it achieves the desired results, satisfaction is immense. A successful rhinoplasty can change one's personality from shy and withdrawn to exuberant and outgoing. When rhinoplasty yields an undesirable result, however, dissatisfaction is equally great. When considering rhinoplasty, you must consider these factors together. There is an 80 percent chance that you will be satisfied, and possibly elated; but there is a 20 percent chance that you will be dissatisfied and possibly seek revision surgery.

Revision Rhinoplasty

If you are dissatisfied with the appearance of your nose following rhinoplasty, this does not necessarily mean that your plastic surgeon performed poorly. If your surgeon agrees that your result is unsatisfactory, agrees that your expectations are realistic, has a specific plan for correcting the problem, and has experience in revision rhinoplasty, you should allow him or her to reoperate. Understand, however, that each procedure on your nose will be much more difficult than the one before. Furthermore, revision surgery is not guaranteed to solve your problem. For the best results in revision rhinoplasty, find a surgeon who is skilled in rhinoplasty as well as revision rhinoplasty—two very different operations.

To minimize your need for revision rhinoplasty, seek an experienced surgeon. Look for one who has performed at least one hundred rhinoplasties over at least ten years. The exact number per year is not as relevant as the doctor's overall experience, which builds over time. The time frame is important, as final results in rhinoplasty may not be evident for two years. As such, surgeons must have the opportunity to assess their own results over time as they modify their techniques. Plastic surgeons who continue to perform rhinoplasties after having performed one hundred over ten years likely do so because of satisfactory results. Those who have unsatisfactory results often abandon this operation before ten years have passed. Plastic surgeons, like most people, enjoy success and avoid failure.

Yet even in the most experienced hands, some surgeries require revision. If you do require revision, wait at least one year following your first operation. Because the appearance of your nose may change over time, the need for revision rhinoplasty may not be evident even for two years. Find out how long your surgeon's policy concerning revision rhinoplasty applies.

Concluding Thoughts

Rhinoplasty modifies the bone and cartilage of your nose to change its appearance. The operation is tailored to the specific needs of the individual. This is the most difficult cosmetic procedure performed by plastic surgeons, because there are elements in healing that simply cannot be controlled. It is critical that you find a plastic surgeon who is highly experienced in this procedure. Cosmetic nose surgery has the potential to create a new appearance and lend new confidence. Just be careful.

Questions to Ask Your Plastic Surgeon

How many rhinoplasties have you performed?

How long have you been performing rhinoplasties?

Can you improve my breathing through surgery?

Do you plan to do open or closed rhinoplasty?

Will you use synthetic material?

Will I have nasal packing?

What is your policy regarding revision surgery, and how long does it apply?

Tips and Traps

- *Know exactly what you want changed and how you want it changed before you see your plastic surgeon. Make a list.*

- *Make sure that you and your plastic surgeon have a clear understanding of the planned changes.*

- *Avoid a surgeon who downplays the difficulty of nasal surgery.*

- *Make sure you and your surgeon examine your chin before surgery. If your surgeon recommends chin implant instead of or in addition to rhinoplasty, listen to that advice.*

- *The older you are, the more difficult it will be for you to adjust to your new nose. Consider this carefully if you are older than forty.*

- *Understand that there is at least a 20 percent chance you will need revision surgery.*

- *Asking your surgeon's revision rate is of little help because many women seek revision from a different surgeon. Your surgeon may not know how many patients have had a second operation.*

- *Avoid all nasal medications for three months before surgery.*

- *Ask your surgeon for a greater palatine block during surgery. This involves injection of local anesthesia in the roof of your mouth and markedly reduces discomfort after surgery.*

- *As swallowing blood during and after surgery markedly increases the incidence of nausea and vomiting, request general anesthesia. Patients under general anesthesia are protected from swallowing blood during the procedure, whereas patients under sedation anesthesia frequently swallow blood throughout the procedure.*

- *For the first two weeks following surgery, use a humidifier and nasal saline spray to keep your nasal passages moist and comfortable.*

- *Sleep in a recliner or with your head elevated on pillows for the first several days to minimize swelling. Apply ice frequently!*

- *If you require revision surgery, wait at least one year after your last nasal operation.*

6

Bringing Out Your Chin and Cheeks

Facial Implants

Facial implants for the chin and cheeks are cosmetic surgical options that are often overlooked. Chin and cheek implants may create a stronger appearance and bring harmony to your face. A properly chosen chin implant can even enhance the appearance of your nose.

Chin and cheek implants, although similar in many respects, differ in three important ways: why people choose to have them, how they are placed, and what might be done instead. After exploring these notable differences, this chapter will focus on the recovery period, costs, risks, and implant options, all of which are similar for chin and cheek implants.

If you are interested only in cheek implants, skip to the next section.

Chin Implants

Together, your chin and nose determine your profile. Look at your profile by using a handheld mirror in conjunction with a wall mirror. Imagine a straight line drawn from your forehead through the forwardmost point of your upper lip. In your mind, extend this line down to the level of your chin (Figure 6-1). If your chin meets the imaginary line, then you have sufficient chin projection. If your chin extends beyond this line, then you have

Gail, a thirty-nine-year-old nurse anesthetist, was self-conscious of her facial contour and profile. Because she did not like the idea of having a synthetic material in her body, she pursued rhinoplasty and neck liposuction, both of which offered some improvement but failed to give her the look she wanted. When she finally underwent chin and cheek augmentation, she achieved the appearance she desired with full, high cheeks and a strong chin.

105

a strong chin. If your chin falls short of this line, then your chin is under-projected. To see this more clearly, have someone take a photograph of your profile and use a ruler to draw the line.

Chin projection affects the appearance of the nose. A weak chin can make an average-sized nose appear large. Strengthening the chin through chin augmentation can make a large nose appear smaller. In Figure 6-1, all noses are the same size. However, in the illustration with a weak chin, the nose appears larger.

Details of Chin Implant Surgery

Chin implantation involves placing a prosthetic material in front of your chin bone (Figure 6-2). Incisions can be made either under your chin or inside your mouth (Figure 6-3). Both are reasonable options. An incision in your mouth avoids a visible scar, but an incision under your chin usually goes without notice. Most surgeons place chin implants through the mouth, unless they are performing a facelift. A facelift usually requires a chin incision, so the same incision can be used to place the implant.

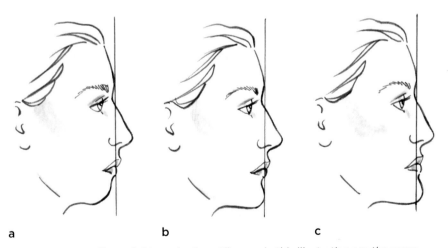

a   b   c

Figure 6-1: *The effect of chin projection. All noses in this illustration are the same size, but they look different. (a) A weak chin that falls behind the vertical line of the face causes the nose to look large. (b) A neutral chin. (c) An overprojected chin causes the nose to look flat. Chin augmentation commonly brings a weak chin into neutral position and can make an apparently large nose look more proportionate.*

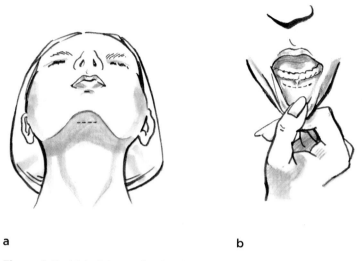

a   b

Figure 6-3: *(a) Incision under the chin. (b) Incision inside the mouth.*

Figure 6-2: *Position of chin implant.*

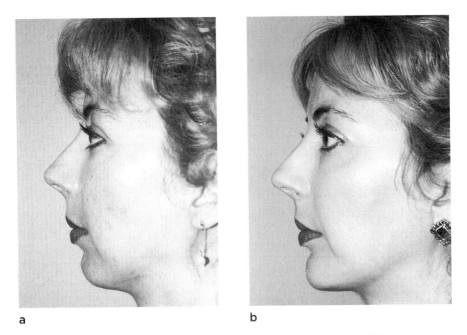

a   b

Chin augmentation. (a) A forty-year-old woman before and (b) after chin implant placement.

Chin Augmentation Without an Implant

It is possible to augment your chin by sliding a portion of your chin bone forward (Figure 6-4). This is known as genioplasty and involves surgically cutting your chin bone, moving it forward, and securing it with screws or wires.

Genioplasty offers the advantage of using your own bone and hence yields slightly lower rates of infection, extrusion, erosion, and migration (see "Complications"). The disadvantages include longer procedure time and recovery. Further, genioplasty is more difficult to modify than chin implantation. So if you are displeased with your result, the bone will need to be rebroken and moved again. Finally, the risk of nerve damage and numbness is greater.

If you are not interested in cheek implants, then skip ahead to "Considerations in Common."

Cheek Implants

Most people consider prominent cheekbones to be attractive, as evidenced by the facial features of successful professional models. Women who have

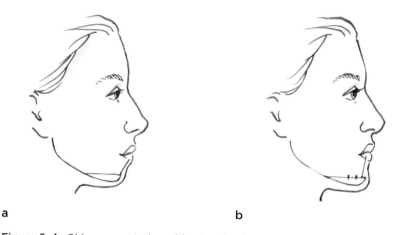

a   b

Figure 6-4: *Chin augmentation without an implant. (a) The chin before surgery. A solid line depicts where the bone will be cut. (b) The chin in its new position with the resultant strengthening of profile. The two small vertical marks indicate wires or plates holding the bone in its new position.*

low or flat cheekbones may seek cheek augmentation to achieve this aesthetic ideal. Because most women who seek cosmetic surgery have other aesthetic priorities, this operation is not as common as some other procedures. Yet when women do choose to pursue cheek augmentation, they are usually quite pleased with the results.

Details of Cheek Augmentation Surgery

Cheek augmentation involves placement of prosthetic material in front of your cheekbones to create the appearance of full, high cheeks (Figure 6-5). The incisions for cheek augmentation are almost always made inside your mouth between the cheeks and gums. These scars are never visible. Other options for the incisions are in your lower eyelids or in front of your ears. These incisions are usually considered only if eyelid surgery or a facelift is performed at the same time.

Your cheek implants can be adjusted in position to suit your goals. If you are most concerned about flatness in the front of your cheeks, the implants can be positioned more anteriorly to give projection there. If you are more concerned about your face being too narrow, your cheek implants can be placed more laterally to give more projection over the side of the cheekbone. For most, a combination provides the best balance.

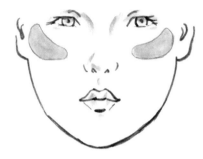

Figure 6-5: *Position of cheek implants.*

Cheek Augmentation Without an Implant

Unlike the chin bone, which can be fractured and moved forward for augmentation, the cheekbones do not lend themselves to such a procedure for purely cosmetic purposes. If you are emphatic about using your own bone for cheek augmentation, a portion of your skull, rib, or hip bone can be used as a graft. The disadvantages of bone grafts are that they must be harvested from separate sites and may shrink after they have been placed. They are also much more difficult to shape. For purely cosmetic cheek augmentation, most surgeons use only implant material.

There is an exception to this rule. If you are having a facelift at the same time, your surgeon may use extra facial tissue, called SMAS, to augment your cheeks. SMAS is a fibrous sheet of tissue located under the skin. It is pulled upward during two-layered facelifts, and the excess is usually discarded. Instead of discarding the extra SMAS, some surgeons use it to create fullness in the cheek area. However, because SMAS is soft tissue, it may thin or droop with time.

Considerations in Common

The rest of this chapter discusses issues that are common to both chin and cheek implants.

Adjusting to Your Implants

Placement of facial implants, like most cosmetic surgery procedures, has a positive impact on self-image of the recipient. However, with facial implants, there is a limit. The older the recipient is at the time of surgery, the less likely she will be pleased with her new facial structure. Over the years, we become accustomed to our basic facial features. Eventually, any change, no matter how attractive, may be unacceptable because it appears different. This difficulty in accepting a new appearance following a structural change is a greater issue following rhinoplasty than chin or cheek augmentation. Following rejuvenating surgeries such as a facelift or blepharoplasty, it is not usually a problem.

Preexisting Asymmetry

Most people have asymmetric facial bones. Minor unevenness is common and usually goes unnoticed. Moderate or severe asymmetry, however, can be troublesome. In these cases, chin and cheek implants can sometimes draw greater attention to preexisting asymmetries. Attempting to correct asymmetries through implant modification can be beneficial, but can also introduce new problems.

Timing for Surgery

Chin and cheek augmentation may be performed once the facial bones are fully developed, which is after the age of fifteen for women.

Complications

When a qualified plastic surgeon performs your operation, both your procedure and recovery are likely to be uneventful. Even in ideal circumstances, however, complications may occur. In addition to the specific complications mentioned here, refer to Chapter 1 for general complications with any procedure.

Sensory Changes

Temporary numbness, pain, and tingling of the chin and cheeks are common, and sensation usually normalizes within two to six weeks. Permanent numbness of the lips can occur if the nerve was injured during surgery.

You may develop delayed numbness several years following surgery if your implant shifts and presses on a nerve. Delayed numbness may be improved by removal of the implant.

Infection

Infection may initially be treated with antibiotics, but if it does not resolve, implant removal is usually necessary. Six months after the infection is resolved, another implant may be placed.

Asymmetry

Asymmetry of the chin or cheeks may occur following surgery if implants are not placed symmetrically, if implants move out of position, or if preexisting asymmetries exist. This may be improved through additional surgery.

What to Expect

- **Anesthesia:** *Sedation or general.*
- **Location of operation:** *Office or hospital.*
- **Length of surgery:** *Thirty minutes for chin implant, forty-five to sixty minutes for cheek implants.*
- **Length of stay:** *Outpatient (home same day).*
- **Discomfort:** *Mild to moderate. Anticipate two to five days of prescription pain medication. Request a long-lasting local anesthetic to help for the first day or so.*
- **Bruising:** *Uncommon.*
- **Swelling:** *Lasts one to two weeks following chin implant and two to three weeks following cheek implants. Reduce swelling through constant head elevation and frequent application of ice.*
- **Bandages:** *Usually none.*
- **Stitches:** *If the incisions are inside your mouth, then absorbable stitches will be used and do not require removal. If skin incisions are used, stitches will be removed in five days.*
- **Makeup:** *May be worn the day after surgery.*
- **Presentable in public:** *You will be presentable in two to five days.*
- **Work:** *You may feel capable of returning within two to five days, but your swelling will be the limiting factor.*
- **Exercise:** *May be resumed in two weeks.*
- **Final result:** *Will be seen between one and two months.*
- **Duration of results:** *Once your implant is in place, the results are usually lasting. Unless you develop complications, further surgery will not be necessary.*

When Can I Stop Worrying About Complications?

As long as your implant is in place, you may never assume that you are clear of complications. Sensory changes, infection, implant displacement, bone erosion, implant detection, and need for further surgery may occur months or years following placement of your implant. Fortunately, once these implants heal into position, complications are extremely rare.

Terry, a forty-seven-year-old sales manager, had undergone chin implant placement eight years earlier by another surgeon. She was initially pleased, but as she aged, her skin thinned, and her implant no longer looked natural. It appeared as a small round knob. Her chin no longer flowed with her jawline. Correction of her button chin involved removing her small implant and placing a longer one.

Implant Displacement

As with any operation involving implants, your surgeon will strive to achieve optimal placement. Yet the forces of healing can drive it out of position. If so, and depending on the severity, you may have an unnatural appearance of your chin or cheeks. Correction of this problem requires surgery to reposition the implant.

Bone Erosion

Occasionally, an implant can become mobile. It may stay in its position, but can move by a fraction of an inch in all directions. When an implant becomes mobile, it generates friction with the underlying bone, which then may cause the bone to be slowly eroded. Chin erosion can be so significant as to affect tooth roots. This is very rare and is treated with removal of the implant.

Detecting the Implant Through Your Skin

You may be able to feel your implant through the skin, depending on the type of implant. This is not necessarily a problem.

Extrusion of Implant

Some implants, if they become mobile, may erode your skin or the lining of your mouth. The implant may then become exposed, greatly increasing the risk of infection. Treatment usually involves removal of the implant.

Need for Further Surgery

If you choose to get an implant, you should expect possible future operations. (This applies not only to plastic surgery implants, but also to artificial joints, pacemakers, and heart valves.) Implants are artificial devices; some may last a lifetime, others will not.

Telltale Signs

There are two classic telltale signs of chin implants: a witch's chin and a button chin. The main telltale sign of cheek implants is a puppet appearance.

Witch's Chin

Witch's chin is chin skin that droops due to the disruption of the attachments between the chin pad and bone (Figure 6-6). Although no surgeon intends this, it occasionally happens, and the reason is not always clear. Attempts to correct this problem through more surgery may not be successful.

Button Chin

An unnaturally small or round chin may result if the implant is too small or narrow. This problem can be avoided or corrected by using a longer, broader implant that extends along the sides of your jaw.

Puppet Cheeks

As with the chin, use of a small implant causes an unnatural appearance of the cheeks, as the implant fails to blend with the existing facial structure. In the cheeks, the appearance is similar to that of a puppet in that a rectangular protrusion is seen over the cheekbones. Using a broader implant that blends with the underlying bone will prevent this.

Figure 6-6: *Witch's chin. This problem is due to a droopy chin pad and is difficult to correct.*

Cost

In the United States, the range of total fees extends from $2,000 to $4,000 for chin implants and $3,000 to $6,000 for cheek implants. The average cost is:

	Chin	Cheeks
Surgeon's fee	$1,800	$2,400
Anesthesiologist's fee	$500	$300
Operating room (facility) fee	$600	$900
Implant fee	$500	$600
Total	$3,400	$4,200

See "Fees" in Chapter 1 for various factors that might affect your own actual cost.

The implant price quoted here reflects the marked-up price. Implants cost between $175 and $1,000 from the manufacturer. (Manufacturer prices are included in the table in the next section.) Your surgeon or the operating facility will mark up that price to cover the cost of ordering, shipping, and stocking implants.

If you are charged more than a 20 percent markup, you should question the price. Only plastic surgeons and hospitals may purchase implants, so you will be limited in your ability to negotiate.

Implant Options

Facial implants are made of several different materials. These materials vary in texture, consistency, firmness, and appearance. Each material has benefits and drawbacks. And each poses certain risks, including infection, asymmetry, displacement, bone erosion, and extrusion. Most surgeons prefer certain implants based on their experiences. (See Table 6-1 for a summary of material properties.)

Silastic

A flexible white or clear plastic, Silastic has been used for decades in pacemakers, artificial joints, and other medical prostheses. It is available in a wide range of sizes and shapes and is relatively inexpensive. It is easily placed and easily removed. The rate of infection is low. For these reasons, Silastic remains the most commonly used implant for chin and cheek augmentation.

Silastic implants also pose some disadvantages. They do not attach to bone and therefore may move out of position after placement or erode underlying bone. You may also be able to feel the edges of the implant through your skin.

Hydroxyapatite

A strong, light ceramic material, hydroxyapatite may be placed as multiple small granules or as a single large piece. Hydroxyapatite is porous like sea coral. This feature allows in-growth of tissue, bone, and blood vessels. In-growth anchors the implant and prevents it from migrating, extruding, becoming infected, or eroding underlying bone. This material may be shaped before placement to correct for pre-existing asymmetries. Once healed, it is more difficult to remove or revise than Silastic.

Overview of Implant Materials

- *Silastic is flexible white or clear plastic.*

- *Hydroxyapatite is a ceramic that resembles sea coral.*

- *Polyethylene is a type of plastic that also resembles sea coral.*

- *Gore-Tex is the material used in high-quality raincoats.*

- *Cadaver bone is bone from deceased human donors.*

- *Proplast is a pliable plastic that resembles chewing gum.*

Table 6-1 Comparison of Chin and Cheek Implant Materials

	Genioplasty (Chin)	Silastic	Hydroxy-apatite	Poly-ethylene	Gore-Tex	Cadaver Bone	Proplast
Risk of infection	Rare	Low	Rare	Rare	Low	Rare	High
Risk of bone erosion	None	Low	Rare	Rare	Rare	Rare	Moderate
Risk of migration or extrusion	Rare	Low	Rare	Rare	Low	Rare	Moderate
Risk of contracting infection from the implant	None	None	None	None	None	Theoretical	None
Cost of chin implant from the manufacturer	n/a	$175	$550	$225	$250	$1,000	n/a
Cost of two cheek implants from the manufacturer	n/a	$225	$800	$400	$350	$1,200	n/a

n/a = not applicable

Questions to Ask Your Plastic Surgeon

Can you correct my facial asymmetry?

Where will the incisions be?

Which implant material do you recommend and why?

Is the implant material associated with bone erosion?

How easy will it be to remove the implant, if needed?

Who pays for implant removal?

Tips and Traps

- *Each implant material offers certain advantages. Surgeons recommend the type of implant they think is most appropriate. Make sure you understand the disadvantages of each implant material.*

- *Anticipate the possible need for future surgery when accepting placement of any type of implant.*

Polyethylene

Polyethylene is a plastic polymer that comes in single large pieces. Like hydroxyapatite, it resembles sea coral and carries the same advantages and disadvantages as implant material.

Gore-Tex

Gore-Tex is a cross between cloth and rubber. Gore-Tex is soft, pliable, porous, and may adhere to surrounding soft tissues. Because it does not attach to bone, it can migrate, become infected, and cause erosion. It is easily modified prior to placement but difficult to modify once in place. The infection and extrusion rates are low if the implant is not near the incision line. But near the incision line, infection and extrusion may occur and pose significant problems.

Cadaver Bone

Cadaver bone is human bone, obtained from donors shortly after death. After being freeze-dried and processed, it can be used for implants without being rejected. Cadaver bone has many advantages. It adheres to your own bone, and your own bone may even grow to replace it. So the implant is stable and resistant to motion, infection, erosion, and extrusion. Disadvantages include high cost, risk of shrinkage, and risk of acquiring an infectious disease from the deceased donor. Some cadaver bone suppliers have been investigated for illegally harvesting bone without consent. If you choose cadaver bone, be certain your plastic surgeon has confirmed the legitimacy of the bone bank.

Proplast

Proplast is like plastic chewing gum. At one time, it was the most popular implant for facial augmentation. But Proplast caused so many complications that it was withdrawn from the market. The edges of Proplast implants curled and became evident through the skin of the face and the lining of the mouth, causing skin to become red, irritated, painful, and infected.

If you already have a Proplast implant, promptly seek the attention of a plastic surgeon when you develop redness or pain in the area of your implant.

Satisfaction

The simplicity with which facial implants can be placed and the magnitude of change they can effect have contributed to their growing popularity. If you have no complications from your implant, then you will likely be satisfied with your result. If you develop complications, you may become rapidly disenchanted with your implant.

Concluding Thoughts

The perfect implant would be inexpensive, easy to place, easy to modify, and easy to remove. It would correct asymmetry, stay solidly in place, and be impossible to feel through the skin. It would never cause infection, never extrude, and never erode bone. Unfortunately, this implant does not exist. Currently available implants, although imperfect, do provide safe, aesthetic augmentation with relatively few problems.

7

Enlarging Your Breasts

Breast Augmentation

Breast augmentation is among the most popular of cosmetic surgery procedures and has been for decades. Yet it also remains among the most highly scrutinized procedures in plastic surgery. Along with the controversy, unfortunately, has come quite a bit of confusion. This chapter will help you sort through the issues and will provide you with the information you need to make the right decisions.

Sonya, a thirty-five-year-old gynecologist, chose her food carefully and worked out four times each week. Her body was trim and shapely, with the exception of her breasts. This was one thing that proper diet and exercise could not fix. She simply wanted her breasts to be in proportion with the rest of her body. Following breast augmentation, she felt balanced for the first time. She found to her surprise that she even stood straighter. Her only regret was that she did not have this surgery sooner.

Breast Augmentation: A Process of Making Choices

A number of important decisions precede your breast augmentation, such as implant type, position, size, shape, volume, and surface. The decisions you and your surgeon make before surgery will affect your risk of postoperative problems and your overall satisfaction. You will see that these decisions are not simple: each option has pluses as well as minuses. You must decide which advantages are most important and which disadvantages you can accept. Effective communication between you and your surgeon is essential for the best outcome.

If your surgeon does not involve you in these decisions, you may ask to be involved—or choose to see another surgeon.

This chapter will lead you through the options and inherent risk of complications. To best understand the close correlation between them, you must first become familiar with the potential complications. Thereafter, the options will make more sense.

Risks and Complications in Breast Augmentation

As with all surgery, certain risks are inherent in breast augmentation. Read this section carefully, as your decisions hinge on your understanding of the risks. An in-depth discussion with your plastic surgeon is also essential to understanding these potential problems.

Capsular Contracture

Scar tissue forms around all implanted materials as a natural part of healing. Scar tissue around a breast implant is not troublesome, unless it tightens. An abnormally tight scar is known as a capsular contracture. It may cause the breast to feel firm, unnatural, or even painful. Capsular contractures may occur at any time, but tend to occur in two waves: early and late.

Early Capsular Contracture

Capsular contractures that occur within the first year of surgery are known as "early." Most of these are thought to be due to a bacteria called *Staphylococcus epidermidis*, which is present on everyone's skin and usually causes no problems. *Staph. epi.*, as it is called, is generally benign unless it is in association with a prosthetic implant, such as an artificial joint, heart valve, pacemaker, or breast implant. Because it is so benign, it does not cause the classic signs of infection: redness, swelling, and fevers. Instead it remains dormant around the implant until it incites the surrounding scar tissue to tighten and contract.

Late Capsular Contracture

Capsular contractures that occur years after surgery are known as "late." These are frequently related to silicone gel implant ruptures, and they occur when the scar tissue around the implant becomes irritated or inflamed in

> ## Risks of Breast Augmentation
>
> - *Capsular contracture*
> - *Interference with mammography*
> - *Implant displacement*
> - *Implant deflation (saline) or rupture (silicone)*
> - *Rippling and wrinkling*
> - *Sloshing*
> - *Infection*
> - *Nipple sensory changes*
> - *Hematoma*

response to silicone gel that has extruded through the implant shell. Saline implants are less likely to cause a late capsular contracture, because saline is absorbed by the body if the implant leaks and does not trigger an inflammatory response. Silicone, however, might cause an inflammatory response if the implant ruptures.

Risk and Prevention

Numerous studies have been published with capsular contracture rates varying between 10 and 50 percent. Perhaps the most meaningful way to interpret these apparently discrepant values is to consider that the risk of severe capsular contracture is close to 10 percent and the risk of mild capsular contracture may be as high as 50 percent. Efforts to prevent capsular contracture include meticulous sterile technique during surgery and implant displacement exercises following surgery. Displacement exercises (Figure 7-1) are thought to stretch surrounding scar tissue, thereby reducing the rate of capsular contracture. Do not begin this until your surgeon advises you to do so.

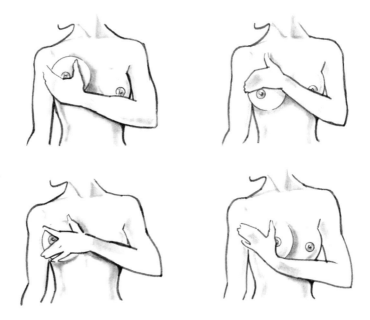

Figure 7-1: *Implant exercises. Women with smooth implants may be instructed to gently but firmly press on each implant in all directions once each day. These exercises may reduce the risk of capsular contracture.*

Treatment

Treatment involves surgical removal of the scar tissue, or capsulectomy, and placement of a new implant. The implant might also be moved to a different plane (i.e., above or below the pectoralis muscle). If you have a moderate or severe capsular contracture, you may choose to undergo this operation. Realize, however, that capsular contracture may recur, as additional surgery is not guaranteed to solve your problem. Therefore, if your contracture is mild, as many are, you might choose to avoid surgery and simply live with it.

Interference with Mammography

Breast implants interfere with the ability of a mammogram to evaluate all breast tissue. Because one in nine women in the United States will develop breast cancer in her lifetime, mammographic screening for early diagnosis is important. The presence of a breast implant may, therefore, delay the diagnosis of breast cancer. A special mammogram method called the Ecklund technique is designed for women with breast implants, and all mammography facilities in the United States are required to offer it.

Implant Displacement

Implants can displace from their original position due to gravity, capsular contracture, muscle pull, the forces of healing, or the weight of the implant.

Interestingly, the nipple will point the direction opposite from where the implant has displaced. For example, if the implant moves upward, the nipple will appear to point downward (Figure 7-2a). Significant displacement can compromise the natural appearance of your breasts and can require an operation to recenter the implant. Due to the forces of gravity, it is much easier to fix an implant that has displaced upward or medially than an implant that has displaced downward or laterally. Efforts to raise low implants are particularly confounded when the implant is very large. Hence, a larger implant that has displaced down-

Closed Capsulotomy

Capsular contractures were previously treated by a procedure known as closed capsulotomy. Closed capsulotomy was a non-surgical procedure in which the surgeon manually squeezed the implanted breast, sometimes with tremendous force. This disrupted the surrounding scar, thereby softening the breast. Plastic surgeons now condemn this procedure because of its propensity to cause implant rupture, implant displacement, hematoma, unnatural appearance, and redevelopment of capsular contracture. If your surgeon suggests closed capsulotomy, you may wisely choose to seek another opinion.

Classification of Capsular Contractures

- **Mild:** *The breast feels slightly firm, and the implant edges can be felt through the skin.*

- **Moderate:** *The breast feels firm, and the implant can be both felt and perceived visually through the skin. The breast may appear unnaturally round or spherical.*

- **Severe:** *The breast is hard, distorted, and painful.*

ward is much more difficult to fix than a small implant that has displaced downward or a large implant that has displaced upward.

Implant Deflation and Rupture

Saline and silicone gel implants both have a shell made of solid silicone. By nature, this shell is soft and pliable, but it may also tear. When a saline implant shell tears, it is called a deflation, because the enclosed saline leaks out and is absorbed by the body, resulting in marked shrinkage of the breast. A rupture occurs when a silicone gel implant shell tears. The enclosed silicone gel might extrude to varying degrees, but the breast does not change in size.

Risk

The risk of saline implant deflation is about 1 percent per implant per year. Silicone gel implant rupture rate is about 3 percent during the first four years, which makes them roughly equivalent to the saline deflation rate during that time frame. Rates thereafter have not yet been determined, but studies are underway.

Treatment

Saline deflations require surgery for placement of a new implant. Silicone ruptures require replacement in addition to capsulectomy, which is the surgical removal of the surrounding scar tissue.

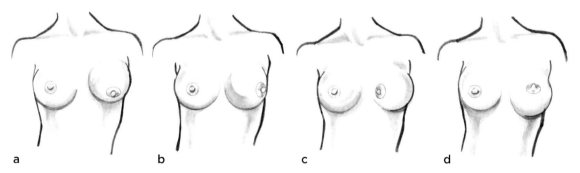

a   b   c   d

Figure 7-2: *Implant displacement. In each illustration, the implant on the left is in good position, while the implant on the right is displaced. Displacement shown is (a) upward, (b) inward, (c) outward, and (d) downward ("dropped down"). In each case, the nipple appears to point in the direction opposite of the implant displacement.*

Rippling and Wrinkling

In a saline implant, the liquid moves freely within the shell and can cause small waves like those seen on the surface of a pond. These waves can be transmitted to the skin, causing the breast to ripple on its inner and upper sides. Rippling gives the breast an unnatural appearance. Thin women are particularly prone to rippling because they have less soft tissue covering their implants.

Wrinkling is the term plastic surgeons tend to use to describe an unnatural scalloping appearance that can occur on the side of the breast or underneath it. Again, thin women and those with saline implants are more prone to this. Be aware that the terms *rippling* and *wrinkling* can be confusing, as some plastic surgeons use them interchangeably.

Sloshing

Because saline has the consistency of water, it may slosh when you move. If so, sloshing usually is only perceived by the woman with the implants. It might be loud or distracting to the woman, but others generally do not hear it. Silicone, because it is more viscous, does not slosh.

Regardless of whether a woman chooses silicone or saline, she may have temporary sloshing within the first few weeks of surgery, but the reason for this is different. As a response to healing after surgery, the human body typically fills the space around the implant with clear liquid called serous fluid, which may slosh. As the body heals, it reabsorbs the serous fluid, and in the process, sloshing resolves.

Infection

Infection, which can occur after any operation, is devastating when it follows breast augmentation. It might require hospitalization, intravenous antibiotics, and removal of the implant. Months (in some cases years) afterward, a new implant can be placed. During that time, your breast asymmetry will be awkward. You will be markedly uncomfortable physically, emotionally, psychologically, and sexually. Fortunately, the risk of infection is less than 1 percent.

If I Treat My Breasts Delicately, Can I Prevent Deflation or Rupture?

Intuitively, it makes sense that doing so might help prevent deflation or rupture, but it does not. You should treat your breasts the same as unimplanted breasts. Do not be guarded or concerned about your significant other handling your breasts. Also, mammograms are not usually associated with deflation or rupture, so you should not defer annual mammography (recommended for women older than forty).

Sensory Changes

Your nipple or breast skin might lose sensation partially or completely following augmentation. As the nerve that conducts sensation to the nipple is typically small and thin, surgeons often do not see it during surgery. As such, it might be stretched, cut, or inadvertently cauterized. If stretched, sensation usually returns. If cut, sensation usually does not return. If cauterized, or burned, the likelihood of sensory return depends upon the extent of cautery.

The risk of permanent nipple numbness is about 15 percent. If loss of nipple sensation is unacceptable to you, you should carefully reconsider this operation. Another option is to ask your surgeon to avoid cautery near the nerve and to use only finger dissection, which confers a lower rate of nipple numbness.

The opposite problem, increased nipple sensation, is also possible and can be very aggravating. If it occurs, it usually resolves within a few weeks.

Breast augmentation does not usually affect nipple erection, which is preserved even if sensation is lost.

Hematoma

A hematoma is a blood collection that can accumulate next to the implant after surgery. Most hematomas appear either within a day of implant placement or about three weeks later. They usually require an additional operation for removal, as untreated hematomas are painful and increase the likelihood of capsular contracture and infection. The overall risk of hematoma is less than 2 percent, but it is higher in those who take aspirin or ibuprofen and in those who return to a physically demanding occupation or resume exercise too soon.

Options in Breast Augmentation

Prior to surgery, a number of decisions must be made, impacting your cosmetic result and your risk of complications. Reaching the best decisions can be challenging. Carefully consider each option by weighing its pluses and minuses (see Table 7-1). Prioritize your goals and base your choices on the issues that are most important to you. Communicate your goals to your

Tracy, a thirty-four-year-old pharmaceutical representative, was relaxing in the tub one evening four years after saline breast augmentation. She became alarmed when she noticed that her right breast was shrinking. There was no obvious cause and no discomfort—simply a shrinking breast for no apparent reason. She was relieved to learn that this problem was not an emergency. One week later, her deflated right implant was replaced with a new one in the operating room. Although the prospect of surgery was less than appealing, the implant manufacturer provided a replacement implant and gave her money to help defray the operating room and anesthesia fees.

Table 7-1 Options for Breast Implant Selection and Placement

Preoperative Decision	Advantages	Disadvantages
Implant Type		
Silicone	Look and feel very natural (provided they do not develop a capsular contracture) Lower risk of rippling Lower risk of displacement	If rupture occurs, it could be silent, so MRI is recommended every 2 years Presumed higher risk of capsular contracture Higher cost by about $1,000 Longer scar
Saline	Shorter scar Lower cost Presumed lower rate of capsular contracture Deflation is usually evident immediately—no need for MRI	Implants can be felt through the skin in thin women Appearance may be less natural than silicone Higher rate of rippling and displacement
Implant Position		
Above the muscle	Less discomfort Less swelling Faster recovery Little or no distortion when flexing pectoralis muscle	Higher risk of capsular contracture More interference with mammography (25% of breast tissue is blocked by implant) Less-natural cosmetic result in women with petite breasts
Below the muscle	Lower risk of capsular contractures Less interference with mammography (10% of breast tissue is blocked by implant) Better cosmetic result in women with petite breasts (vs. above muscle)	More discomfort More swelling Lengthier recovery Expect breast distortion with use of the pectoralis muscle

Preoperative Decision	Advantages	Disadvantages
Implant Surface		
Smooth	Lower risk of rippling and seroma Cost $100 less per pair than textured implants	
Textured	Necessary if selecting teardrop implants	Higher risk of rippling and seroma Cost $100 more per pair than smooth implants
Implant Shape		
Round	Rotation will not affect the appearance of breast Cost is less than teardrop Available in both saline and silicone implants	Round appearance of upper half of breast in some women
Teardrop	May provide better cosmetic result in selected women	May rotate, creating an abnormally shaped breast Cost about $200 more than round implants Must be textured Available only in saline, as of 2007
Implant Profile		
Low	Best for women who choose a small implant volume relative to their breast diameter	
Medium	Best for women who choose an implant volume that is proportionate to their breast diameter	
High	Best for women who choose an implant volume that is large relative to their breast diameter	
Implant Fill		
Fill to capacity	None	Higher risk of deflation Higher risk of rippling and sloshing
Overfill	Lower risk of deflation Lower risk of rippling and sloshing	None

(continued)

Table 7-1 Options for Breast Implant Selection and Placement *(continued)*

Preoperative Decision	Advantages	Disadvantages
Site of Incision		
Under breast	Scar is hidden by the breast	If scar heals poorly, it may be visible when you are unclothed
	Any revision surgery can be performed through this scar	
	Allows your plastic surgeon the best visibility during surgery	
	Any size silicone implant can be placed	
Around nipple	Scar can be camouflaged around the nipple	Because the nipple is the focal point of the breast, any imperfection will be highly visible
		May alter nipple sensation
		Large silicone implants cannot be placed through this incision
Underarm	Well-hidden scar except in sleeveless tops or swimming suit	Requires endoscopic equipment
		Least favorable visibility for your surgeon
		Revision surgery may require an additional incision (under breast or around nipple)
		Large silicone implants cannot be placed through this incision
Belly button	Well-hidden scar	Silicone implants cannot be used
		Implants must be placed over the muscle
		Revision surgery cannot be performed through the same scar, so an additional scar around the areola or under the breast is required

Breast-Feeding

Neither breast-feeding ability nor milk content is altered following breast augmentation. The greatest potential problem associated with pregnancy following breast augmentation is the appearance of the breast. (See "Postpartum Droop" later in this chapter.)

The Implant Shell

Breast implants are similar to water balloons. The shell of the balloon is made of a durable, pliable plastic called solid silicone. This is true whether the implants are filled with saline or liquid silicone gel. Solid silicone is a very different substance than silicone gel, which fills silicone gel implants. Solid silicone, or Silastic, has been implanted in millions of people in pacemakers, artificial joints, heart valves, penile implants, and artificial lenses for the eye.

surgeon, who will guide you through these decisions. The decisions include the following:

Implant type	Saline or silicone gel?
Implant position	Above or below the muscle?
Implant surface	Smooth or textured?
Implant shape	Teardrop or round?
Implant volume	How big?
Implant profile	Low, medium, or high profile?
Implant fill	Underfill or overfill?
Site of incision	Under the breast, around the nipple, under the arm, or through the belly button?

Saline Versus Silicone Gel

In saline implants, the shell is filled with sterile salt water; in silicone gel implants, the shell is filled with liquid silicone gel, which has the consistency of molasses.

History of Saline and Silicone Gel Implants

Both types of implants have been used since the 1960s. In 1992, the U.S. Food and Drug Administration (FDA) issued a moratorium on silicone gel implants based on concern that they might cause autoimmune diseases such as lupus and rheumatoid arthritis in some women.

From 1968 when silicone gel implants were introduced to 1992 when silicone gel implants were banned by the FDA, they were the overwhelmingly most popular type of implant due to their extraordinarily natural look and feel in most women. From 1992 to 2006, saline-filled implants with solid silicone shells, also known as saline implants, were the only option available to women in the United States seeking breast augmentation. Throughout that time, silicone gel remained the implant of choice for women in Europe, South America, and Canada.

In 2006, the FDA lifted the restriction on silicone gel breast implants after substantial evidence showed that silicone gel implants did not cause such diseases. The evidence determined that a woman's risk of developing autoimmune diseases is the same whether she has silicone gel implants or no implants.

Pros and Cons of Silicone Gel Implants

The advantage of silicone gel implants is primarily aesthetic: they look and feel so soft and natural that they typically cannot be distinguished from breasts without implants, provided they do not develop a capsular contracture. They also have a lower rate of rippling and wrinkling. Hence, thin women with modest breast tissue may choose to have them placed in the subglandular plane (see the section "Above the Muscle"). If the same women chose saline implants, they would most likely be advised to have them placed in the subpectoral plane to reduce the risk of rippling. Also, because silicone is lighter than saline, the risk of downward displacement due to gravity is lower.

The disadvantages of silicone gel breast implants include higher cost (by about $900–$1,000) and a typically longer scar. The longer scar is usually necessary, as silicone gel implants are prefilled by the manufacturer and must be able to fit through the incision. In general, larger implants require longer scars. Also, the risk of capsular contracture is higher with silicone. This is because silicone implants might incur a late capsular contracture due to implant rupture, whereas saline implants do not form capsular contractures in response to rupture or deflation.

Finally, silicone gel implants might rupture "silently," such that there is no outward evidence that a rupture has occurred. Physical examination by your plastic surgeon will identify only 30 percent of ruptures, whereas magnetic resonance imaging (MRI) will identify about 90 percent of ruptures. So women with silicone gel breast implants are encouraged to have an MRI scan every two years, beginning three years after surgery.

Pros and Cons of Saline Implants

The advantage of saline implants is a presumed (studies currently are underway) lower rate of revision surgery than silicone gel, as saline implants tend to get mostly early capsular contractures, rather than both early and late. Further, the scar is usually shorter, as saline implants can be filled after they are placed, allowing a smaller incision. The primary disadvantages of saline

Other Options for Breast Augmentation

Efforts to find other options for breast implant materials have been met with disappointment. Oil-filled implants have turned rancid, leading to unpleasant body odors. Fat injections (from hips or thighs) cause calcifications, which can confound the detection of breast cancer. Some plastic surgeons advocate fat injections for augmentation, but others remain concerned about their interference with mammography. Plastic surgeons continue to seek other alternatives.

implants are that they tend to look round and feel stiff and unnatural, particularly in thin women with modest breast tissue. In addition, large saline implants have a higher rate of downward displacement than silicone, as they are heavier than their silicone counterparts.

Recommendations

Thin women with a modest amount of breast tissue tend to select silicone gel implants, as the cosmetic advantages are substantial and easily offset the known disadvantages and risks. Heavy women and those with a more generous amount of breast tissue enjoy less of an aesthetic advantage with silicone, as both silicone and saline tend to feel soft and natural in women with more breast tissue. Hence, the disadvantages of silicone implants are not warranted, and saline is often selected. An exception here is with larger implants. If a large implant is selected, silicone offers the advantage of a lower rate of downward displacement.

Women with an intermediate amount of breast tissue find themselves caught in the middle of this decision. For these women, I recommend they decide which is most important: optimal cosmetic result (silicone) or lower rate of revision surgery, shorter scar, lower cost, and avoidance of routine MRI scans (saline). Once they make this decision, the choice is clear.

Implant Position

Implants can be placed in one of two positions: between the breast and the pectoralis muscle, or between the pectoralis muscle and the ribs (see Figure 7-3). Either way, they are centered under each breast and nipple.

Above the Muscle

Position of the implant above the pectoralis muscle is known as subglandular placement (Figure 7-3b) and offers several advantages. This operation involves less discomfort and faster recovery because the pectoralis muscle itself is not disturbed. Your breasts immediately appear attractive because swelling is minimal. In athletic muscular women, it causes less distortion of the breast when the pectoralis muscle is flexed.

Gummy Bear Implants

One of the two main silicone gel implant manufacturers touts that its silicone gel breast implants are made with cohesive *silicone gel. Being cohesive, the gel supposedly has a tendency to stay together rather than disband in the event of a rupture. They have been likened to Gummy Bears, the soft candy that feels as though it is filled with liquid, yet its contents do not run out if cut open. The other large implant manufacturer argues that all silicone gel implants are cohesive in nature and that the first company uses the term* cohesive *as a marketing ploy. Whether and to what extent cohesiveness confers an advantage has yet to be proven. Studies are underway but may not be complete until 2010–2020.*

Women with ample breast tissue might be more likely to select subglandular placement than women with very modest breasts, as larger breasts offer more of a cushion between the implant and the skin.

Disadvantages include a higher risk of capsular contracture and greater interference with mammography than subpectoral placement. Women with thin skin, low body fat, or petite breasts are very likely to feel the implants through the skin and are more likely to have rippling and wrinkling. Large implants are more likely to displace downward, and the risk of nipple numbness is slightly higher.

Below the Muscle

Implant position below the muscle (Figure 7-3c), also known as submuscular or subpectoral placement, offers the advantages of a lower rate of capsular contracture, less interference with mammography, lower rate of rippling, and less likelihood of downward displacement. Thin women with petite breasts may obtain the best cosmetic result with the implant placed under the muscle, which provides more padding between the implant and the skin.

Disadvantages include greater postoperative pain, greater swelling, and a longer recovery period. Swelling can be profound and may persist for weeks to months. During this time, the upper portion of the breast appears unnaturally full. And after swelling subsides, flexing the pectoralis muscles, such as during exercise, may cause the breasts to move and look distorted.

Terminology for Implant Placement

Other Names for Subglandular
Above the muscle
Over the muscle
Under the breast
Between the breast and muscle

Other Names for Subpectoral
Submuscular
Under the muscle
Below the muscle
Between the muscle and rib

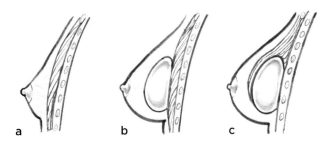

Figure 7-3: *Implant position. (a) A nonaugmented breast. (b) An implant above the muscle. (c) An implant below the muscle.*

Bodybuilders and Other Thin Athletic Women

Bodybuilders tend to be thin and muscular. As thin women benefit from implant placement under the muscle, and as muscular women have greater muscular distortion with implants placed under the muscle, bodybuilders found themselves in a quandary when only saline implants were available. Now that silicone is an option, bodybuilders and other thin athletic women usually choose silicone implants over the muscle. Being silicone, these implants have a lower rate of rippling, even in thin women. Being over the muscle, there is less distortion with the flexion of the pectoralis muscles. Prior to the availability of silicone, these women often had disappointing cosmetic results.

Implant Surface

The outside surface of an implant can be either smooth or textured. The surface of the implant is indiscernible following surgery.

Textured

Textured implants have a surface that feels like dull sandpaper. They were developed because they were thought to impose a lower risk of capsular contracture. This has not turned out to be true. Textured implants are more prone to rippling than smooth implants and are also more likely to cause seromas, or fluid collections, around the implant. For these reasons, very few surgeons use textured saline implants.

One situation in which textured implants might be important, however, is in the selection of teardrop-shaped silicone gel implants. Although these implants were not approved by the FDA as of 2007, plastic surgeons are working with the FDA to achieve approval. Teardrop-shaped silicone gel implants are filled with silicone gel that is stiffer than that in round silicone gel implants. They offer the benefits of maintaining their shape while feeling soft and natural. Because they are filled with stiffer silicone gel, their likelihood of rippling is significantly reduced in spite of being textured. All teardrop implants are textured to help prevent rotation of the implant sideways or upside down. Hence, if teardrop silicone implants are selected, a textured surface is the only option.

Smooth

Smooth implants offer the advantage of a lower rate of rippling and fluid accumulation. Most plastic surgeons use smooth implants for these reasons.

Implant Shape

Implants may be teardrop-shaped or round. Round implants are shaped like a hamburger bun (Figure 7-4a). Teardrop implants have greater fullness in the lower half and less fullness in the upper half (Figure 7-4b).

Teardrop

Because the breast has greater fullness toward the bottom, some plastic surgeons prefer teardrop implants. They have found that teardrop implants provide a more natural result. Other surgeons think that the teardrop shape makes no difference, particularly with regard to saline implants, because as the body heals, it forces the implant into a round shape regardless of how it started.

Because of their design, teardrop implants must be oriented under the breast with the fullest portion at the bottom of the breast. One problem with teardrop implants is that they may rotate following surgery. This results in a sideways or upside-down appearing breast. To reduce the risk of rotation, teardrop implants are textured; however, risk of rotation is still about 10 to 20 percent. Teardrop implants cost about $200 more than round implants. Because of these drawbacks, the plastic surgeons who use teardrop implants tend to reserve them for women with extremely little or no breast tissue, as these women might otherwise appear too "round" in the upper half of their breasts.

Round

Round implants have several advantages. They may rotate freely under the breast without aesthetic consequences, they may be textured or smooth, and their cost is lower. Because the contents gravitate to the lower pole of the implant when a woman stands, the lower pole will naturally become fuller, thus negating the need for a teardrop implant.

"Complete" Submuscular Controversy

Some plastic surgeons tout "complete" submuscular placement, as opposed to partial submuscular placement. In complete submuscular placement, the implant is purportedly 100 percent covered by muscle: the pectoralis muscle covers the upper, inner half; the serratus muscle covers the outer quarter; and the rectus muscle covers the lower quarter. In contrast, partial submuscular placement, also known as subpectoral placement, involves muscle coverage of only the upper, inner half of the implant by the pectoralis muscle.

Those who promote complete submuscular placement claim that complete coverage confers more cushion between the implant and skin, thereby making the implant more difficult to see or feel, particularly in the lower, outer half.

Other plastic surgeons challenge that complete submuscular placement is not anatomically possible, pointing out that attempting to join all three muscles over the implant causes distortion and unnatural breast shape.

The truth probably lies somewhere in between.

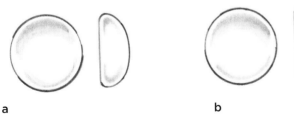

a

b

Figure 7-4: *Implant shape. (a) A round implant viewed from the front and side. (b) A teardrop implant viewed from the front and side.*

Anatomic Implants

Teardrop implants were previously called anatomic implants. In response to a lawsuit alleging that the term anatomic *created falsely elevated expectations for recipients, this term has been abandoned in favor of the term* teardrop.

Cup Size Is Not Standardized

One day, a woman saw me in consultation for breast augmentation. Her breasts were so modest in size that there was no discernible crease beneath the breast. I could not tell where the lower border of the breast was because she was literally flat. Yet she told me she wore a C-cup. My next patient, on the same day, was a woman in whom I had placed 350 mL implants. She was distraught that she was still wearing an A-cup. That day I decided never again to discuss cup size with patients. I now tell them that if they can select sizers that make them look the size they want to be, then I can select similar implants. But I still will not know the cup size, as it is not standardized.

Implant Size

Deciding upon the right implant size can be the most challenging part of this operation. This is because cup size is not standardized. It varies among bra manufacturers and also among a single manufacturer's products. For example, the cup of a 32C bra is smaller than the cup of a 34C bra, even when made by the same company. So telling your surgeon which cup size you desire may be of limited help. Some surgeons may ask your desired cup size to get a general idea of your goals. Do not misinterpret this as a guarantee of the final size.

Typically, implant sizes range from six to eighteen fluid ounces, or 200–600 mL, although larger and smaller implants are available. Implants are manufactured in 25–30 mL increments. As the volume of the implant grows, so does its diameter and projection.

Tips for Selecting Size

There are a number of factors to consider when selecting implant size.

• It might be useful to discuss proportion with your surgeon. Many women seek augmentation to make their breasts proportionate to the rest of their bodies, in which case your surgeon may measure your breast diameter to select an implant size that provides a proportionate augmentation. Others might want their final size to be either larger or smaller than the proportionate size. Of course, one drawback of this approach is that your concept of proportion may be very different than your plastic surgeon's.

• Ask your surgeon for breast implant samples or sizers. You can place these in your bra to help you determine the best volume. You may also use water balloons that are filled to various volumes (a more arduous task). If your plastic surgeon has sizers, be sure to wear a tight sports bra (or two), as doing so makes the sizers more accurate. Incidentally, plastic bags filled with rice are not very useful for sizing, as they do not conform to the shape of the breast.

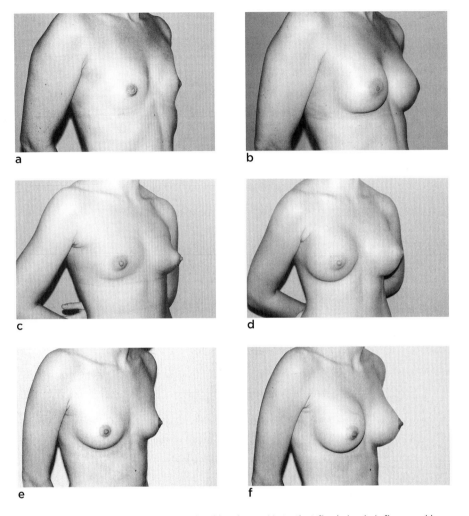

Breast augmentation with various sized implants. Note that final size is influenced by implant size, preoperative breast size, and body size. (a and b) A forty-three-year-old woman who is 5 feet 2 inches and 115 pounds before and after placement of saline implants under the muscle: both 240 mL. (c and d) A twenty-three-year-old woman who is 5 feet 2 inches and 128 pounds before and after placement of saline implants under the muscle: 310 mL right, 280 mL left. (e and f) A twenty-year-old woman who is 5 feet 8 inches and 130 pounds before and after placement of saline implants under the muscle: both 360 mL. (g and h) A twenty-one-year-old woman who is 5 feet 1 inch and 107 pounds before and after placement of saline implants under the muscle: both 375 mL. (i and j) A twenty-three-year-old woman who is 5 feet 6 inches and 125 pounds before and after placement of silicone implants over the muscle: both 500 mL high profile. (k and l) A thirty-one-year-old woman who is 5 feet 4 inches and 135 pounds before and after placement of saline implants under the muscle: both 510 mL. (m and n) A thirty-two-year-old woman who is 5 feet 10 inches and 135 pounds before and after placement of saline implants under the muscle: both 650 mL.

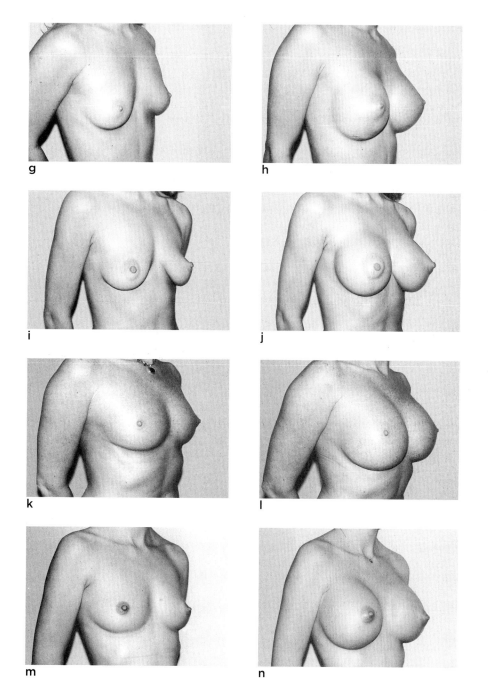

• If you seek large breasts, do not hesitate to say so. The only way your surgeon can provide you with your desired result is if you are open about your goals. Now is not the time to be modest. Be aware, also, that very large implants (especially saline) are more likely to displace downward. You must balance these issues if you seek very large implants.

• Although 30 mL sounds like a lot, it is not. It is merely a fluid ounce. So if, for example, you are struggling between a 360 mL implant and a 390 mL implant, you should stop torturing yourself. They are so similar that if you like one, you will also like the other. Conversely, if you end up deciding (after surgery) that the 360 is too small, then the 390 would also have been too small. Once you have narrowed your selection down to two or three sizes, I recommend you choose the largest among them, as this is associated with greater satisfaction in the end.

• The following is an extremely rough guideline for the volume required to change a single cup size. Multiply by two or three for multiple cup size changes. Based on variation among bra manufacturers, please do not hold me or your plastic surgeon accountable if these volumes are not accurate in your case.

Bra Circumference	Volume Needed to Increase by One Cup Size
32	100–200 mL
34	150–250 mL
36	200–300 mL
38	250–350 mL

Pitfalls in Size Selection

The following are not necessarily useful ways to select implant size:

• Avoid relying on photos of other women: this can be very misleading, especially when height, weight, and chest diameter are different from your own.

Nadine, a thirty-six-year-old corporate attorney, did not want breasts so large that they were a distraction when she was in a business meeting, but she wanted them large enough so that the surgery was worthwhile. She liked several sizes and selected the largest of these. The diameter of the selected implants also matched her breast diameter, and she was very satisfied with her final size.

Janet, a twenty-eight-year-old mechanical illustrator, spent a great deal of time selecting the appropriately sized implant. Yet immediately following surgery, she felt that her breasts were far too large and that a mistake had been made. She was assured that the agreed-upon implant size had been used, that swelling accounted for some of her volume, and that most of her reaction was due to the sudden dramatic change in size for which no one can truly be prepared. She reluctantly agreed to let time pass before making her final judgment. Four weeks later, she said that she had become accustomed to them, but that they actually seemed too small. She was again convinced to wait. Two months later, she was finally satisfied with the size she had chosen.

- Avoid lingerie ads: there is no way to tell which size implant will give the size proportionate to that seen in an ad.
- Do not request the same size implant as a friend whose implanted breasts appear aesthetic to you: this simply does not work unless you are identical twins.
- Do not select a smaller implant than you desire with the hope that "no one will notice." Those who do often later complain, "But no one noticed!"
- Do not select a size larger than you like because "everyone on the Internet said they wished they had gone larger." Be honest with yourself while trying sizers, and you will most likely select an appropriate size.

Implant Profile

Round implants are made roughly in the shape of a jelly doughnut. They also come in three different variations of the doughnut shape: low, medium, and high profile. For any given volume, a low-profile implant has a greater diameter and lower projection than the same-sized high-profile implant. The medium-profile implant is somewhere in between.

Letting Your Surgeon Decide Size: A Double-Edged Sword

The advantage of letting your surgeon select the size is that your plastic surgeon can use your measurements to select implants that are proportionate to your body. The disadvantages are that you might want to be either larger than or smaller than what your plastic surgeon considers proportionate. Plus, some women's breast diameters are not proportionate to the rest of their bodies, which creates an opportunity for getting the size wrong. Finally, some plastic surgeons tend to make all of their patients a size the plastic surgeon feels is aesthetic, without considering that not all women share the same ideas for breast aesthetics.

Alternatively, selecting a size yourself can be a daunting task, as you most likely have never done this before. Perhaps the best option is for you to have an idea of the size you want to be (in mL, not cup size) and then let your plastic surgeon guide you within that range. Your input is needed, as I have observed that, for example, ten women with similar bodies and breasts can all select different sizes.

Communication is critical. The more honest you are with yourself and your plastic surgeon regarding your desired size, the more likely you will be pleased with your result. But remember, final breast size and cup size cannot be guaranteed.

The profile most appropriate to you is objectively determined by the volume you select and the diameter of your breast. As an objective issue, this is best left to your plastic surgeon. For example, if your breast diameter is 13 cm, and you select 400 mL implants, you will be well suited to a medium-profile implant of that volume, as the diameter is about 13 cm. If you selected 550 mL, then you would be well suited to a high-profile implant, as its diameter is also about 13 cm. The difference is that it has more projection to accommodate the larger volume. If you selected a 250 mL implant, then you might be well suited to a low-profile implant. Again, because this is an objective issue, it is best left to your plastic surgeon. In general, about 80 to 90 percent of implants selected are medium profile. About 10 percent are high profile, and less than 5 percent are low profile.

Implant Fill

Saline breast implants are empty when they arrive from the manufacturer. During surgery, your surgeon will fill each implant to the desired volume. The amount within each implant can be adjusted by 25–30 mL before concluding the procedure. Filling to the maximum recommended volume, also known as overfilling, reduces deflation, rippling, and sloshing. Hence, implant manufacturers encourage overfilling. Filling beyond the recommended overfill volume is not usually advocated by the manufacturers, as doing so might increase the risk of deflation.

Deflation

Implants that are filled to the recommended minimum capacity have a higher risk of deflation than those filled to their recommended maximum capacity. The former's edges fold repeatedly and weaken just as a piece of paper folded along the same line repeatedly will thin and tear easily. That is why implant manufacturers recommend that implants be filled to the recommended maximum fill volume.

Adjustable Implants

Because of the difficulty in determining the desired final breast size, some surgeons use adjustable saline implants. Adjustable implants have a small port (for adding or removing saline) that is placed under the skin near the breast. After surgery, your surgeon can easily and painlessly add or remove saline from your implant. The main drawback is that your desired size may still not be achieved. Your surgeon will have at most a 50 mL leeway in adjusting the volume. Adding or removing 50 mL does not alter breast size much. So you and your surgeon must still identify an implant size that is close to your desired size. A final disadvantage is that you will eventually require another operation to remove your ports. Because of these disadvantages, most surgeons do not use adjustable implants.

Implant Profile Terminology and Confusion

Manufacturer	Term for Low Profile	Term for Medium Profile	Term for High Profile
Inamed (Allergan)	Low profile	Moderate profile	High profile
Mentor	Moderate profile	Moderate profile plus	High profile

Note that Mentor uses the term moderate profile *to describe their lowest profile implant, whereas Inamed (Allergan) uses* moderate profile *to describe their medium profile implants. This has created a "moderate" amount of confusion among patients and physicians.*

Rippling and Sloshing

If you have a waterbed, you may have noticed that the amount of water in the mattress alters its degree of rippling and sloshing. The same is true for saline breast implants. Both effects can be reduced by overfilling the implants.

Breasts of Different Sizes

If your breasts are different sizes, this can be addressed in one of three ways. Your surgeon will recommend the best option for you.

1. Have implants of different sizes placed. Because the implants will have different diameters, you may be introducing a new asymmetry. But if your breasts vary in size by more than 20 mL that is the best option.
2. Have identical implants placed and filled to different volumes. This option is most appropriate for volume discrepancies of less than 20 mL and can only be achieved with saline implants, as silicone implants arrive prefilled and cannot be altered by the surgeon.
3. Have identical implants filled to the same volume. Your present size discrepancy will be less noticeable when both breasts are larger. This is best for asymmetries less than 20 mL that do not bother the patient.

Note that regardless of the option you select, your size discrepancy will be less obvious after surgery, as both breasts will be larger. Other breast asymmetry issues are discussed later in this chapter.

Site of Incision

Incisions may be placed under the breast, around the nipple, under the arm, or through the belly button (Figure 7-5).

Under the Breast

An incision under the breast, also called inframammary incision, is hidden along the natural skin crease, in the shadow of the breast. It often heals inconspicuously and affords the surgeon excellent visibility for surgery. But if it heals poorly, it will be visible when you are wearing no clothing. If your surgeon needs to lower your breast crease for optimal positioning of the implant, your scar might end up on the undersurface of the breast, rather than in the crease. Women who have asymmetric breast creases before surgery should expect asymmetrical positions of their scars after surgery. One of the chief advantages of this incision location is that it allows your surgeon

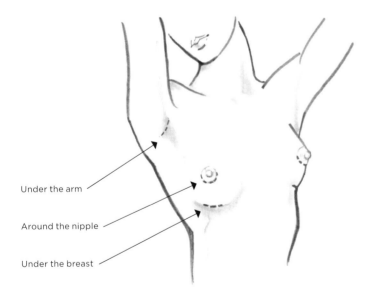

Under the arm

Around the nipple

Under the breast

Figure 7-5: *Incision options. The three common incisions used are under the arm, around the nipple, and under the breast. Each is shown with a dashed line. Only one incision is necessary for each breast.*

to lower the implants (if needed) while they are in place. This may help your surgeon achieve better breast implant position symmetry.

Around the Nipple

An incision around the nipple is designed to camouflage the scar by placing it at the junction of the nipple skin, called the areola, and the surrounding skin. Typically the incision goes halfway around the areola. Because of the natural color transition in this area, the scar is not easily seen. Many surgeons use this incision, also called the periareolar incision, with good results. However, because the nipple is the focal point of the breast, any imperfection, no matter how small, will be obvious. Also, this incision imposes a slightly higher risk of nipple numbness than the other incisions. Finally, because areola size limits incision size, women with small areolas or large silicone implants may not be candidates for this incision, as implant placement might not be technically possible.

Under the Arm

Using an endoscope, which is a pencil-sized rod with a fiber-optic camera on its tip, surgeons have achieved good cosmetic results with an incision under the arm, also called the transaxillary incision. Because silicone implants arrive prefilled from the manufacturer, large silicone implants may be difficult to place through this incision, thereby rendering this incision ill-advised in women seeking large silicone implants.

The scar is well hidden. But if the scar remains noticeable after healing, it will be visible in evening gowns, tank tops, and bathing suits. It will be especially visible in women with olive or brown skin. It can also be a telltale sign, particularly for women who participate in aerobics.

Through the Belly Button

Also called transumbilical breast augmentation (TUBA), placement of implants can be performed through a small incision inside the belly button. It is only an option for saline implants, as silicone implants are too large to fit through the incision. Also, it is used mostly for subglandular placement, as subpectoral placement through the belly button is fraught with implant malposition and hematomas. Because subglandular saline implants present several aesthetic disadvantages (e.g., rippling, wrinkling), many women find this option has more disadvantages than advantages.

Length of Scar

Because saline implants are filled after they are placed, your surgeon can use a small (3–5 cm) incision. Because silicone implants are prefilled by the manufacturer, the incision must be long enough to accommodate the implant. Small implants (less than 350 mL) can often be placed through a 3–5 cm incision. Medium implants (350–500 mL) can often be placed through a 4–6 cm incision. Large implants (greater than 500 mL) often require a 5–8 cm incision.

Scar Visibility

Usually, scars from breast augmentation fade. Occasionally, they become wide or unsightly. The final visibility of your scar depends more on your healing process than on your plastic surgeon's technique. It may take one to two years for your scar to mature.

Aesthetic Issues

In addition to implant size and shape, a number of other aesthetic issues are associated with breast augmentation.

Breast Asymmetry

All women have breast asymmetry. One breast may be higher, larger, or shaped differently than the other. The nipples may be uneven in size, shape, position, or height. The breast crease is often asymmetric in position or shape. Your surgeon will probably point these asymmetries out to you prior to surgery. It is important that you recognize them and understand that, with the exception of breast size discrepancy, most asymmetries will not be improved or corrected by breast augmentation. In fact, some asymmetries may become more obvious simply because you will spend more time looking at your breasts after surgery. (Breast size discrepancy is addressed in the section titled "Implant Fill.")

Marked Asymmetry

Some women have such significant asymmetry that their breasts vary in size by several cups. Many options exist for attaining symmetry in these

Do Implants Really Drop?

Internet chat rooms and message boards are flooded with discussion of implants "dropping" a few weeks after surgery. In most cases, this is not what is happening. Realize that after surgery, especially following subpectoral placement, your body will weep serous fluid into the implant pocket, causing marked swelling above and around the implant, resulting in a bulge above the implant. Some assume this bulge is the implant, but it is usually the serous fluid. As the swelling (serous fluid) resorbs, it will appear as though the implant has dropped, but it has not. It is most likely in the same position as it was all along.

What to Expect

- **Anesthesia:** *Sedation or general.*

- **Location of operation:** *Office or hospital.*

- **Length of surgery:** *One to two hours.*

- **Length of stay:** *Outpatient (home same day).*

- **Discomfort:** *Mild to moderate following implant placement over the muscle, and moderate to severe following implant placement under the muscle. Anticipate three to seven days of pain medication. Ask your surgeon to inject long-lasting local anesthetic during surgery to make your first night more comfortable. Muscle relaxants also help, especially with subpectoral implants.*

- **Bruising:** *Improves in five to ten days. Many have no bruising.*

- **Swelling:** *Peaks around three to five days after surgery. During this time, your breasts might feel as though your breast milk has "come in" following pregnancy. Swelling is typically greater following subpectoral implant placement than after subglandular. Within ten to fourteen days of surgery, 50 to 75 percent of your swelling will resolve. 75 to 90 percent of your swelling will be resolved within a month, and the remainder will resolve over the next month or two. Swelling may be worse if you are athletic or if you resume heavy exercise.*

- **Numbness:** *Temporary numbness, if it occurs, lasts anywhere from two weeks to two years. Permanent numbness occurs in 15 percent.*

- **Bandages:** *Removed in one to seven days.*

- **Stitches:** *Most plastic surgeons use absorbable stitches that are buried under the skin and never require removal. If your surgeon uses nonabsorbable stitches, they will be visible outside the skin and will be removed in five to seven days.*

- **Support:** *You will wear a sports bra or Ace wrap for one to four weeks. Avoid an underwire bra until your surgeon approves it.*

- **Work:** *You may return to work in three to seven days if the implants were placed over your muscle, and five to ten days if the implants were placed under your muscle. If your job requires heavy lifting, wait two to four weeks and obtain your surgeon's approval.*

- **Exercise:** *May be resumed in two to four weeks.*

- **Final result:** *Will be seen within one to four months depending on swelling.*

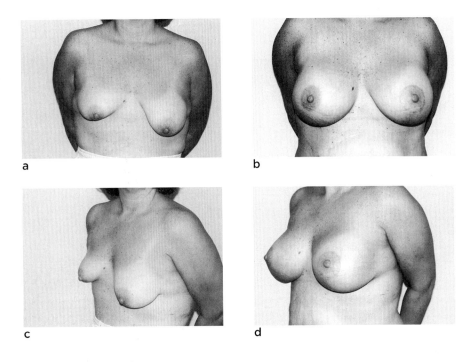

Breasts with marked asymmetry. (a and c) A thirty-six-year-old with tuberous breasts, droop, and a smaller right breast. (b and d) Six months after a left breast lift, bilateral augmentation (550 mL left and 750 mL right), and bilateral release of tuberous breasts. Note that in spite of grade II–III droop preoperatively on the right, this woman did not require a right breast lift, as release of the tuberous breast was all that was required in her case.

instances. First, you must decide your desired breast size. Do you want both breasts smaller than the small breast or larger than the large breast? Would you rather have both breasts match the size of one of your existing breasts? Or would you want them somewhere in between? Regardless of what you choose, a combination of augmentation, lift, and reduction can be applied to improve your symmetry—often with amazing results.

Cleavage

Cleavage refers to the distance between the breasts, not to breast size. By way of cultural values, when the breasts are close together, they are considered to have attractive cleavage. For this reason, many women hope to gain cleavage as a result of breast augmentation. Unfortunately, this is not always possible. The likelihood of attaining tighter cleavage depends somewhat upon preoperative cleavage and whether the implants are placed under or over the pectoralis muscle. Women who start with widely spaced breasts before surgery and who choose subpectoral placement of implants should expect little or no improvement in cleavage, as the attachments of the pectoralis muscle to the ribs and sternum typically prevent tight cleavage. Implant placement over the muscle is more likely to yield tight cleavage. Note that one potential consequence of trying to attain tight cleavage is symmastia (see "Telltale Signs").

Breast Droop

Breast droop is defined and explained in detail in the next chapter. In short, breast droop refers to the condition whereby the nipple has sagged down to or below the breast crease. Breast implants do not affect nipple height. As such, they will not raise droopy nipples. However, because implants can lower the breast crease, they can affect the relative position of the nipple to the crease, thereby making breast droop less obvious or less severe in cases of mild droop. Yet the most definitive treatment for breast droop remains breast lift (see Chapter 8).

Stretch Marks

Breast augmentation will not improve stretch marks on the breasts. It might cause new stretch marks to form, but this is uncommon.

Breast Shape

Breast augmentation mainly affects breast volume, not shape. Some breast shapes require more than simple augmentation. One example of this is a tuberous breast, which is narrow and long. If your plastic surgeon tells you your breast is tuberous, its shape can be improved through implant placement, but surgical division of the fibrous bands within your breast that cause this shape is also required.

Adjusting to Your "New" Breasts

Getting used to your new breast size may be easy or difficult. Some women are immediately pleased with their size. Others may take months to adjust. Some women are disconcerted that their inner arms brush against their breasts during normal movement. This is to be expected. It is not uncommon for a woman to initially be concerned that her breasts are too large, only to be disappointed after the swelling has resolved. The best way to prepare yourself for this is to choose the largest size that you find acceptable and also antici- pate that you might initially perceive yourself as too large. Be patient, and stop staring at your breasts in the mirror.

Telltale Signs

There are a number of telltale signs of breast augmen- tation that you should be aware of.

Spherical Breast

Moderate or severe capsular contractures can cause the breasts to appear unnaturally round. Severely affected breasts can resemble coconuts. If you peruse *Sports Illustrated*'s swimsuit issue, you are likely to see a variety of examples. (See the section "Capsular Con- tracture" for treatment of this problem.)

Postpartum Droop

During pregnancy, breast skin stretches to accom- modate the enlarging breast. Following pregnancy, the breast returns to normal size. If the skin does not regain its tone, the breast droops. Because the implant does not droop, the breast may appear to have fallen off the implant (Figure 7-6). A breast lift is required to restore the breast to its natural position (see Chapter 8).

Not all women who become pregnant following augmentation suffer this cosmetic problem. Those who have modest change in breast size during pregnancy and those with good skin tone are less likely to have postpartum droop. Be aware that droop following pregnancy is due to the pregnancy, not the implants. Hence, if it occurs, it likely would have done so whether or not implants were involved—it just looks worse when implants are in place.

Breast Augmentation Without Surgery

With all of the previously mentioned risks and potential problems with breast implants, it is no wonder that some women seek an alternative that does not require surgery or implants. It is called the Brava system and involves wearing plastic suction domes over each breast for ten hours each day for 10 to 14 weeks. Risks are low, and results are modest, with most women achieving an average size increase of about 100 grams (the equivalent of a 100 mL implant), which correlates to about three ounces or one-half cup size. Cost is $2,500. The greatest problem women encounter with this program is compliance, as the plastic domes can be large, cumber- some, and uncomfortable. Those who are compliant with the system and con- servative in their expectations have been pleased. The Brava system is available only through physicians.

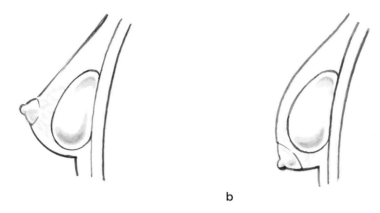

a   b

Figure 7-6: *Postpartum droop. (a) An augmented breast prior to pregnancy. (b) Following pregnancy, the breast droops, but the implant holds position. This creates the appearance of the breast falling off the implant.*

Symmastia

Symmastia is the merging of the breasts into an indistinct mass (Figure 7-7). It occurs if the skin between the breasts loses its attachment to the breastbone during or after surgery. This can be the consequence of trying to achieve tight cleavage for women who have widely spaced breasts. This is a challenging problem to fix, and revision surgery may not be successful. Fortunately, symmastia is rare. More common is a condition known as bread-loafing, in which the breasts appear separate and distinct unless they are being manually pushed toward one another, at which time the distinction is lost.

Cost

In the United States, the range of total fees for breast augmentation extends from $5,000 to $10,000. The average cost is:

	Saline	Silicone
Surgeon's fee	$3,400	$3,700
Anesthesiologist's fee	$700	$700
Operating room (facility) fee	$900	$900
Implant fee	$1,300	$2,200
Total	$6,300	$7,500

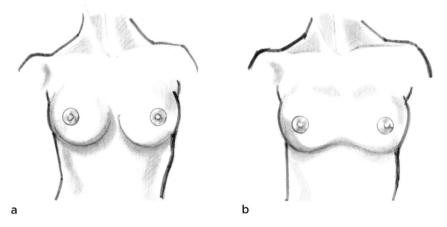

a

b

Figure 7-7: *Telltale sign symmastia. (a) Natural breasts, which are distinct and separate. (b) Breasts with symmastia, which are unnaturally merged together into an indistinct mass.*

See "Fees" in Chapter 1 for various factors that might affect your own actual cost.

Saline implants cost $900 to $1,100 per pair from the manufacturer. Silicone implants cost $1,600 to $2,200 from the manufacturer. Your surgeon or the operating facility will mark up that price to cover the cost of ordering, shipping, and stocking. If you are charged more than $1,400 for saline or $2,400 for silicone implants, you should question the price. Only plastic surgeons and hospitals may purchase implants, so you are limited in your ability to negotiate.

Duration of Results and Need for Further Surgery

The Internet is flooded with claims that breast implants last ten years, at which time they must be replaced. This simply is not true. Whether your implants are ten, twenty, or thirty years old, you need not replace them unless there is a problem. Many of the problems that lead to revision or replacement are usually evident within the first three months (e.g., infection, hematoma, asymmetry, displacement, malposition). So if these problems do not occur within the first few months, they might never occur. Other problems, such as rippling and wrinkling, can become evident early on, after weight loss, or as you age. Rupture for silicone implants, deflation for saline implants, and capsular contracture for any implant can occur at

The Ten-Year Rumor

Most likely, the rumor that implants need to be replaced every ten years evolved due to the thin-shelled silicone gel implants that were used in the 1970s and 1980s. These implants had such thin shells that rupture and resultant capsular contractures were very common within ten years of placement. Silicone implants that have been in use since the silicone ban was lifted in 2006 have much thicker shells and are expected to have much lower rates of rupture and capsular contracture.

Questions to Ask Your Plastic Surgeon

Do you recommend placement above or below the muscle?

Do you recommend silicone gel or saline?

Do you recommend smooth or textured? Round or teardrop?

Where will the incisions be?

Do you plan to overfill the implants (if saline)?

May I have muscle relaxants after surgery?

What is your policy regarding revision surgery?

any time and are the primary things you need to be concerned about as you and your implants age. Yet if none of these things occurs, you need not have revision surgery or new implants. Of course, some women seek revision for a change in size as they age, but this is not due to a problem with the implant. Finally, some problems, such as persistent numbness or pain, do not lend themselves to surgery, as surgery does not improve them.

Not all women with implants require further breast surgery, but it is prudent to assume that sooner or later, revision surgery will be required for one of the preceding reasons.

Changing Your Mind

Breast implants can be removed at any time. However, you may find your natural breasts have changed due to breast shrinkage and skin stretch. Breast shrinkage, or atrophy, occurs to varying degrees in response to aging and pressure exerted on your breast by the implant. Do not expect this to improve following implant removal.

After breast augmentation, your skin may stretch to accommodate the new implant. Following removal of the implant, your skin may tighten somewhat or not at all. The degree of skin tightening depends on your age, the length of time the implant was in place, and the volume of the implant. An older woman with large implants placed decades earlier should expect little tightening of breast skin. A younger woman with smaller implants can expect more tightening. If spontaneous tightening does not occur to a satisfactory degree within six months, breast lift is an option (see Chapter 8).

Satisfaction

Breast augmentation is one of the most requested procedures in plastic surgery. As with all cosmetic surgery, there are no guarantees regarding outcome or satisfaction. If you understand and accept the risks of this opera-

Tips and Traps

- *Round implants are appropriate for most women. Compared to teardrop implants, they provide an aesthetically similar result, do not restrict options regarding type of implant surface, obviate the potential problem of implant rotation, and cost less.*

- *Request overfilling of saline implants to reduce the risk of deflation, rippling, and sloshing.*

- *Do not expect tight cleavage if your breasts are widely separated and you choose subpectoral augmentation. Implants do not change the position of your breasts—only the volume.*

- *Anticipate that small breasts with saline implants will look and feel somewhat stiff. If this is not acceptable, choose silicone implants.*

- *If you do not want others to suspect that you had breast augmentation, stuff your bra progressively for a few months prior to surgery and wear tight clothing. Afterward, wear loose baggy clothing and complain about weight gain.*

- *Expect that you will be required to have a mammogram before surgery if you are older than thirty-five.*

- *Women whose mothers or sisters had breast cancer should recognize that they are at increased risk for breast cancer and that implants do interfere with mammography. These women should have their implants placed below the pectoralis muscle, which poses least interference.*

- *Women unwilling to accept the potential loss of nipple or breast sensation should not have breast augmentation.*

- *Women unwilling to accept the potential need for further surgery should not have breast augmentation.*

- *If you are prone to chest acne, request a prescription for Bactrim from your plastic surgeon and start taking it one week before surgery to clear your chest acne. As acne is associated with bacteria, this might reduce your risk of capsular contracture or infection.*

- *Avoid exercise for three to four weeks after surgery to minimize swelling and the risk of seroma and hematoma.*

- *As lifelong follow-up is important, find out if your surgeon charges for visits after surgery.*

- *Ask your plastic surgeon to use bupivacaine, a long-lasting local anesthetic, during your procedure to take the edge off your pain as you recover. Although it only lasts eight to twenty-four hours, reducing initial pain upon waking results in overall less discomfort long after the bupivacaine has worn off.*

- *Following surgery, ask your surgeon for a copy of the typed operative report in addition to an implant identification card, provided by the manufacturer. As most physicians keep records for only seven years, you will want to have copies of these important documents.*

Lori, an uninhibited thirty-three-year-old computer salesperson, was so pleased with her implants that after a few drinks at a large family picnic, she proudly pulled open her shirt to show off her new breasts. Subsequently two family members sought breast augmentation, and one male cousin sought pectoral implants.

tion and still choose to proceed, you most likely will be glad you did.

Concluding Thoughts

The decision to proceed with breast augmentation is not a simple one, particularly in light of the fact that those who receive implants should anticipate future revision. Although breast implants do not cause medical illnesses, numerous risks are associated with their placement. Those who understand these issues and choose to proceed with breast augmentation are among the most satisfied patients in any plastic surgery practice.

8

Raising Droopy Breasts

Breast Lift

reast lift (also called mastopexy) affects the position of the breasts without affecting size. It is an entirely different operation than breast augmentation. Mastopexy is for women whose breasts have sagged as a result of pregnancy, weight loss, or time. But like so many plastic surgery procedures, mastopexy has its drawbacks. This chapter will help you decide whether this operation will be worthwhile for you.

Augmentation Versus Lift

Breast augmentation makes breasts larger but does not raise the nipple or lift the breast. A breast lift raises the nipple but does not affect breast size. These are two very different operations for two very different purposes. In women who wish to address both size and droop, both operations can be performed on the same patient at the same time, as explained later in this chapter.

Causes of Breast Droop

Breast droop is an unfortunate by-product of breast size, age, gravity, and pregnancy. Each of these causes contributes to stretching of breast skin. Because breast skin is solely responsible for holding the breast in position, its laxity will give way to breast droop, also called breast ptosis (pronounced *toe-sis*).

If your breast skin is tight and has good tone, it will hold your breast high. If your skin is loose or stretched, it will allow your breast to droop.

Size, Age, and Gravity

Breast size is the greatest determinant of droop. As breasts enlarge, gravity pulls them downward. The overlying skin stretches and loses its tone. Age also contributes to breast droop, because skin thins with age and becomes less resistant to the effects of gravity. Yet size is a more important factor than age. For example, an eighteen-year-old with large breasts will usually have greater droop than a fifty-year-old with small breasts.

Pregnancy

During pregnancy your breasts enlarge, causing the skin to stretch. Following pregnancy your breasts may diminish in size, but the overlying skin might not. It often loses tone and allows droop. Because each pregnancy can cause this, you should defer a breast lift until after your last child is born.

Degrees of Breast Droop

Plastic surgeons gauge droop based on the position of the nipple compared to the breast crease, also called the inframammary crease (Figure 8-1). The ideal position for the nipple is above the inframammary crease, but with time, age, and gravity, the breast descends.

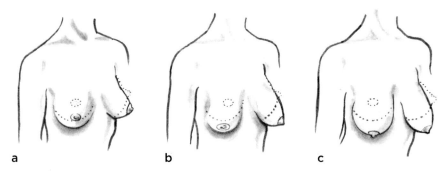

a   b   c

Figure 8-1: *Degrees of breast droop. Dotted lines show ideal breast position. (a) Mild droop: the nipple is level with the inframammary crease. (b) Moderate droop: the nipple is below the inframammary crease. (c) Advanced droop: the nipple is on the lowest part of the breast, pointing downward.*

How Plastic Surgeons Fix Breast Droop

Because loose skin causes breast droop, the treatment is to remove excess skin. The remaining, tighter skin then holds the breast in a higher position. The greater the droop, the more skin must be removed—and the more extensive will be the scars. The operation also reduces nipple size for those who have undesirably large nipples.

As droop improves at the cost of new scars, a breast lift involves trading one cosmetic problem for another. Because of this, many women are unwilling to consider this operation unless their droop is moderate or advanced.

The following are general guidelines. Ask your plastic surgeon which procedure is most appropriate in your case.

Mild Droop

Correction of mild droop usually involves removal of skin around the nipple, which leaves a scar around the areola. If it heals well, the scar is relatively well hidden. (Figure 8-2).

Moderate Droop

Surgeons usually correct moderate droop by removing skin both around and below the nipple (i.e., from the nipple to the inframammary crease), resulting in scars in both areas (Figure 8-3).

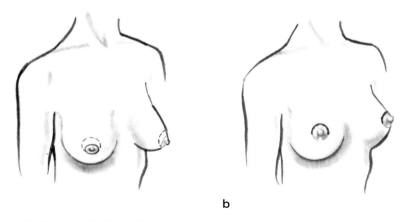

a   b

Figure 8-2: *Breast lift for mild droop. (a) Breasts with mild droop, with the anticipated incision (dashed line). (b) Following surgery, the breast is lifted and the
scar is above the nipple (solid line). For correction of mild droop, the scar often
extends all the way around the nipple.*

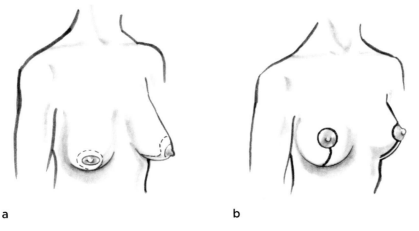

a   b

Figure 8-3: *Breast lift for moderate droop. (a) Breasts with moderate droop, with the anticipated incision (dashed line). (b) Following surgery, the breasts are lifted and the scar is present around the nipple and from the nipple to the inframammary crease (solid line).*

Advanced Droop

Correction of advanced droop usually involves skin removal and scars in three areas: around the nipple, below the nipple (i.e., from the nipple to the inframammary crease), and along the inframammary crease (Figure 8-4).

Purse-String Breast Lift

Another alternative is a purse-string mastopexy, in which a doughnut of skin is removed from around the nipple, regardless of the extent of droop. This limits the scar to the area around the nipple, but drawbacks include flattening of the breasts, widening of the areola (i.e., the pigmented skin around the nipple), development of stretch marks, and bunching of skin around the areola. Further, the scars that are omitted with this technique, from the areola to the inframammary crease and along the inframammary crease, are often less visible than the scar around the areola. Because these issues are magnified in cases of moderate or severe droop, this technique is typically limited to cases involving mild droop.

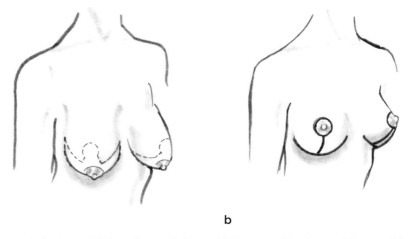

a   b

Figure 8-4: *Breast lift for advanced droop. (a) Breasts with advanced droop, with the anticipated incision (dashed line). (b) Following surgery, the breasts are lifted and the scar is more extensive (solid line). These incisions may be used for moderate droop as well.*

Cosmetic Limitations of a Breast Lift

As you decide if a breast lift is right for you, it is important to keep in mind the cosmetic limitations of the procedure.

Scars

A breast lift is designed to keep all scars at or below the nipple level. They will not be visible in clothing and most swimwear. Immediately following surgery, the scars may be red, firm, and raised. The scars mature, fade, and soften over the course of months or years. As with any scar, breast lift scars may fade and become nearly invisible, or they may become wide and raised. Final scar appearance cannot be predicted prior to any surgery.

Scars are permanent. Not all women consider the scars to be acceptable, even when well healed and barely visible. Many women with mild droop who initially seek breast lift surgery reconsider after learning about the scars. Women who are more willing to accept the exchange of droop for scars tend to be those who have moderate or advanced droop.

Breast Shape

Whereas a breast lift alone will definitely raise the nipple and tighten the skin, it may not restore shape to the upper half of the breast, which might still appear hollow following a lift alone. If this is your concern and if you want your breasts larger, then you should consider augmentation along with your lift.

Breast Height

Whereas a breast lift will raise the nipple, it does not raise the inframammary crease, which is the crease below the breast. Women who have low creases will continue to have this issue after a breast lift. Because the position of the crease dictates how high the nipple can be repositioned, these women might never achieve results they feel are acceptable. Women who

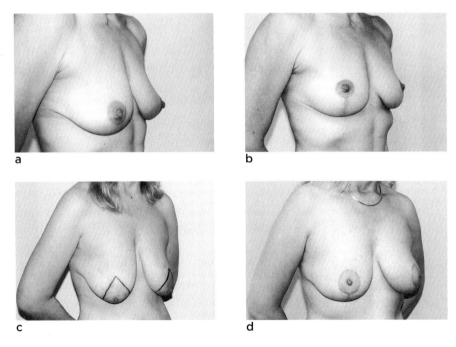

a

b

c

d

Upper pole (upper half of the breast mound) appearance after a lift alone. Following a lift alone, women with firm breasts may have an aesthetic fullness in the upper half of the breast, whereas women with flaccid breasts tend to look hollow. (a and b) This woman had grade II droop and flaccid breasts before surgery. After a breast lift, her nipple position is good, but the upper half is flat. (c and d) This woman had grade III droop and very flaccid breasts before surgery. After a breast lift, the upper half of the breast appears hollow or concave. An implant can improve this.

have had substantial weight gain and loss are more likely to fall into this category.

Large Breasts

Because recurrent droop following a breast lift is closely tied to size, women who have large breasts have a greater likelihood and degree of recurrent droop than those with small breasts. In the worst-case scenario, a woman with very large breasts who undergoes a lift might find herself three months later with breasts just as low as before surgery—but also with scars. These women might be best suited to a breast reduction, in which the breasts are both raised and reduced in size.

Breast Augmentation Instead of Breast Lift

Some women optimistically and erroneously believe that breast implants will raise their droopy breasts. This is not true. Implants do increase the projection of the breast and nipple, but they do not raise the nipple higher. In some cases, breast implants can lower the breast mound and thus cause the nipple to appear relatively higher, but the actual nipple height does not change.

Augmentation Alone in Cases of Mild Droop

Because augmentation does not affect nipple height, women who choose augmentation alone must be prepared for persistently low nipples after surgery. Because most women with mild droop would prefer low nipples over the scars of a lift, this is a reasonable option, provided they understand these issues.

Augmentation Alone in Cases of Moderate or Advanced Droop

In cases of moderate or advanced droop, augmentation alone often results in unfavorable cosmetic results (as Figure 8-5). Because the nipple in these cases is so low, it might appear as though the nipple and natural breast tissues are hanging off the implant and that the implant is causing an unnatural bulge in the upper half of the breast (Figure 8-5b).

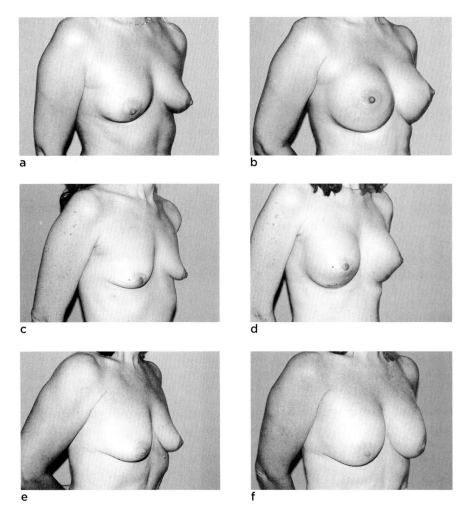

Women with different degrees of droop who chose augmentation without a lift. Note that implants do not raise the nipples in any of these women. Also note that there are no cases of grade III droop here, as implants alone invariably appear unacceptable in these cases. (a and b) A thirty-four-year-old woman with grade I droop before and after placement of 510 mL saline implants under the muscle. She has neither a bulge in the upper half of the breast nor a double-bubble in the lower portion of the breast, although either of these could have occurred. (c and d) A thirty-five-year-old woman with grade I–II droop before and after placement of 375 mL silicone implants under the muscle. She has mild upper pole bulging. (e and f) A forty-three-year-old woman with grade II droop before and after placement of 360 mL (left) and 390 mL (right) saline implants under the muscle. She has upper pole fullness and low nipples, both of which would be improved with a lift. In cases such as this, some women choose to have a lift, whereas others choose to accept their low nipples and upper pole fullness in order to avoid scars associated with a lift.

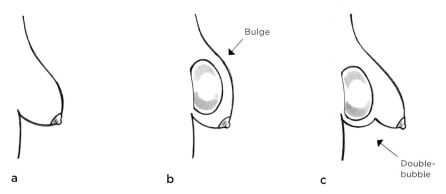

Figure 8-5: *Possible outcomes of augmentation (without a lift) on a moderately or severely droopy breast. (a) Droopy breast without an implant. (b) If the droopy breast receives an implant (but not a lift), then the implant might cause an unnatural bulge in the upper half of the breast. (c) If the implant is lowered to avoid bulging in the upper half, then it might cause a double-bubble of the lower half of the breast.*

In an effort to avoid this appearance, you might think that lowering the implant farther will solve the problem. Unfortunately, lowering the implant in cases of moderate or severe droop can cause a double-bubble (Figure 8-5c).

Recommendation

Bulging of the upper half of the breast or double-bubble of the lower half can occur in mild droop, but they are more likely with increasing degrees of droop. Even so, women with moderate or advanced droop can still choose to have augmentation alone—provided they want to increase breast size and they understand these issues. If after an augmentation alone, they are dissatisfied with the appearance of their breasts and wish to have a lift, they may do so. Because a secondary lift more easily remedies the problem of upper bulging than lower double-bubble, I recommend that women choosing to have an augmentation alone proceed with the goal of implant placement as low as possible, while not so low as to cause a double-bubble. If in doing so an upper bulge exists, it can either be accepted or remedied with a lift.

Breast Augmentation in Combination with Lift

Women who desire both larger and higher breasts may seek to combine breast augmentation and lift. Most plastic surgeons perform both procedures concurrently. One distinct advantage of having both a lift and augmentation is that the implants can lend an aesthetic shape to the upper half of the breasts, whereas a lift alone often leaves the upper half of the breasts hollow.

Complications

When a qualified plastic surgeon performs your operation, both your procedure and recovery are likely to be uneventful. Even in ideal circumstances, however, complications may occur. In addition to the specific complications mentioned here, refer to Chapter 1 for general complications that may follow any procedure.

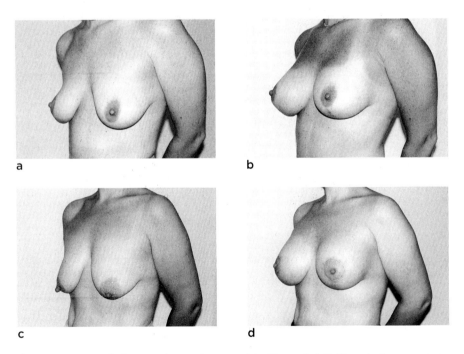

a

b

c

d

Augmentation and lift. (a) A thirty-one-year-old with grade I–II droop before surgery. (b) Two months after a lift and augmentation with 300 mL saline implants under the muscle. (c) A thirty-three-year-old with grade III droop before surgery. (d) Three months after a breast lift and augmentation with 330 mL saline implants under the muscle.

Skin Death

Skin death is a potential complication of a breast lift. It is a great risk for smokers, which is why most plastic surgeons mandate that smokers cease smoking and all nicotine aids several weeks before and after surgery. Yet even in nonsmokers, skin death may occur as a result of a hematoma, from excessive tension on the skin, or for no apparent reason. If skin death occurs, you will develop an open wound, usually in a small area below the nipple. The wound will heal within weeks, depending on its size. Final appearance cannot be predicted; some open wounds actually heal more discreetly than do scars.

Nipple Problems

Loss of nipple sensation, change of nipple color, and partial nipple death may occur. This is uncommon, but it is more likely among those with

What to Expect

- **Anesthesia:** *General or sedation.*
- **Location of operation:** *Office or hospital.*
- **Length of surgery:** *One to three hours (three to four hours if performed with augmentation).*
- **Length of stay:** *Outpatient (home same day).*
- **Discomfort:** *Mild to moderate. Anticipate two to seven days of prescription pain medication.*
- **Swelling and bruising:** *Improve in three to ten days.*
- **Bandages:** *Will be removed in one to seven days.*
- **Stitches:** *Most plastic surgeons use absorbable stitches that are buried under the skin and never require removal. Nonabsorbable stitches, if used, will be removed in five to seven days.*
- **Support:** *Wear a sports bra or Ace wrap for one to four weeks. Avoid an underwire bra until your surgeon approves it.*
- **Work:** *You may return to work in three to seven days.*
- **Exercise:** *May be resumed in two weeks.*
- **Final result:** *Will be seen after the scars have matured, which will be about six to eighteen months.*

severely droopy breasts. If numbness occurs, nipple sensation usually returns within six months. Color changes and irregularities may never improve.

Telltale Signs

The main telltale signs of breast lift are scars, which have been fully discussed throughout this chapter. The other telltale sign is an unnaturally high nipple.

High Nipple

If your nipple is too high after surgery, it will look unnatural (Figure 8-6). It might even worsen over time because your breast mound will descend in response to gravity, but your nipple will not. Attempts to correct this problem can result in new scars above the nipple.

Cost

In the United States, the range of total fees for breast lift extends from $4,000 to $9,000. The average cost is:

Surgeon's fee	$4,000
Anesthesiologist's fee	$900
Operating room (facility) fee	$1,200
Total	$6,100

If you combine breast augmentation and lift, expect to pay $9,000 to $12,000. See "Fees" in Chapter 1 for various factors that might affect your own actual cost.

Satisfaction

A breast lift exchanges the aesthetic problem of droop for the aesthetic problem of scars. Those who have a clear understanding of this drawback and choose to proceed with surgery are usually satisfied with their results. Disappointment is generally due to complications, misconceptions about scars, or recurrence of droop.

Questions to Ask Your Plastic Surgeon

Will a breast implant alone solve the problem of my droopy breasts?

Will you show me where the scars will be on my breasts?

How long will a breast lift last in my case?

Large Nipples

Large, or hypertrophic, nipples are nipples that have become so large (typically in response to breast-feeding) that they flop down over the areola. This condition ironically seems to be more common in women with smaller breasts. Correction involves surgically recessing the nipple into the areola by trimming redundant skin around the nipple. This can be performed under local anesthesia. If bupivacaine, a long-lasting local anesthetic, is used, you may return to work on the same day. Average total cost is $1,500.

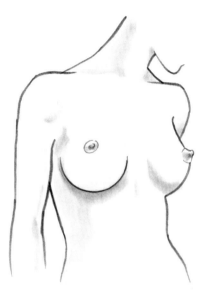

Figure 8-6: *Both nipples are high and appear to point upward. If your nipple is placed too high, you may have this undesirable telltale result.*

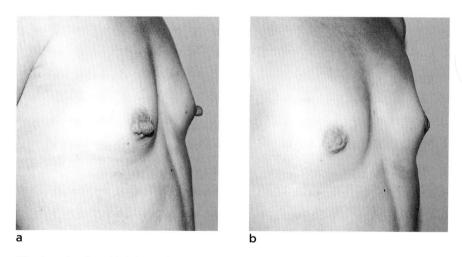

a   b

Nipple reduction. (a) A forty-three-year-old woman with hypertrophic nipples before surgery. (b) Four months after nipple reduction.

Tips and Traps

- *Anticipate scars. As a general rule, the more extensive your droop, the more extensive will be your scars.*

- *Scars can be limited to the area around the nipple if droop is mild. If droop is moderate or advanced, limiting your scars to this area may impose further trade-offs such as flattening of the breast and stretch marks.*

- *Wait until you are done bearing children before considering a breast lift.*

- *Quit smoking and nicotine aids for two to four weeks.*

- *Anticipate recurrent droop if your breasts are large. The larger your breasts are, the more droop you can expect, and the sooner you can expect it.*

Concluding Thoughts

A breast lift offers the opportunity to turn back time to an extent, providing youthful breast position without affecting size. If you desire larger breasts, a breast lift can be performed together with augmentation. The main drawback of a breast lift is scarring. Because scars represent a different cosmetic problem than droop does, each woman must decide if this trade-off is worthwhile.

9

Tightening Your Loose Body Skin

Tummy Tuck, Inner Thigh Lift, Outer Thigh and Buttock Lift, Body Lift, and Arm Lift

Many women deal with the consequences of weight gain and weight loss at some point in their lives. Oftentimes, it is related to pregnancy. Regardless of the cause, weight change results in loose skin of the abdomen, thighs, and buttocks. Women eager to address this problem typically turn to diet and exercise, only to find that these efforts—even if successful—fail to tighten their loose skin.

Fortunately, cosmetic surgery has something to offer. If your problem is a protruded abdomen or loose abdominal skin, a tummy tuck may be appropriate. For loose inner thigh skin, an inner thigh lift may be the operation of choice. If your buttocks and outer thighs have descended, lifting these areas can help. Those with hanging arm skin may choose an arm lift. Those with concerns in multiple areas may consider a total body lift, which combines a tummy tuck, an inner thigh lift, and an outer thigh and buttock lift. Following a tummy tuck, a thigh lift, a buttock lift, or a body lift, you will find that your skin is tighter and your body appears leaner and younger.

Liposuction Versus Lift

Liposuction removes some fat, but it plays only a minor role in skin tightening. As a rule, liposuction that removes only fat will make your body appear thinner, whereas a body lift that removes both fat and loose skin will make your body look thinner and younger.

These operations, however, are not appropriate for all women. Each procedure involves major surgery, poses significant risks, and is worthy of serious consideration. To determine the right operation for you, consult a plastic surgeon who is experienced in body contour surgery.

169

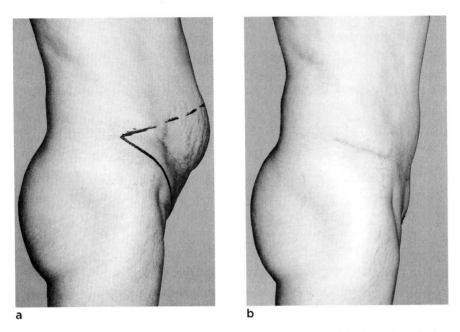

a   b

Abdominoplasty. (a) A forty-seven-year-old before surgery. The black marks indicate the estimated amount of skin to be removed. (b) Five months after abdominoplasty.

Tummy Tuck

A tummy tuck, also called abdominoplasty, is an operation for women who have been pregnant or who have undergone weight gain and loss. Both conditions stretch the abdominal wall and can result in a flabby and protruded abdomen.

The term *tummy tuck* is deceptive and implies a simple, risk-free operation. A tummy tuck is neither simple nor risk-free. It is a serious operation with potentially serious consequences. If a surgeon tells you that a tummy tuck is minor surgery, go elsewhere.

Tummy Tuck or Liposuction

Women often question whether their lax abdomens would be best improved by a tummy tuck or by liposuction. The

Tightening Loose Skin Without Surgery

Radio-frequency treatments have been used with some success to tighten loose facial skin, thereby avoiding or postponing a facelift (see Chapter 2). Efforts to apply the same technology to loose skin of the body have been generally disappointing thus far. It is possible, however, that as this technology advances, radio-frequency treatments may someday be very effective for loose skin of the arms, legs, and trunk.

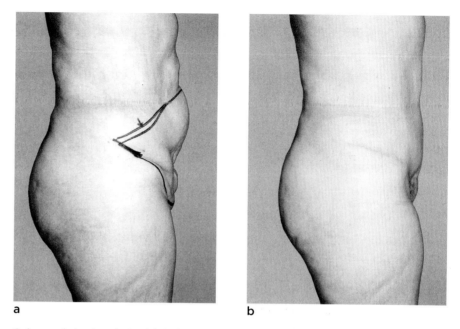

a   b

Salvage abdominoplasty. (a) A sixty-nine-year-old woman who underwent abdominal liposuction by another surgeon in spite of very loose skin. She predictably had skin irregularities. (b) Nine months after abdominoplasty.

answer depends on whether the problem is due to loose skin, excess fat, a lax inner girdle, or a combination of these. In order to determine your problems, work through the "Abdominal Self-Assessment" sidebar.

Angie, a thirty-nine-year-old mother of three, was often asked her due date by strangers who assumed she was pregnant. Although she had a protuberant abdomen, she was not pregnant, and these episodes were embarrassing and depressing to her. After a tummy tuck, she could fit into clothing four sizes smaller and no longer worried about looking pregnant.

Tummy Tuck Versus Liposuction

A tummy tuck can improve loose skin, excess fat, and lax fascia. Liposuction only reduces excess fat. If you have excess skin, poor skin tone, or lax fascia, then you would be disappointed with the results of liposuction. A tummy tuck is more appropriate.

Tummy Tuck Combined with Liposuction

A tummy tuck removes the fat of the lower abdomen only. If you have significant excess upper abdominal fat as well as lax fascia and loose skin, you may need both a tummy tuck and liposuction. However, performing abdominal liposuction and a tummy tuck simultaneously may increase the risk of complications in some women. For this reason, many surgeons will not perform both at the same time and recommend separating the operations by at least three months.

Some surgeons will perform limited liposuction of the abdomen at the same time as a tummy tuck, but most will avoid extensive abdominal liposuction. Concurrent liposuction of other areas such as the hips or thighs does not increase the risk of abdominal skin complications.

Abdominal Self-Assessment

Stand in front of your mirror and evaluate your bare abdomen. Do not tighten your muscles. Relax. You will assess three characteristics: skin, fat, and inner girdle.

Skin
Pinch the skin of your lower abdomen. See if you can get the skin near your belly button to meet the skin near your pubic hair. If so, you have significantly loose skin.

Fat
Tighten your abdominal muscles by trying to flatten your tummy. With your abdomen tight, pinch your skin and fat. If you can gather more than a fistful, you probably have excess fat. Tightening your abdomen helps you distinguish between excess fat and a loose inner girdle.

Inner Girdle (Also Known as Fascia or Gristle)
Both your inner girdle and your abdominal muscles (the rectus muscles) affect the tone and appearance of your abdomen. Your inner girdle is made of fascia, which is the dense, white gristle found on steak. A broad sheet of fascia extends from your rib cage to your pubic bone. The purpose of fascia is to keep the abdominal contents, such as the stomach and intestines, inside the abdomen. Whereas exercise can tone the rectus muscle, it does not affect the tone of the gristle.

During pregnancy, your inner girdle stretches to accommodate the growing fetus. Following pregnancy, your rectus muscle may or may not regain the tone it once had, depending on how distended your abdomen became, how old you were during pregnancy, and how many pregnancies you have had. Younger mothers have a better opportunity to regain fascia tone. In some women, excellent muscle tone can compensate for lax fascia.

Stand with your profile toward the mirror and tighten your abdomen. You will see the effects of muscle tone on the appearance of your abdomen. When your abdominal muscles relax, the appearance of your

Stretch Marks

During periods of rapid weight gain, skin stretches to accommodate increased body volume. Because skin is elastic, it tolerates significant stretching over a short period of time, such as during pregnancy. At some point, however, the skin reaches a limit, and the deepest layer tears instead of stretching further. When the deep layer tears, the overlying skin remains intact but appears thin and streaky. These streaks are called stretch marks. Once stretch marks occur, they are permanent.

abdomen is determined mostly by your inner girdle (Figure 9-1). The visible difference between a relaxed abdomen and a tightened abdomen reflects the degree of weakness in your abdominal fascia. If there is a significant difference, you likely have significant laxity of your fascia. This is a critical point to assess. If you have a lax inner girdle, tightening it through a tummy tuck is one of the keys to a more aesthetic abdomen, as liposuction does not address this problem.

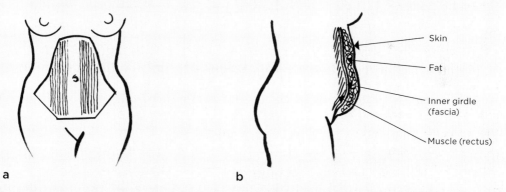

a   b

Figure 9-1: *Abdominal self-assessment for skin, fat, and fascia. (a) A frontal view showing the inner girdle beneath the skin. The vertical lines indicate the position of the paired rectus muscles under the inner girdle. (b) A side view showing that a bowed inner girdle can cause the skin and fat to bow forward also.*

Finally, ask a close friend to use his or her open hands to try to press your abdomen flat. If the person is able to do so, it is a sign that you might be able to achieve a flat abdomen following a tummy tuck, provided your fascia quality is reasonable. If the person cannot make your abdomen flat with this maneuver, then you probably have excessive internal fat, and a tummy tuck definitely will not make you flat.

Julia, a thirty-five-year-old mother of three, wanted to regain the taut, flat abdomen of her youth. Following her pregnancies, she had developed loose skin, a lax inner girdle, and significant excess abdominal fat. It was evident that liposuction alone would not be adequate, because it would not improve her lax fascia and loose skin. A tummy tuck alone would not be adequate, because it would not address the problem of excess upper abdominal fat. To achieve the desired results safely, she underwent a tummy tuck followed by liposuction four months later. Although she would have preferred to have both procedures simultaneously, she was grateful for an uncomplicated recovery and a satisfying final result.

Anna, a forty-three-year-old data processor, sought laser removal of stretch marks on her lower abdomen. She was surprised and disappointed to learn that lasers were not successful in removing stretch marks. During her consultation, she also complained about her protrusive abdomen. After examination, it was apparent that a tummy tuck would improve both problems. A tummy tuck removed all the excess skin below her belly button, both removing her stretch marks and flattening her abdomen.

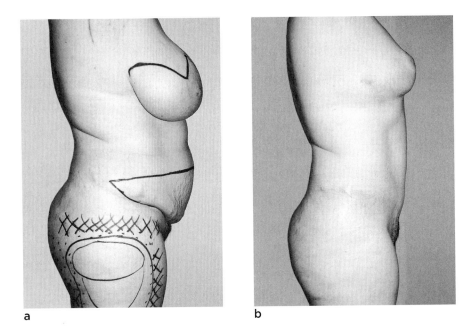

a   b

Abdominoplasty. (a) A thirty-eight-year-old woman with stretch marks of her lower abdomen. (b) Nine months after abdominoplasty (also had liposuction of the outer thighs and breast reduction). Note that her scars have faded significantly and her stretch marks have been removed.

Cindy, a thirty-nine-year-old free-lance photographer, requested liposuction of her abdomen. Upon examination, however, she had excess fat, a lax inner girdle, loose skin, and therefore was better suited to a tummy tuck. She insisted on liposuction because she thought tummy tucks were too extensive and the scar would be too long. She sought liposuction from another surgeon and, not surprisingly, continued to have a bulging abdomen and loose skin. She finally had a tummy tuck and has been satisfied since. In looking back, she regrets that she had not listened to the original advice.

Lower abdominal stretch marks are removed during a tummy tuck. Those around and above your belly button usually are not. Fortunately, most stretch marks occur on the lower abdomen.

Hips

Standing in front of a mirror, look at your hips objectively. Does your silhouette follow a single gentle curve from your waist, around your hips, and down your thigh? Or do your hips and thighs form bulges, much like the silhouette of a cello (Figure 9-2)?

A tummy tuck may narrow your waist, because it will tighten your fascia (Figure 9-3). However, it will not narrow your hips. As a result, your hips may appear larger in comparison to your tightened waist. Your plastic surgeon may recommend liposuction of your hips in addition to a tummy tuck. Do not be offended, and do not assume your plastic surgeon is pitching unnecessary surgery. If your hips are generous, you might want to consider having both procedures for the best outcome.

Laser Removal of Stretch Marks

Although some physicians claim that lasers improve stretch marks, there is no scientific evidence to support this. Lasers are effective in removing, vaporizing, and breaking down tissues. They do not generally repair tissues. Stretch marks represent torn tissue. Hence, improvement should not be expected from laser treatment. Laser technology is evolving, so there may someday be a laser that is effective for stretch marks. In the meantime, beware. Stretch mark removal is an arena in which false claims prevail.

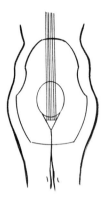

Figure 9-2: *The cello silhouette. If you have this type of silhouette, your hips form the upper bulge, and your outer thighs the lower bulge.*

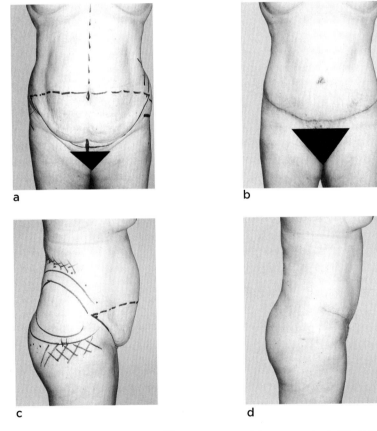

Abdominoplasty. (a and c) A fifty-seven-year-old woman who is 5 feet 3 inches and 145 pounds before surgery. (b and d) Three months after abdominoplasty. She also had liposuction of her hips. Her waistline and overall contour have improved. The scar can be positioned higher or lower than shown, according to patient preference.

Waistline Problems

While most women enjoy a narrower waistline after abdominoplasty, a small but distinct number of women report that their waists are actually larger after a tummy tuck. One possible explanation is swelling, which can be substantial. Another possibility is that in some women, lower abdominal protrusion might be tightened more than the mid- or upper abdomen, thereby pushing the abdominal contents higher and creating slightly more fullness near the waistline.

Tummy Tuck: The Operation

There are several ways to perform a tummy tuck. The most common technique is called a full tummy tuck or full abdominoplasty and involves four steps (Figure 9-3):

1. Removing most of the skin and fat between your belly button and your pubic hair in a horizontal oval
2. Tightening the fascia with permanent sutures
3. Repositioning your belly button (your belly button does not actually move, but the skin surrounding it does)
4. Sewing together the remaining skin above your pubic hair

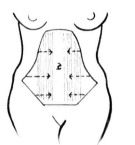

a Frontal view before surgery

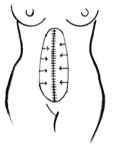

b Frontal view after surgery

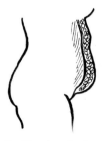

c Profile view before surgery

d Frontal view after surgery

Figure 9-3: *Tummy tuck. (a) Before surgery, the muscles are widely separated. Arrows show the direction the fascia will be pulled together and tightened. (b) After surgery, a zipperlike seam is shown where the fascia has been sewn together and tightened. The waist is narrowed, and the abdomen appears flat. (c) Before surgery, the fascia is lax and skin is loose. (d) After surgery, the tightened fascia no longer bows forward.*

Incisions and Scars

Scars can be designed to fall within the bikini line. Because bikini styles have changed over the years, be sure to bring yours to your appointment if this is an important issue for you. Scars may extend from hip to hip, but they can be shorter in some women. As with all surgery, the final visibility of scars varies significantly from person to person. If the skin around your belly button was repositioned, there will be a scar around it (see Figure 9-4). In addition, there may be a small vertical scar just above your pubic hair if all lower abdominal skin could not be removed.

Modified Techniques

Some modifications of the standard tummy tuck have evolved to address the issues of women with different concerns.

The Myth of Tightening the Muscle

Some plastic surgeons tell patients that they "tighten the muscle" during a tummy tuck, because it is easier for them to say this than to explain what fascia is. These plastic surgeons are simply tightening the fascia. Doing so does pull the underlying muscles closer to the midline, but the surgeon is not actually tightening the muscle. The muscle is not even exposed during the operation.

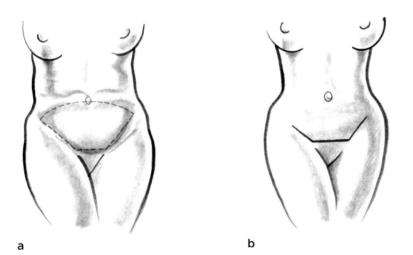

a   b

Figure 9-4: *Tummy tuck incision and scars. (a) The skin to be removed (dashed line). (b) The scars will be around the belly button and may be designed higher or lower than shown.*

1. **Mini tummy tuck.** This procedure removes loose skin of the lower abdomen, but it does not reposition the skin around the belly button or tighten loose upper abdomen skin. It may or may not tighten the fascia of the lower abdomen. It is best suited to thin women with firm inner girdles who have loose lower abdominal skin. A mini tummy tuck uses shorter incisions and avoids scars around the belly button, but it does not improve the upper abdomen.

2. **Panniculectomy.** A pannus is skin and fat that hangs below the abdomen in the shape of an apron. Women who have a pannus are commonly very overweight. Because of their weight, a full abdominoplasty poses substantial healing risks, so a panniculectomy (pannus removal) might be recommended instead. This operation removes hanging skin of the lower abdomen and does nothing with the fascia or the skin above the pannus. A panniculectomy and a mini tummy tuck are similar in that they both limit surgery to the lower abdomen. But mini tummy tucks are performed most often on thin women who do not have upper abdominal concerns, whereas panniculectomies are performed on obese women who are not good candidates for an abdominoplasty due to healing concerns.

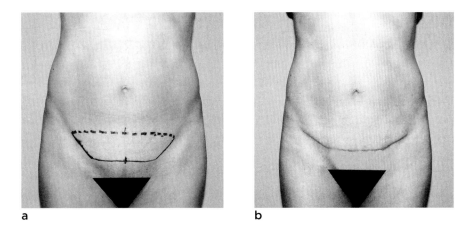

a   b

Mini tummy tuck. (a) A thirty-seven-year-old woman who is 5 feet 4 inches and weighs 106 pounds with loose skin of the lower abdomen before surgery. The black marks indicate the estimated amount of skin to be removed. (b) Six months after mini tummy tuck. Note the scar is still very visible and is expected to fade.

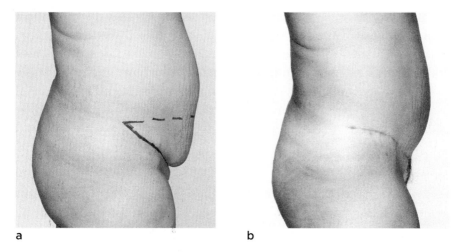

a   b

Panniculectomy. (a) A thirty-five-year-old woman who is 5 feet 6 inches and 190 pounds before surgery. Because she was a smoker and could not quit, she was not a candidate for a full abdominoplasty, which would have given her the best result. (b) Four months after panniculectomy. Note that the hanging skin is gone, but the abdominal protrusion is not improved. This result is expected.

3. *Conservative abdominal liposuction with a full tummy tuck.* This procedure is performed by some surgeons and is most appropriate for women who desire conservative liposuction of their upper abdomens and flanks. Because of possible healing complications, aggressive abdominal liposuction should not be performed at the same time as a full tummy tuck.

4. *Endoscopic tummy tuck.* In this technique, your surgeon uses an endoscope to tighten your fascia, but the surgeon does not remove skin. Liposuction of the abdomen may be more thorough than the other techniques because the incision is small and thus the blood supply is less interrupted for healing. Scar length is only a few inches. This operation is best for women with lax fascia but no loose skin. Because most women with lax fascia also have loose skin, this technique is not commonly indicated.

Complications

When a qualified plastic surgeon performs your operation, both your procedure and recovery are likely to be uneventful. Even in ideal circumstances, however, complications may occur. In addition to the specific complications mentioned here, refer to Chapter 1 for general complications that may follow any procedure.

What to Expect: Tummy Tuck

- *Anesthesia:* General.
- *Location of operation:* Office or hospital.
- *Length of surgery:* Two to three hours.
- *Length of stay:* Outpatient or overnight.
- *Discomfort:* Moderate to severe. The tighter your surgeon makes your fascia, the greater your discomfort will be. Anticipate three to seven days of prescription pain medication.
- *Bruising:* Does not usually occur.
- *Swelling:* Will peak in one to three weeks. Most swelling will improve within four to six weeks, but may take months to improve completely.
- *Numbness:* Abdominal numbness is expected and may last for six months or longer. The skin between your belly button and pubic hair is likely to regain some sensation, but may never feel normal. Most do not find this bothersome.
- *Bandages:* Removed in one to four days.
- *Stitches:* Many plastic surgeons use absorbable stitches under the skin that do not require removal. If your surgeon uses nonabsorbable stitches, they will be visible and will be removed in seven days.
- *Drains:* Will be placed at the time of surgery to prevent postoperative fluid collections called seromas. The drain tubes are plastic and will be connected to small reservoirs the size of tennis balls. You will go home with drains and will be instructed to empty them several times daily. Your surgeon will remove your drains between two days and two weeks following surgery. The drains are not painful, but their removal causes temporary discomfort.
- *Support:* You may be given an abdominal binder following surgery. It is a broad elastic band that should be worn continuously for two to six weeks. The binder will provide extra comfort and support as you heal.
- *Presentable in a bathing suit:* Your abdomen will immediately look better in most one-piece bathing suits than it did prior to surgery. However, a two-piece bathing suit may not conceal your scars. You may need to choose your swimwear carefully. Because sun exposure can result in scar discoloration, protect your scar from direct sun exposure or tanning bed exposure until the redness has faded (one to two years).
- *Work:* You may return to work once you have stopped taking prescription pain medication. For most, this is in one to two weeks. If your job requires lifting or manual labor, wait four weeks.
- *Driving:* May be resumed in seven to fourteen days, if you have stopped taking prescription pain medication.
- *Exercise:* May be resumed in four weeks.
- *Final result:* Is seen after your scar has matured, approximately one to two years.

Skin Death

During the course of an abdominoplasty, your abdominal skin will be lifted off of the underlying fascia (or gristle, inner girdle). In the course of lifting the abdominal skin, the blood vessels between these two layers will be cut, tied off, or cauterized. Because these blood vessels are responsible for a significant portion of the circulation to the overlying skin, that skin must rely on circulation from the surrounding skin and fat, which is less robust and might be inadequate for sustaining the healing tissues. If this is the case, there will be skin and fat death.

If skin death occurs, it usually involves the skin between your pubic hair and belly button, just above the scar. Depending on the size of the affected area, it may heal on its own within a few weeks, or it may require further surgery.

Smokers, diabetics, and obese women have greater circulatory problems and are at significant risk of skin death, although it may occur in anyone. If you are at high risk for skin death, your surgeon may either advise against a tummy tuck or may choose to remove less skin so that the remaining skin is closed without tension to ease circulation. If the latter is chosen, your aesthetic outcome may be compromised.

Hematoma

A hematoma is a collection of blood under the skin. If it develops, it usually does so within a day of surgery. Even if identified and treated quickly, it may block circulation enough to cause skin death. Hematomas following a tummy tuck usually require an operation for removal if they are large.

Seroma

A seroma is a collection of fluid under your skin. Drainage tubes are used to prevent seromas, but they may occur anyway. Seroma fluid can be removed by your surgeon in the office through a needle and syringe. This is not painful, because your abdominal skin will be numb for several months following the tummy tuck. Sometimes fluid requires repeated removal. Seroma accumulation is one of the most common problems following a tummy tuck, but it does not usually alter the final cosmetic result.

Suture Rupture

If the suture that tightens your inner girdle breaks, you may rapidly redevelop lax fascia. Correction requires reoperation with placement of a new suture. The risk of suture rupture is minimized by avoiding abdominal strain during the first four weeks after surgery.

Belly Button Death

Your belly button skin may lose its circulation and die. If this happens, the area develops a scar. Because a normal belly button resembles a scar, the new scar is usually cosmetically acceptable.

Reasons to Avoid or Postpone a Tummy Tuck

I advise my patients to avoid or postpone a tummy tuck for any of the following reasons:

Future Pregnancies

Defer your tummy tuck until you are done bearing children. If you bear a child after a tummy tuck, you may require another operation to correct recurrent lax fascia and loose skin.

Previous Abdominal Scars

If you have a horizontal scar across your upper abdomen, you are at high risk for healing problems. Your surgeon will either advise against a tummy tuck or will suggest a modification of surgery that incorporates this scar. In this case, your scar will be higher.

Obesity

If you are obese, the circulation to your abdominal skin and fat may be too poor for proper healing following a tummy tuck. You will be at high risk for skin death, infection, and wound separation. If you are obese and have droopy skin, a better approach may be panniculectomy.

Smoking

If you smoke, you have a greatly increased risk of healing problems, and you will be advised to quit before surgery. If you are unable to quit, your surgeon may cancel your surgery or choose to remove less skin than would be considered optimal.

Breast Cancer

If no family members have had breast cancer, your lifetime risk is one in nine. If your mother or sister had breast cancer, you are at even higher risk. Breast cancer is sometimes treated by breast removal, also called mastectomy. One of the most common techniques for breast reconstruction following mastectomy is called a TRAM (transverse rectus abdominis myocutaneous) flap, which uses abdominal skin and fat. If you have had a tummy tuck, you will not be a candidate for this type of breast reconstruction later. On the other hand, you may never get breast cancer, you may not need mastectomy if you do, and other options are available for breast reconstruction.

Telltale Signs

A number of telltale signs are associated with a tummy tuck.

Scars

Following your tummy tuck, you may have a visible scar around your belly button. Your belly button may also become distorted. Your scar may be visible when you wear your swimsuit—even with a one-piece bathing suit. As swimwear fashions change periodically, many women who undergo abdominoplasty are bound to encounter this sooner or later.

Dog Ears

Puckered skin, called a dog ear, may occur on either end of the scar if there is more skin on either side of the suture line. Puckering sometimes can be avoided if your surgeon gathers the excess skin in the middle or extends the incision to your hip bones or beyond. If your surgeon originally recommended a total body lift, but you chose to have only a tummy tuck, your risk of dog ears is probably higher. They may be removed through an office procedure, but that often requires extension of the scar.

Pubic Hair Lift

The upper border of your pubic hair becomes lifted following a tummy tuck. This is not usually a problem unless you wear low-cut bikinis. If you do and wish your pubic hair not to be raised, mention this to your plastic surgeon, who can make a lower incision that removes more of your pubic hair. This results in a lower scar but might also result in a vertical scar in the lower midline, which corresponds to the skin that used to be around the belly button.

Cost

In the United States, the range of total fees for a tummy tuck extends from $6,000 to $10,000. The average cost is:

Surgeon's fee	$4,800
Anesthesiologist's fee	$800
Operating room fee	$1,100
Total	$6,700

See "Fees" in Chapter 1 for various factors that might affect your own actual cost.

Satisfaction

Patient satisfaction following surgery is high if expectations are realistic and complications are avoided. Because the results are lasting (in the absence of weight gain), most women's greatest regret is that they did not seek it sooner.

Concluding Thoughts

Women with excess skin or lax fascia may try diet and exercise, only to discover that weight loss and improved muscle tone do not solve these problems. A tummy tuck offers these women an opportunity to regain the tighter, flatter abdomen they had in youth—but not without risk. Tummy tuck is a deceptively innocuous name for a major operation. Recovery is not easy, and potential complications are serious. As long as these issues are fully understood, a tummy tuck can be a gratifying procedure.

Inner Thigh Lift

An inner thigh lift, also called a medial thigh lift, was designed for women with sagging inner thigh skin. Standing in front of a mirror, use your thumb and forefinger to pinch the skin of your inner thigh near your groin. Now lift it upward. This shows you the effect of an inner thigh lift. Note that the improvement you see is greatest in the upper half of your thigh and least in the lower half. Women with loose skin of the knees gain little improvement from an inner thigh lift.

Lift Versus Liposuction

Liposuction makes one look thinner, while a lift makes one look younger. Liposuction reduces fat volume, but it may worsen the appearance of your inner thighs if your primary problem is loose skin.

Loose inner thigh skin typically has poor tone; thus it will not reliably contract following liposuction. If your main problem is loose skin, an inner thigh lift is the procedure for you. If your problem is both loose skin and excess fat, you may attempt liposuction and hope for some skin tightening. Understand, however, that an inner thigh lift may be necessary, also. Some plastic surgeons perform inner thigh lift and liposuction together. Others do not because of the increased risk of healing complications.

Inner Thigh Lift Procedure

An inner thigh lift removes loose skin and anchors the remaining skin to your pubic bone area. Your scar most likely will be in your groin crease and hopefully will heal undetectably (Figure 9-5). Women with markedly loose or hanging skin throughout the inner thigh might be advised to have skin removed in an ellipse from the inner knee to the groin. This is called a vertical thigh lift, which results in a more visible scar and is usually reserved for those with extremely loose skin.

Complications

When a qualified plastic surgeon performs your operation, both your procedure and recovery are likely to be uneventful. Even in ideal circumstances,

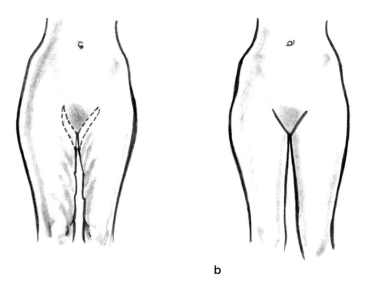

a   b

Figure 9-5: *Inner thigh lift. (a) The incisions (dashed lines). (b) The scars within the groin creases (solid lines).*

What to Expect: Inner Thigh Lift

- *Anesthesia:* General.

- *Location of operation:* Office or hospital

- *Length of surgery:* Two to four hours.

- *Length of stay:* Overnight.

- *Discomfort:* Moderate to severe. Anticipate two to seven days of prescription pain medication.

- *Swelling:* Will peak at three days. As thigh swelling improves, you may notice swelling in your knees and ankles. All swelling should improve within two to six weeks. Keep your legs elevated to expedite this process.

- *Bandages:* Removed in two to four days.

- *Stitches:* Most plastic surgeons use absorbable stitches that do not require removal. If your surgeon uses nonabsorbable stitches, they will be removed in seven to ten days.

- *Drains:* If drains are placed, they will be removed in one to five days.

- *Presentable in a bathing suit:* Two to three weeks.

- *Work:* You may return to sedentary work in one to two weeks if you have stopped taking prescription pain medication. If you are able to keep your feet elevated at work, you may return sooner.

- *Driving:* May be resumed in one to two weeks, if you have stopped taking prescription pain medication.

- *Exercise:* May be gradually resumed in four weeks.

- *Final result:* Is seen after your scars have matured in approximately one to two years, although your new contour will be evident immediately.

however, complications may occur. In addition to the specific complications mentioned here, refer to Chapter 1 for general complications that may follow any procedure.

Healing Complications

Healing problems may lead to infection or wound separation. If so, you may require hospitalization and intravenous antibiotics. Fortunately, most wound problems are relatively minor. Healing problems are more common in smokers and diabetics. If the surgeon removed too much skin or closed it too tightly, healing complications are also more likely.

Persistent Swelling

Because lymphatics, which are responsible for draining normal body fluid, are located in the region of thigh lift surgery, they might become disrupted following surgery. If so, you might have persistent swelling in your leg or legs, which might or might not improve with time. Support hose and leg elevation can help significantly.

Downward Drift of Your Scar

If the anchoring sutures rupture or if too much skin was removed, your scars may descend down your thighs. Then they will no longer be hidden in your groin creases. Worse, your vaginal opening may be widened, possibly causing pain during intercourse or persistent discomfort.

Reanchoring the thigh skin to the pubic bone may improve cases in which the anchoring sutures ruptured. If too much skin was removed, the problem may be difficult to remedy through further surgery.

Telltale Signs

Scars are the telltale signs of an inner thigh lift. They may be visible with some swimwear, especially if the scars drift downward.

Cost

In the United States, the range of total fees for an inner thigh lift extends from $4,000 to $8,000. The average cost is:

Surgeon's fee	$4,000
Anesthesiologist's fee	$900
Operating room (facility) fee	$1,200
Total	$6,100

See "Fees" in Chapter 1 for various factors that might affect your own actual cost.

Satisfaction

Because diet and exercise do not improve loose inner thigh skin, women who suffer from this problem become frustrated. If and when they choose to proceed with an inner thigh lift, they are highly gratified. Usually, the looser the skin before surgery, the more they are rewarded afterward, particularly when the loose skin is in the upper thigh rather than near the knees.

Concluding Thoughts

An inner thigh lift offers the potential to reduce baggy inner thigh skin and restore a more youthful appearance. It is, however, a major operation with significant medical risks that you must weight against its potential benefits.

Outer Thigh and Buttock Lift

The outer thigh and buttock lift (also called buttock lift) was designed for women with sagging skin in these areas. Standing in front of a mirror, place one hand on the outside of each thigh at the level of your hip and lift upward. This demonstrates the effects of an outer thigh lift. Now, with your back to the mirror, hold a hand mirror so that you can see your buttocks. Place your remaining hand above one buttock at the hip level and lift it up. This shows you the effect of a buttock lift.

This procedure is most commonly performed in conjunction with abdominoplasty, as women who have loose skin of the buttocks and outer thighs nearly always have the same problem with the abdomen. The combination of a tummy tuck and an outer thigh and buttock lift is sometimes called belt lipectomy, as the scar is circumferential.

Cellulite

Inelastic fibers tether your skin to your bone or underlying muscle fascia. In some people, the skin around these fibers droops over time, creating the puckers called cellulite. Most people believe it is due solely to fat, but it is not that simple. Cellulite is due to a combination of fat, fibrous tissue, and gravity. An outer thigh and buttock lift takes tension off the tethered fibers and may relieve cellulite in some women.

When you perform your self-evaluation in front of a mirror, note whether you have cellulite. If you do, pay attention to whether it improves while you lift your thigh and buttock skin. If it does, it may also improve following a thigh and buttock lift. Even so, be guarded in your expectations. Cellulite is also explained in Chapter 10.

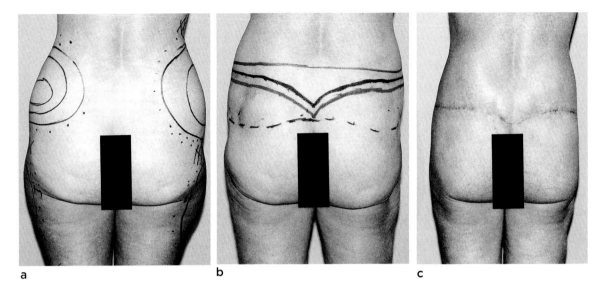

a   b   c

Staged liposuction and an outer thigh and buttock lift. (a) A fifty-four-year-old woman with excess fatty deposits of the hips and outer thighs before surgery. She also has loose skin. Because skin was not excessively loose (hanging), liposuction alone was a reasonable option. (b) Ten months after liposuction, the volume of her hips and thighs has diminished, but loose skin has predisposed her to irregularities. The middle solid line and the lower dashed line indicate the estimated skin to be removed during an outer thigh and buttock lift. (c) Four months after the outer thigh and buttock lift, the skin is smoother than it was after liposuction alone. The scar is immature and expected to fade.

Outer Thigh and Buttock Lift Operation

The outer thigh lift and buttock lift is one procedure. Prior to surgery, your surgeon will mark the areas of skin to be removed (Figure 9-6). After the removal of loose skin, the remaining skin is pulled upward and anchored in position with sutures.

Incisions and Scars

Following this operation, you will look better in clothing and in most swimwear. When you are unclothed, however, your scar will be obvious. It will extend from hip to hip across the top of your buttocks (Figure 9-6b). The final appearance of your scar is difficult to predict. Your scar may fade and flatten, or it may widen and become unsightly. Do not expect this scar to become invisible; it does not heal as well as scars in other areas. It can be

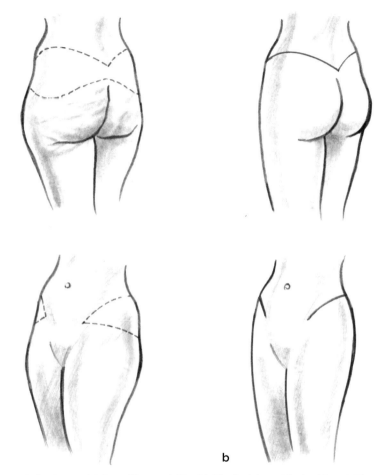

Figure 9-6: *Outer thigh and buttock lift. (a) The incisions (dashed lines). The area between the dashed lines is the skin to be removed. (b) The position of the resulting scars (solid lines).*

hidden by a one-piece bathing suit, but it may be visible with a bikini. If scar position is important to you, ask your plastic surgeon if he or she can design your incisions such that the scar is hidden by your swimming suit. Most will.

Complications

When a qualified plastic surgeon performs your operation, both your procedure and recovery are likely to be uneventful. Even in ideal circumstances,

What to Expect: Outer Thigh and Buttock Lift

- *Anesthesia: General.*

- *Location of operation: Hospital.*

- *Length of surgery: Three to five hours.*

- *Length of stay: One to two nights.*

- *Discomfort: Moderate to severe. Anticipate five to ten days of prescription pain medication.*

- *Swelling: Improves in two to four weeks.*

- *Bandages: Removed in one to four days.*

- *Stitches: Most plastic surgeons use absorbable stitches that do not require removal. Nonabsorbable stitches will be removed in seven to ten days.*

- *Drains: If drains are placed, they will be removed in one to ten days.*

- *Presentable in a bathing suit: Two to four weeks. Be certain to wear sunscreen (SPF 15–40) for at least one year on any scars that may be exposed to the sun, as sun exposure may cause scar discoloration.*

- *Work: You will be able to return to work in one to three weeks if you have stopped taking prescription pain medication. If your job requires lifting, you should wait four weeks.*

- *Driving: May be resumed in two weeks, if you have stopped taking prescription pain medication.*

- *Exercise: May be resumed in four to six weeks.*

- *Final result: Will be seen after scar maturation, in approximately one to two years.*

however, complications may occur. The risks described for an inner thigh lift also apply to the outer thigh and buttock lift; yet the risks of complications are higher for the outer thigh and buttock lift.

Telltale Sign

The scar is a telltale sign for outer thigh and buttock lift.

Cost

In the United States, the range of total fees for an outer thigh and buttock lift extends from $5,000 to $8,000. The average cost for an outer thigh and buttock lift (OTBL) alone and in combination with a tummy tuck (TT) follow:

	OTBL Alone	OTBL and TT
Surgeon's fee	$4,200	$7,500
Anesthesiologist's fee	$1,000	$1,300
Operating room (facility) fee	$1,300	$1,800
Hospital fee for overnight stay	$600	$600
Total	$7,100	$11,200

See "Fees" in Chapter 1 for various factors that might affect your own actual cost.

Satisfaction

Satisfaction following surgery is closely tied to the degree of droop before surgery. So if your droop is mild before surgery, you may be unimpressed with your result and unhappy with your scars. If your droop is moderate to severe, you will most likely be pleased with your result and consider the procedure worthwhile.

Concluding Thoughts

An outer thigh and buttock lift can raise droopy buttocks and restore more youthful contours to the outer thighs. Some women also gain an improvement in cellulite. If you seek this procedure, you must be prepared for major surgery and extensive scars. In the end, you will probably be pleased with your choice and satisfied with your new appearance.

Total Body Lift

A total body lift includes a tummy tuck, an inner thigh lift, and an outer thigh and buttock lift (Figure 9-7). Surgery is extensive; however, the results are gratifying in properly selected patients. The procedure may take five to eight hours and mandate a one- to three-night hospital stay. Blood loss may be enough to merit transfusion. You may return to sedentary work in two to six weeks.

Because a total body lift entails having a tummy tuck, an inner thigh lift, and an outer thigh and buttock lift at the same time, the risks applicable to all components must be considered, and the recovery is lengthy. You and your surgeon should decide together whether you are a candidate for this procedure, or if you should undergo each component separately to

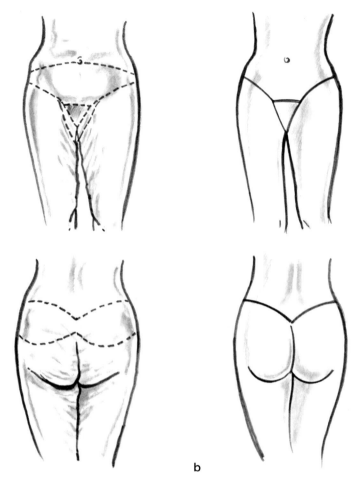

a   b

Figure 9-7: *Total body lift. (a) The incisions (dashed lines). The skin between the dashed lines will be removed. (b) The resultant scars (solid lines). A total body lift is the combination of a tummy tuck, an inner thigh lift, and an outer thigh and buttock lift.*

minimize risk. Given the magnitude of this operation, some surgeons advise performing it in stages.

Cost

In the United States, the range of total fees for a total body lift extends from $8,000 to $20,000. The average cost is:

Surgeon's fee	$10,000
Anesthesiologist's fee	$1,800

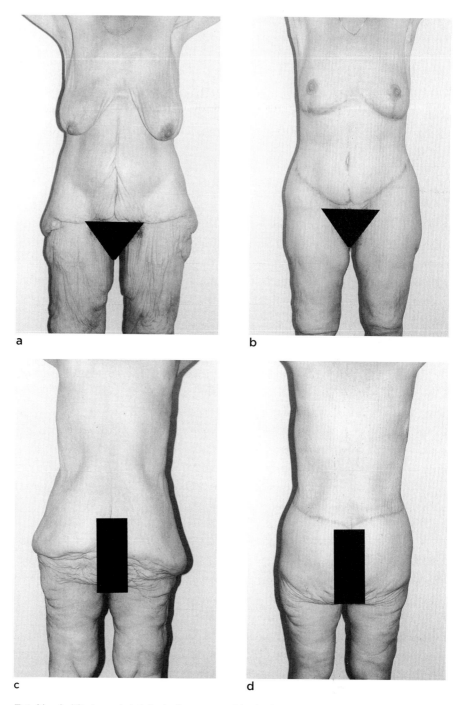

Total body lift. (a and c) A forty-four-year-old who lost 200 pounds after gastric bypass and weighed 150 pounds at the time of body lift surgery. (b and d) Seven months after an abdominoplasty, an outer thigh and buttock lift, and an inner thigh lift. She also had a breast lift.

Operating room (facility) fee	$2,200
Hospital fee for overnight stay	$1,000
Total	$15,000

See "Fees" in Chapter 1 for various factors that might affect your own actual cost. For example, if you plan to have this procedure in New York, expect to pay an average of $20,000 in total fees, with a range from $15,000 to 25,000.

Concluding Thoughts

A total body lift is a serious operation. Do not underestimate the enormity of this procedure. You must be prepared for extensive surgery and a lengthy recovery. If you proceed, you must keep these issues in mind and be willing to accept potential complications. If you do have this procedure and emerge without complications, you will probably be satisfied.

Arm Lift

An arm lift, also known as brachioplasty, involves the removal of loose skin from the upper arms. The removal of skin leaves a scar along the inside of the arm from the armpit to the elbow. An alternative option for those with minimal excess skin involves removing skin near the armpit only, thereby limiting the scar to the armpit area.

When the main problem is fat, rather than loose skin, liposuction is recommended instead.

Complications

When a qualified plastic surgeon performs your operation, both your procedure and recovery are likely to be uneventful. Even in ideal circumstances, however, complications may occur. The risks described elsewhere in this book also apply here: infection, bleeding, hematoma, delayed healing, numbness, and fluid collections (seromas) are all possible complications, but they are generally uncommon.

Gwen, a fifty-three-year-old socialite with a flamboyant personality, grabbed her buttocks in the exam room, pulled them up, and exclaimed, "I need this lifted." She wanted an outer thigh and buttock lift, which we proceeded to discuss. As I rose to leave, she said, "Oh, and I need this tucked, too," as she grabbed her lower abdomen, pinched it together, and pulled it outward. We proceeded to discuss a tummy tuck. As I again began to exit, she stopped me, pulled her inner thigh skin up, and said, "Can you do this, too?" A total body lift was born.

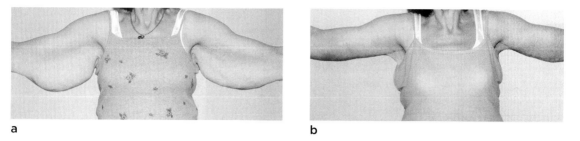

a   b

Arm lift. (a) A fifty-three-year-old woman who lost 225 pounds through diet and exercise weighed 145 pounds at the time of arm lift surgery. (b) Two months after surgery.

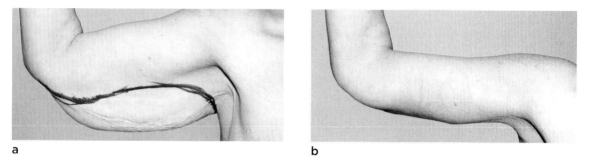

a   b

Arm lift. (a) A forty-six-year-old woman who once weighed 310 pounds and lost 145 pounds over five years through dieting. The black marks indicate the estimated amount of skin to be removed. (b) Four months after the arm lift.

Telltale Sign

The scar is the telltale sign for an arm lift.

Cost

In the United States, the range of fees for an arm lift ranges from $4,000 to $6,500. The average cost is:

Surgeon's fee	$3,500
Anesthesiologist's fee	$700
Operating room (facility) fee	$900
Total	$5,100

What to Expect: Arm Lift

- **Anesthesia:** *General or sedation.*

- **Location of operation:** *Office or hospital.*

- **Length of surgery:** *One to three hours.*

- **Length of stay:** *Outpatient (home same day).*

- **Discomfort:** *Mild to moderate. Anticipate two to five days of prescription pain medication.*

- **Swelling:** *Upper arm, forearm, and hand swelling may worsen for the first week. Wearing a compression garment or compression sleeves (ask your plastic surgeon where to get these) will help considerably. Swelling will improve over two to four weeks and is usually resolved within four to eight weeks.*

- **Bandages:** *Removed in one to four days.*

- **Stitches:** *Most plastic surgeons use absorbable stitches that do not require removal. Nonabsorbable stitches will be removed in seven to ten days.*

- **Drains:** *If drains are placed, they will be removed in one to ten days.*

- **Presentable in a bathing suit:** *Two to four weeks. Be certain to wear sunscreen (SPF 15–40) for at least one year on any scars that may be exposed to the sun, as sun exposure may cause scar discoloration.*

- **Work:** *You will be able to return to work in one week if you have stopped taking prescription pain medication. If your job requires lifting, you should wait two to four weeks.*

- **Driving:** *May be resumed as soon as you have stopped taking prescription pain medication.*

- **Exercise:** *May be resumed in two to four weeks.*

- **Final result:** *Will be seen after scar maturation, in approximately one to two years.*

Satisfaction

An arm lift, like a breast lift, exchanges one cosmetic problem (hanging skin) for another (scars). As such, satisfaction following an arm lift is closely tied to the degree of excess skin before surgery. So if your excess skin is mild before surgery, you may be unimpressed with your result and unhappy with your scars. If your excess skin is moderate or severe, you will most likely be pleased with your result and consider the procedure worthwhile.

Gabby, a thirty-eight-year-old photo lab technician and mother of three, had undergone gastric bypass and lost 128 pounds. To her disappointment, however, she still felt like an overweight person because of her loose hanging skin. She began to evolve a new self-image after a body lift and a breast lift. But it was the arm lift that finally enabled her to leave her old self-image behind.

Concluding Thoughts

The arm lift is one of the most sought-after procedures following significant weight loss. Women who have undergone other skin-tightening procedures often report that the arm lift was the most gratifying procedure because it removed flabby arm skin, which had been a constant reminder of their previous weight. A number of women state that only after the arm lift were they able to adopt a new view of themselves as being thinner, healthier people. Further, compared to other procedures for loose body skin, an arm lift involves a shorter procedure, less discomfort, fewer

Questions to Ask Your Plastic Surgeon

Will my cellulite be improved?
Will you be able to remove my stretch marks?
Where will my scars be?

Tips and Traps

- *Diet and exercise will not tighten your loose skin.*

- *If you seek a tummy tuck, wait until you have finished bearing children.*

- *If you have a tummy tuck, then your abdominal tissue will not be available for future breast reconstruction. This is relevant only if you later require mastectomy for breast cancer.*

- *If your hips are wide, consider hip liposuction at the same time as a tummy tuck.*

- *If you have thick abdominal fat, lax skin, and loose fascia, your surgeon may recommend both a tummy tuck and abdominal liposuction.*

- *Beware of the surgeon who advocates thorough abdominal liposuction at the same time as a tummy tuck. This can disrupt circulation and predispose you to healing problems.*

- *An outer thigh and buttock lift may or may not improve cellulite.*

risks, and a faster recovery. As such, some women are now favoring the arm lift as the first cosmetic surgery procedure after massive weight loss, rather than the final procedure. Although this procedure can be performed on anyone with loose upper arm skin, those who have had extreme weight loss tend to be the most pleased with the results, as they had the most to benefit.

10

Defining Body Contour and Smoothing Cellulite

Liposuction, Endermologie, and Mesotherapy

L iposuction remains among the most popular cosmetic procedures performed in the United States for its ability to target excess fat. The problem of localized fatty deposits affects women of all ages, body types, and fitness levels. Liposuction is particularly well suited to women who are at or near their ideal body weight and still have fat deposits.

Surgeons perform various types of liposuction. The most common type of liposuction is traditional liposuction. This chapter discusses both basic questions and sophisticated concerns regarding liposuction. Newer liposuction techniques also are discussed, and the various types of liposuction are compared and contrasted. As liposuction is not ideal for all types of fat deposits, this chapter also includes a discussion of alternative fat-removal techniques that are better suited for smoothing cellulite.

Liposuction: The Easy Way Out?

Some erroneously contend that those who choose liposuction are "taking the easy way out." Although liposuction can be performed on people who are overweight, the best candidates for liposuction are those who are already at their ideal body weight and still have problem areas of fat. In such cases, the weight loss required to lose a stubborn fat bulge often causes loss of fat elsewhere, possibly resulting in a gaunt face that appears unnatural. For these women, liposuction is not the easy way out, but the only way out.

Candidates for Liposuction

The best candidates for liposuction are those who are near their ideal body weight but have fat deposits that are resistant to diet and exercise. For those who are slightly or moderately overweight, liposuc-

201

tion can provide incentive for weight loss. Liposuction alone, however, is not recommended as a method of weight control. It is not a substitute for diet and exercise.

Liposuction also is not a treatment for obesity. True, if you seek liposuction for weight control, you are likely to find a doctor willing to perform the procedure. Unfortunately, you are unlikely to have a pleasing or lasting result.

Liposuction Requires a Steady Weight

The best time to consider liposuction is after you have stabilized your weight through diet and exercise. If you have been gaining weight prior to surgery, you most likely will continue to gain weight and develop new fat deposits in the area treated with liposuction. If you have been losing weight, you should wait until it has stabilized. Otherwise, you may undergo unnecessary liposuction in some areas.

Good Skin Tone

Having good skin tone is one of the keys to attractive results following liposuction. The better the skin's tone, the better it will contract to fit the newly contoured fat after surgery. Several factors influence skin tone:

Good Skin Tone	Poor Skin Tone
Tight skin	Loose skin
Younger patients	Older patients
Thick skin, such as outer thighs	Thin skin, such as inner thighs
Stretch marks absent	Stretch marks present
Minimal prior sun exposure	Extensive prior sun exposure

Thus a young woman seeking treatment of her outer thighs will have better results than an older woman seeking treatment of her inner thighs.

Mandy, a twenty-four-year-old sales representative, was proud of her diligent diet and exercise. Despite her attractive body, she was self-conscious because of her large thighs. Plus, her clothes never fit right. When she bought pants to fit her waist, they were too tight for her thighs, and when she bought pants to fit her thighs, they were too loose for her waist. Following thigh liposuction, she was more comfortable, and she had an easier time finding clothes that fit.

Karen, a thirty-nine-year-old data-entry specialist, sought evaluation for liposuction. She said that her metabolism had changed and she was gaining weight. Her weight had recently increased by fifteen pounds, and she continued to gain slowly. Diet and exercise had not helped. She was certain that liposuction would solve her problems. However, I told her that because of her recent pattern of weight gain, she was not a good candidate for liposuction. She sought a second opinion and proceeded with liposuction through that surgeon. She was initially pleased but continued her steady weight gain. Not surprisingly, one year later she weighed even more and was frustrated with her previous decision to have liposuction.

Fat Facts

Everyone is born with a genetically de-termined number of fat cells. Through-out childhood and adolescence, the size and number of fat cells increase, even if you remain at the ideal body weight for your height and age. After adolescence, further fat accumulation increases the size of the fat cells. But new fat cells are not formed, unless you approach morbid obesity, which is twice your ideal body weight.

What If I Gain Weight After Liposuction?

No one can predict where your new fat will be deposited, as your pattern of fat deposit most likely will have changed as a result of liposuction. Some women gain in the area of previous liposuc-tion, whereas others gain in new areas. Women who gain weight after hav-ing undergone extensive liposuction sometimes gain fat in unusual areas such as the hands or feet. Fortunately, this is very unusual. Interestingly, when men gain weight after liposuction, they usually deposit it in the area that was suctioned.

Of course, exceptions abound, but all five factors affecting skin tone must be taken into account.

Best Body Areas for Liposuction

Certain areas of the body have good skin tone in most women (Figure 10-1, speckled areas). These include the outer thighs, hips, and knees. Thus these areas tend to yield good liposuction results.

Body Areas That Yield Mixed Results

Not all body areas are equally amenable to liposuction (Figure 10-1, crosshatched areas). Some areas yield favorable results only if the skin tone happens to be good. Likewise, areas with only superficial fat yield satisfactory results only under certain conditions. Areas with natural skin creases are likely to yield poor results unless certain conditions are met.

Areas with Poor Skin Tone

If the skin is loose and thin, it will fail to tighten after liposuction—and it may appear looser and baggier. In these cases, removal of excess skin is more appropri-ate than liposuction. For example, women with poor skin tone of their inner thighs may get a better result following an inner thigh lift than liposuction. Simi-larly, loose abdominal skin with stretch marks does not contract well following abdominal liposuction; women with these skin features should instead con-sider a tummy tuck.

Areas with Only Superficial Fat

Most areas of the body have two layers of fat: a thin, superficial layer and a thicker, deep layer. Liposuction is primarily aimed at removing deep fat, because suction of superficial fat may lead to skin irregularities, dimpling, and puckering.

The calves, unlike most other areas of the body, have only a superficial layer of fat. Therefore, calf liposuction runs a greater risk of skin irregulari-ties. Yet when performed by an experienced plastic surgeon, it can be safe

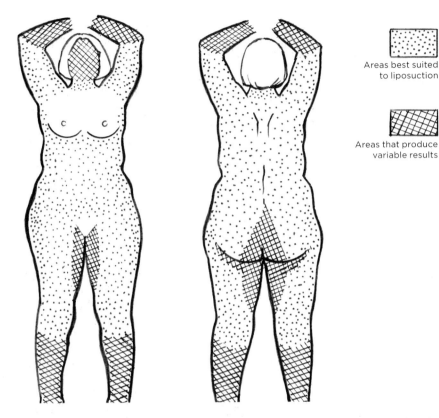

Figure 10-1: *Speckles indicate areas that are best suited to liposuction. Crosshatches indicate areas where liposuction results vary.*

and effective. Calf liposuction also leads to marked swelling. Bed rest and leg elevation are recommended for several weeks following surgery, which most women consider impractical.

A minority of surgeons do perform superficial liposuction routinely. Presumably they have extensive experience with it and have not found an increased risk of complications. If you seek superficial liposuction, choose a surgeon with experience in this technique. Ask how many superficial lipo-suction procedures your surgeon has performed. (Superficial fat is further discussed in "Beyond Liposuction: Cellulite Treatments.")

Areas with Natural Creases

Liposuction of the crease between the buttock and thigh can disrupt the fibrous bands between the skin and bone that maintain the crease. If so,

Name Game

In referring to the outer thighs, plastic surgeons also use the terms saddlebags *and* trochanters. *In referring to the hips, plastic surgeons also use the terms* flanks, love handles, *or* iliac crests. *This causes some confusion, but your familiarity with these terms will help you in communicating with your plastic surgeon. If you have any doubts about the areas your surgeon plans to target during liposuction, outline your areas of concern with your finger and ask your plastic surgeon to confirm by outlining the areas with an erasable marker.*

this causes the buttock to droop. Therefore, most surgeons avoid liposuction of the buttock crease.

A noteworthy exception is the fat roll, often called the banana roll, immediately below the buttock crease. Superficial liposuction here usually will not disrupt the fibrous bands above it.

Hips, Thighs, and Harmony

For many women, the hips and thighs cast a cello-like silhouette (Figure 10-2a and b). If you have a cello silhouette and undergo liposuction of your hips alone, your outer thighs may look larger by comparison (Figure 10-2c). If you proceed with liposuction of your outer thighs alone, then your hips may look larger by comparison (Figure 10-2d). The best result is obtained by suctioning both the hips and outer thighs, but not the depression between them, to bring your entire contour into harmony (Figure 10-2e). Surgeons avoid performing liposuction in such areas of natural concavity, as doing so brings your hips and outer thighs into alignment with these depressions (Figure 10-3a). Otherwise, you might just go from a cello to a violin (Figure 10-3b).

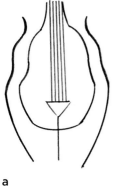
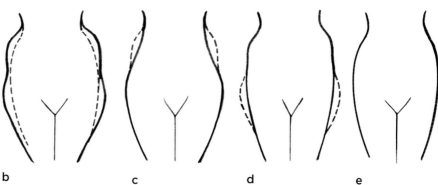

a   b   c   d   e

Figure 10-2: *The cello silhouette. (a) Cello silhouette with cello inside. (b) Cello silhouette with dotted line showing desired contour. The depression between the hips and the thighs should not be suctioned. (c) Cello silhouette following liposuction of hips only. Wide thighs appear wider. (d) Cello silhouette following liposuction of the thighs alone. Wide hips appear wider. (e) Silhouette following liposuction of hips and thighs.*

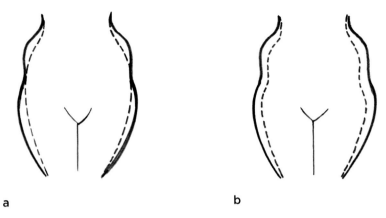

a   b

Figure 10-3: *Avoid liposuction of the natural depression between the hips and the outer thighs. (a) A cello silhouette (solid line). The dashed line shows the desired contour. The depression between the hips and the thighs needs no liposuction to accomplish the desired result. (b) After liposuction of the depression is performed along with liposuction of the hips and thighs, a smaller cello or violin results.*

Liposuction Versus Other Surgery

It can sometimes be tricky to tell whether your problem areas can best be corrected by liposuction or by a different surgery altogether. Here are some general guidelines to follow.

Lift

The inner thighs, outer thighs, buttocks, and neck may lend themselves to either liposuction or lift. Sometimes it is difficult to know which technique will yield the best results. If your problem involves loose skin with poor tone, a lift is best. If your problem is excess fat, then liposuction is most appropriate. As a rule, liposuction makes you look thinner, whereas a lift makes you look younger. (See Chapter 9 for more information on body lifts and Chapter 2 for more information on facelifts.)

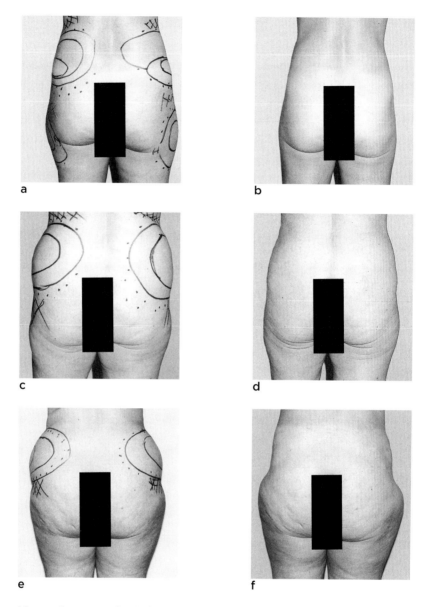

Liposuction can maintain harmony or create disharmony. (a and b) A thirty-two-year-old woman before and after liposuction of her hips and outer thighs. As hips and outer thighs were equally problematic, it was appropriate to have liposuction of both areas. She was size 8–10 before surgery and size 4 after. (c and d) A fifty-seven-year-old woman before and after liposuction of her hips. As her hips were significantly more problematic than her outer thighs, it was appropriate for her to have liposuction of her hips alone. (e and f) A thirty-eight-year-old woman before and after liposuction of hips alone. As the hips and the outer thighs were equally problematic, it would have been best to have liposuction of both areas. Instead, the patient opted for hip liposuction alone, which by comparison makes her outer thighs appear larger.

Tummy Tuck

Many women with flabby abdomens seek liposuction. Liposuction, however, does not always yield much improvement. This is because your abdomen's appearance depends on your skin tone and on more than just fat. Your skin and inner girdle are also factors. The inner girdle is a sheet of tough connective tissue. It extends from your ribs down to your pubic bone, and it functions to keep your internal organs inside your abdomen. After being stretched during pregnancy, it often fails to regain tone. For women with lax inner girdles or loose skin, a tummy tuck is better suited than liposuction. (See Chapter 9 for a self-assessment to determine your needs.)

Cellulite Removal

Liposuction will not help with cellulite. For cellulite treatment and removal, see the section "Beyond Liposuction: Cellulite Treatments."

How Liposuction Works

Traditional liposuction can be performed through small incisions, often less than one-fourth inch each. Usually, two incisions are needed to adequately treat each area. When possible, your incisions will be hidden, such as in your pubic hair, inside your belly button, or in natural skin creases. Some areas, such as the hips, upper abdomen, and outer thighs, may require incisions that cannot easily be hidden. Because the scars are small, they usually are not obvious once they mature.

Day of Surgery

When you arrive for surgery, your surgeon will mark the areas to be suctioned and may mark areas to avoid. This is done with you standing, because the areas shift when you recline. The marks help guide your surgeon during the operation. After you are sedated or asleep, your surgeon will make several tiny incisions around the areas to be treated and inject tumescent fluid into your fat layer.

Tumescent Fluid

Tumescent means "overblown, ballooned, or inflated." Tumescent fluid is so named because it temporarily stiffens fat deposits, making the fat easier to suction during liposuction.

Tumescent fluid contains saline, lidocaine (a local anesthetic), and adrenaline. It reduces blood loss and improves the final result. Almost all plastic surgeons use tumescent fluid during liposuction. If your surgeon does not plan to do so, you may wish to seek another opinion.

Following the infusion of tumescent fluid, your surgeon will use a liposuction rod to remove fat cells (Figure 10-4). The rod has one or more holes at the end and is attached to a suction machine or syringes, which produce a vacuum. Your plastic surgeon will then move the liposuction rod through your fat, systematically suctioning your deep fat.

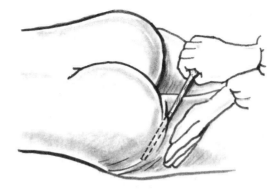

Figure 10-4: *Liposuction technique. The metal rod is moved methodically through the deep fat to evenly and effectively remove it.*

Liposuction Garments

In order to achieve maximum results after surgery, it is essential to wear a liposuction garment for several weeks following surgery. Liposuction garments provide firm pressure and support to suctioned areas, facilitate skin retraction, and optimize your final contour. These garments are designed to be worn continuously for several weeks, but they may be removed daily for bathing. They are made of wash-and-wear material similar to spandex.

Your plastic surgeon may provide you with a garment or may ask you to order a garment by telephone or online prior to surgery. If you purchase it in advance, check the fit. Your garment should be very tight. If it seems to be a size too small, then it is probably the correct size. Garments cost $50 to $100 each, and you should purchase two if possible so you can wear one while washing the other.

Liposuction garments are similar to girdles and vary in style according to the areas suctioned. Garments usually extend from below the lowest suctioned area to above the highest suctioned area. For liposuction of the hips alone, your garment will resemble bicycle shorts. If you have liposuction of your hips, abdomen, and thighs, your garment will extend from your knees to your ribs.

The Liposuction Rod

Liposuction rods, or cannulas, are long, thin, and available in a variety of diameters. The larger the rod, the more efficiently fat can be suctioned and the quicker the procedure can be performed. But because large rods are more likely to result in irregularities, lumpiness, uneven results, seromas, and fat emboli, most plastic surgeons prefer medium and small rods.

Small rods: 2–3 millimeters in diameter

Medium rods: 4–5 millimeters in diameter

Large rods: 6–10 millimeters in diameter

To take a shower, remove your garment only if you are certain that you can get it back on afterward. This task will not be easy, because you will be swollen and sore and the garment will be tight. If you anticipate difficulty replacing your garment, wear it in the shower and blow-dry it afterward. Garments may be machine laundered. If your garment is loose, the dryer will shrink it. If your garment is tight, allow it to air-dry.

Volume of Fat Removed

Your plastic surgeon knows when to stop suctioning based on the volume of fatty fluid suctioned and the appearance of the area. Before finishing an area, your surgeon lightly suctions the adjacent fat to blend the treated and untreated areas. This creates a smooth and natural transition between the areas of liposuction and the surrounding areas.

The typical volumes removed from each area are:

Neck	25–100 mL
Abdomen	150–2,500 mL
Hip (each)	200–2,000 mL
Outer thigh (each)	300–2,000 mL
Inner thigh (each)	150–800 mL
Front of thigh (each)	200–1,200 mL
Knee (each)	50–100 mL

For rough equivalents in U.S. liquid units of measure, 500 mL is about one pint, and 1,000 mL is about one quart. The volumes shown include both fat and tumescent fluid.

Large-Volume Liposuction

Women with marked fatty deposits may be candidates for the removal of 5,000 mL or more. However, large-volume liposuction carries greater risk, and many plastic surgeons choose not to perform it. It involves longer operating times, increased amounts of tumescent fluid, increased intravenous fluid, and increased blood loss. It also imposes a higher total dose of anesthetic agents.

Large-volume liposuction can be safe, provided the procedure is performed in an accredited operating room and that the patient is monitored closely following surgery, including a one-night stay in a hospital.

What to Expect

- **Anesthesia:** *General or sedation.*
- **Location of operation:** *Office or hospital.*
- **Length of surgery:** *Thirty minutes to five hours, depending on the extent of fat to be removed.*
- **Length of stay:** *Outpatient for small and medium volume; overnight for large volume.*
- **Discomfort:** *Varies from mild to severe. Anticipate two to seven days of prescription pain medication.*
- **Bruising:** *Lasts for two to ten days.*
- **Swelling:** *Peaks within three to five days and dissipates over two to eight weeks. As swelling resolves, it settles to lower parts of your body. For example, following liposuction of your thighs, your knees and ankles will swell temporarily. Following liposuction of your abdomen, your genitalia will swell.*
- **Numbness and tingling:** *May occur in suctioned areas and is due to damaged or irritated nerve endings. Sensation will return, and tingling will abate over weeks or months. Regular self-massage of suctioned areas will expedite this process.*
- **Bandages:** *Will be removed in one to four days.*
- **Stitches:** *Will be removed in five to ten days.*
- **Drains:** *If drains are placed, they will be removed in one to three days.*
- **Support:** *A liposuction garment must be worn continuously for several weeks.*
- **Presentable in a bathing suit:** *You will be presentable once your bruising has resolved, your swelling has improved, and your plastic surgeon has allowed you to discontinue wearing your liposuction garment.*
- **Work:** *Most can return to work in five to fourteen days, if they have stopped taking prescription pain medication. If your job requires lifting, wait two to three weeks.*
- **Driving:** *May be resumed once you have stopped taking prescription pain medication.*
- **Exercise:** *May be resumed in two to four weeks. Exercise within two weeks of liposuction will increase swelling and postpone your final result.*
- **Final result:** *Is seen after swelling subsides. Expect four to eight weeks or more.*
- **Duration of results:** *Provided you maintain a stable weight, your results will be lasting.*

New and Alternative Liposuction Techniques

The popularity of liposuction has led to modifications of the traditional technique with the goals of better results and fewer complications. Two techniques incorporate ultrasound waves into liposuction treatments.

Recovery following liposuction varies significantly from person to person. **Andie,** a twenty-seven-year-old product design consultant, underwent a three-liter liposuction of her thighs and hips. She stopped taking pain medication in three days and was back to work within a week. Nina, Andie's twenty-six-year-old friend, underwent a one-liter liposuction of her outer thighs and was incapacitated for two weeks.

Traditional Liposuction (Tumescent Liposuction)

Traditional liposuction began in the 1970s. It remains the most common technique for cosmetic fat removal. The technique for liposuction described earlier in this chapter is for traditional liposuction.

Advantages

Traditional liposuction has been practiced for nearly thirty years, and it yields consistent and satisfying results when performed by experienced plastic surgeons. No long-term negative medical consequences have been identified. Nearly all plastic surgeons who perform liposuction have experience with this technique. More experience translates into better results. Because high-tech equipment is not needed, it may cost less than newer techniques.

Disadvantages

Traditional liposuction may result in greater blood loss than techniques that employ ultrasonic energy. This matters most in large-volume liposuction, where blood loss might be a concern.

Power-Assisted Liposuction (PAL)

Power-assisted liposuction is a modification of traditional liposuction whereby the liposuction cannula oscillates, or vibrates, as the surgeon moves it back and forth through the fat. This enables the cannula to move through the tissue with more ease. Some plastic surgeons report their patients have less discomfort, less swelling and bruising, and smoother results.

What's in a Name?

Traditional liposuction may also be called

Liposuction	*Wet liposuction*
Tumescent liposuction	*Lipoplasty*
Super-wet liposuction	*Standard lipoplasty*
Traditional lipoplasty	*Liposculpture*
Tumescent lipoplasty	*Standard liposculpture*
Traditional liposculpture	*Suction lipectomy*
Tumescent liposculpture	*Tumescent suction-assisted*
Suction-assisted lipectomy (SAL)	*lipectomy*
Standard liposuction	*And other names*

Ultrasonic liposuction (UL) may also be called

Ultrasound-assisted	*Standard-ultrasonic*
liposuction (UAL)	*liposuction*
Ultrasonic lipoplasty	*Ultrasound-assisted lipoplasty*
Ultrasonic liposculpture	*Ultrasound-assisted liposculpture*
Ultrasonic lipectomy·	*Ultrasonic-suction lipectomy*
Ultrasound-assisted	*And other names*
suction lipectomy	

Some plastic surgeons use alternative terms for liposuction, such as lipoplasty, liposculpture, or lipectomy. They are not offering a new or better technique, but they may be trying to convince you they are.

Ultrasonic Liposuction (UL)

UL was developed in Europe in the 1980s and was first used in the United States in the early 1990s. It became widely available in the United States in 1995. UL combines the application of high-frequency sound waves with low-level suctioning.

First, tumescent fluid is instilled, as in traditional liposuction. Second, a rod capable of emitting ultrasonic waves is inserted into the fat. The waves liquefy the fat, which is then evacuated with low-level suction.

Advantages

Compared to traditional liposuction, UL results in less blood loss. Some plastic surgeons also note less pain, swelling, and bruising and speedier recovery.

Disadvantages

Because the equipment needed is expensive, UL may not be available everywhere, and some surgeons charge more for UL. The incisions are slightly larger than in traditional liposuction. In addition, you may sustain a skin burn near a treated area, although burns are rare and usually are prevented through proper technique. Fluid collections called seromas are more common following UL than traditional liposuction. Seroma incidence may be reduced by drain placement at the time of surgery. The drain can then be removed a few days later. Following UL, patients are more likely to develop painful tingling, which may persist for several months. Ultrasonic liposuction takes longer, which may translate into higher cost and greater surgical risks.

External Ultrasound-Assisted Liposuction (EUAL)

In EUAL, ultrasonic energy is delivered to the skin overlying the fat. Then liposuction is performed. When compared to traditional liposuction, EUAL, like UL, may offer the advantages of less blood loss, less swelling, less discomfort, and faster recovery. When compared to UL, EUAL may also offer decreased risks of seromas, burns, and painful postoperative tingling. EUAL is more expensive and time-consuming than traditional liposuction.

Assessing the Techniques

If after reading the preceding information you are divided over which technique is the best, you are in good company. Plastic surgeons, too, are divided. Because each plastic surgeon tends to use the technique that has worked well for him or her, you should feel comfortable following the recommendation of your plastic surgeon. Do not make the mistake of trying to convince your plastic surgeon to perform a technique that he or she does not usually employ.

Complications

The media have deluged the public with horror stories of complications following liposuction performed by inexperienced or unqualified doctors. When a qualified plastic surgeon performs your operation, your chances of an uneventful recovery increase.

Even in ideal circumstances, however, complications may occur. The risk of complications increases as the volume suctioned increases. In addition to the specific complications mentioned here, refer to Chapter 1 for general complications that may follow any procedure.

Death

An estimated 25 to 50 people die each year in the United States from complications related to liposuction. Because the number of people having liposuction is 250,000 to 500,000 per year, the risk of death is about 1 in 10,000. Some deaths have been due to puncture of internal organs with liposuction rods. This complication is often related to surgeon inexperience. Other complications may occur regardless of your surgeon's experience.

Fat Embolus

During liposuction, small fat globules may migrate into blood vessels and gather into a larger mass of fat. If this mass then travels into the lungs, it can interfere with respiration. Severe and potentially fatal problems may result. Fortunately, this occurs in less than 0.1 percent of liposuction patients. Even when it does occur, consequences are usually mild and improve with hospitalization and supplemental oxygen. Use of large-diameter liposuction rods have been linked to this complication.

Deep Vein Thrombosis (DVT)

A DVT is a blood clot in the deep veins of the thighs. It can travel through blood vessels and lodge in the lungs, leading to potentially life-threatening breathing problems and debilitating leg problems. DVT risk is increased in overweight patients, in those taking birth control pills, and in those who remain sedentary after surgery.

Following surgery, a swollen or painful thigh may be a sign of a DVT. However, everyone who has thigh liposuction gets swollen, painful thighs. If one leg is more swollen than the other, an ultrasound scan can rule out a DVT. Be aware, however, that asymmetric swelling is common following liposuction and does not necessarily mean a DVT is present. If you have any concerns about a possible DVT, call your surgeon at once. If a DVT is found, you will most likely be admitted to the hospital for treatment and observation.

Heart Failure

During liposuction, you may be given several liters of tumescent fluid and intravenous fluid. Most healthy people can tolerate this extra fluid load. However, if the load is extreme or if you have a weak heart, the fluid burden may cause your heart to fail. Normally this is easily treated with diuretics. But because heart failure can be fatal if severe or unrecognized, women with weak hearts should not have liposuction. Following large-volume lipo-suction, which involves significant fluid loads, even healthy people require close monitoring during and after surgery.

Bleeding

Blood loss depends on the amount of liposuction performed. About 1 to 5 percent of the suctioned fluid is blood. Hence, liposuction of four liters may result in blood loss of 50 mL to 200 mL, which is less than the amount you donate to the blood bank in one sitting. Most healthy people can handle this amount of blood loss with ease, but it may cause others to feel weak and anemic.

Irregularities, Dimples, Puckers, and Divots

One goal of liposuction is to create symmetric body contours with smooth and natural skin. Liposuction may, however, lead to permanent skin irregu-larities, dimples, and depressions even when performed competently. Fat injection can improve this problem.

Discoloration

Skin may become temporarily or permanently discolored in the area of liposuction. The overall risk is less than 5 percent. Discoloration usu-ally improves on its own within three to twelve months. Topical creams that contain hydroquinone are available by prescription and can expedite resolution.

Kala, a twenty-eight-year-old high school social studies teacher, had liposuction of her thighs and hips with good initial results. She gained weight afterward and returned one year later looking no different than she had looked before liposuction. During our discussion, she reached down, grabbed her hips, and said, "What's this? I thought you removed all this fat. I thought it was permanent." She requested touch-up liposuction. I explained that her weight gain had caused fat to reaccumulate and that further liposuction was not warranted. I encouraged her instead to use diet and exercise to control her weight. As expected, she left the office unhappy.

Telltale Signs

Irregularities, dimples, puckers, and divots, as described in the section on complications, may serve as telltale signs of liposuction. However, many people who have not had liposuction may have these problems due to previous trauma or other surgeries. Therefore, these problems are not reliable indications of previous liposuction.

Cost

The average total fees for liposuction in the United States are shown in Table 10-1. These averages are rough guidelines. Nowhere in cosmetic surgery do costs vary more widely. See "Fees" in Chapter 1 for various factors that might affect your own cost.

Charges may be based on the volume suctioned, specific areas suctioned, number of areas suctioned, or time spent suctioning. In general, the more you have suctioned, the more you will pay.

Table 10-1 Average Cost of Liposuction

	One Area	Three Areas	Five Areas
Surgeon's fee	$2,200	$4,600	$7,000
Anesthesiologist's fee	$500	$900	$1,200
Operating room (facility) fee	$800	$1,100	$1,400
Hospital fee for overnight stay	$0	$0	$600
Total	$3,500	$6,600	$10,200

Note: Typically, each of the following counts as a single area: neck, abdomen, both hips, both flanks, both outer thighs, both inner thighs, or both knees. Some surgeons further subdivide areas, such as upper versus lower abdomen.

Revision Liposuction

About 5 to 15 percent of those who have liposuction seek revision. This is appropriate when asymmetric fat deposits persist after six months. Surgeons usually perform revision using sedation or local anesthesia, suctioning the larger area until it matches the smaller side.

Revision liposuction may be needed regardless of your surgeon's experience. This is partly because liposuction is performed when you are lying down. If your surgeon could perform your liposuction with you in a standing position, many cases of revision might be avoided. Obviously, this is not possible. Therefore, your plastic surgeon cannot with certainty give you the result you expect. Further, your surgeon may perform your liposuction smoothly, but factors beyond his or her control might cause you to heal irregularly.

If you do need revision, you should usually wait at least six months. Many surgeons will waive the surgeon's fee if performed within a certain period.

Beyond Liposuction: Cellulite Treatments

Cellulite is a common but unattractive dimpling and puckering of skin. Cellulite is caused by a combination of fibrous bands and superficial fat. These inelastic fibrous bands connect the skin to the deep layer of fat, passing through the superficial layer of fat. When superficial fat compartments become distended with fat, dimpling occurs where the fibrous bands tether the skin (Figure 10-5). Cellulite only occurs in the areas that have fibrous bands, such as the buttocks and thighs. Interestingly, men do not get cellulite.

Contrary to popular belief, neither liposuction nor laser will improve cellulite. Three options are available to address cellulite: endermologie, mesotherapy, and a body lift.

Endermologie

Endermologie is a nonsurgical procedure that theoretically stimulates the breakdown of fat and cellulite. In it, a technician uses a machine to apply gentle pressure and suction to your skin. The machine looks and sounds somewhat like a handheld vacuum cleaner, and its application feels similar to a deep massage. Sessions last forty minutes and are conducted one to two times per week until a point of diminishing improvement is reached. Those

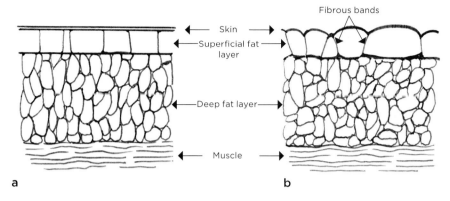

Figure 10-5: *Cellulite. (a) Superficial and deep fat layers without cellulite. (b) The superficial layer of fat becomes distended, causing the fat to bulge around the skin-tethering bands. This creates the dimpled appearance of cellulite.*

who benefit begin to see results within ten sessions and plateau between the fifteenth and twentieth session. Thereafter, monthly sessions are required to maintain the result.

Advantages

Endermologie is generally affordable. Each treatment costs $50 to $100, with a typical fee of $65. The average cost to achieve a plateau is between $975 and $1,400. Maintenance is then about $65 per month. There is no pain and no recovery time. In addition to improvement in cellulite, many see tighter skin and a decrease in fat volume.

Disadvantages

Even though the price seems low compared to liposuction, the final outcome depends on several factors and is not guaranteed. One key factor is the skill of the technician who performs the procedure. Other important factors are diet and exercise, which are necessary to achieve benefit from endermologie. Metabolism must be geared toward fat breakdown in order for endermologie to be effective. If diet and exercise are not followed, little improvement results. Women who cannot commit to regular treatments, diet, and exercise should not pursue endermologie.

Monthly maintenance sessions cost about $780 per year. Within three to five years, you will return to your original state before endermologie, despite strict adherence to maintenance sessions, diet, and exercise. You must then resume weekly sessions to regain your previous plateau.

Other Applications for Endermologie

Endermologie may be used before and after liposuction. Some surgeons perform endermologie in the operating room immediately prior to liposuction. They think it softens fat, aids suctioning, and smooths the final result. Other surgeons ask their patients to have endermologie sessions following liposuction, as endermologie may optimize the result of liposuction by smoothing fat and stimulating skin retraction. I liken it to ironing out the fat.

Mesotherapy

Mesotherapy involves injecting fat with pharmacologic agents that stimulate fat breakdown. A variety of agents in various combinations have been shown to be effective, such as hyaluronidase, phosphatidylcholine, aminophylline, caffeine, carnitine, and others.

Cellulite Versus Deep Fat

When injected very superficially, mesotherapy can improve cellulite, as cellulite is composed of superficial fat. When injected into deep fat, mesotherapy can reduce fat volume, but it does not affect cellulite. Because only a limited amount of mesotherapy agent can be safely injected during one session, patients with both problems (fat volume and cellulite) are usually asked to select one issue to target with each treatment.

Procedure and Recovery

Mesotherapy may be performed by a physician or nurse. It involves numerous tiny shots—up to two hundred or so. The shots take only a few minutes to administer and are not usually painful. In mesotherapy, discomfort often occurs following completion of the procedure as the fat-dissolving, or lipolytic, agents begin to work. As they stimulate fat breakdown, the body usually mounts an inflammatory response, such that the treated areas become firm, red, and very tender. This may last hours or days depending on the amount and type of lipolytic agents injected and the response to them. Often, the greater the response, the better the result. You can return to work the next day, unless your response was marked. If that is the case, less agent can be injected during your next session.

Results

Final results are seen about two to three weeks after each session, and results tend to be subtle. Following injection for cellulite, improvement ranges from 20 to 50 percent with each session, hence several sessions are usually required. Following injection for deep fat volume, improvement ranges from 5 to 20 percent with each session; hence it may be somewhat hard to see a difference. Whereas most see at least some improvement following each session of mesotherapy for cellulite, the results for fat volume are less impressive and less predictable. In some cases, little if any improvement is seen, even after several sessions, which is why mesotherapy is best suited to those who are at their ideal body weight and have subtle areas of localized excess fat or cellulite. Mesotherapy is generally not a substitute for liposuction, but it can be an adjunct.

Cost and Risks

Mesotherapy costs $200 to $600 per session with a typical fee of $400. Risks include infection, irregularities, dimples, failure to see improvement, and fat necrosis, a painful lump of dead fat under the skin. Fat necrosis usually resolves spontaneously but can take months to do so.

Body Lift

If the cause of your cellulite is droopy thigh or buttock skin, then a body lift will help. See Chapter 9 and follow the self-assessment to help you make this determination.

Realistic Expectations

As with other cosmetic surgeries, it is important to have realistic expectations about liposuction and other fat-removal operations before undergoing any operation. Do not expect all fat to be removed from treated areas. Not only would this look unnatural, but it is impossible. The right amount of fat to remove is that which brings your contour into harmony with the rest of your body. If your silhouette looks like a cello, expect that your convex and concave curves will be smoothed, as noted with the dotted line in Figure 10-3a. You may likely discover that your measurements have improved, and you might even wear smaller clothing by one or more sizes. Weight is sometimes reduced—but not always. In fact, don't be surprised if your weight is temporarily increased due to fluid retention.

Satisfaction

Satisfaction following liposuction, endermologie, and mesotherapy is closely tied to expectations. If you expect significant weight reduction or improvement in cellulite following liposuction, you will be disappointed. If you expect a more harmonious body contour and understand the limitations, you probably will be pleased.

Concluding Thoughts

Several liposuction and other fat-removal techniques exist to help you achieve your desired results. Among plastic surgeons, there is no consensus regarding the optimal liposuction technique. When you seek to remove excess fat, follow the advice of your plastic surgeon, who will recommend the technique that yields the best results in his or her hands.

Liposuction reduces specific areas of fat that are otherwise resistant to diet and exercise. It involves permanent removal of fat cells from the body. Provided there is no weight gain, results are lasting. For these reasons, liposuction has remained among the most popular procedures in cosmetic surgery.

Questions to Ask Your Plastic Surgeon

What size liposuction rods do you use?

Do you use tumescent fluid?

What is your revision rate?

What is your revision policy?

Which liposuction technique do you recommend, and why?

Tips and Traps

- *Wait until your body weight has been stable for at least six months before seeking liposuction.*

- *Do not expect liposuction to improve your cellulite. It may actually worsen it. Instead, consider endermologie or mesotherapy.*

- *Maintain stable weight following liposuction for the best results.*

- *You cannot predict where you will gain weight following liposuction. You may regain weight in the area of liposuction, or you may develop fat deposits in other places.*

- *If you seek large-volume liposuction, find a surgeon who is experienced and anticipate an overnight hospital stay.*

- *Consider a lift or tuck rather than liposuction if you have significantly loose skin.*

- *To maintain or achieve harmonious body contour, surgeons sometimes wisely recommend liposuction of adjacent areas, such as the hips or thighs.*

- *Avoid liposuction of buttock creases and calves, unless your surgeon is experienced in liposuction of these areas.*

11

Simple Solutions for Aged and Sun-Damaged Skin

Skin Care, Superficial Peels, Intense Pulsed Light, Fillers, and Botox

Dull skin seems to be an inevitable part of aging. It does not have to be. Fortunately, relatively simple options are available to improve rough, lifeless, blotchy, wrinkled skin, and new treatments become available regularly. The solutions aim to brighten the complexion, smooth the skin, revitalize the face, equalize color, and improve fine wrinkles—all while allowing immediate recovery, imposing little risk, and being relatively inexpensive.

Of course, anything that sounds too good to be true probably is. Such is the case with simple solutions for wrinkles, as each approach has limitations and requires multiple treatments. Most simple solutions mentioned in this chapter must be performed regularly for best results. Skin care, for example, should be performed twice daily at home. Superficial peels should be performed twice each month for three months and then maintained every six weeks for the best results. Filler injections and Botox also require regular maintenance.

Helen, a forty-three-year-old home-maker, won a recipe contest that was sponsored by a local television show. She was both elated and panicked when she was invited to appear on the program. She wanted to look her best, but with just two weeks to prepare, her options were limited. Two superficial peels and Botox injections for her forehead, frown lines, and crow's feet were timely solutions that helped her feel her best the day the show was filmed.

223

No Such Thing as a Healthy Tan

Before considering any skin problem or treatment, it is critical that you first understand the damaging effects of ultraviolet light. Ultraviolet light, whether from the sun or tanning beds, accelerates and compounds the aging process. The effects are cumulative and delayed. If you have significant sun exposure during your teens, you may not see sun damage for decades. But by that time, avoiding the sun will not prevent accelerated aging. The greater your lifetime total ultraviolet light exposure, the greater the damage to your skin. The term *photoaging* is often used to describe the changes that occur to sun-damaged skin over time.

Most important, exposure to ultraviolet light increases your chance of developing skin cancer. The greater your lifetime exposure, the greater your risk. Melanoma, a particularly aggressive type of skin cancer, may be fatal even when diagnosed and treated early. Clearly, you have many reasons to protect yourself from the damaging effects of the sun.

Meg, a forty-year-old sun worshipper, lived in the Sunbelt and prided herself on her deep tan. When work and weather kept her from the sun, she went to tanning beds. By the age of thirty, her skin looked like that of a forty-year-old. By the age of thirty-five, her skin looked like that of a fifty-year-old. She finally realized that her sun exposure must stop. She was shocked, however, to see that her accelerated aging did not. By the age of forty, she had the skin of a sixty-year-old. Skin does not forget its previous sun exposure, and the full effects of sun damage may be delayed by years.

Identify Your Skin Problems

To begin your quest for youthful skin, first take inventory of your specific problems. This will help you select the treatment(s) most appropriate for you.

Loss of Skin Vitality

Skin vitality is a feature that is difficult to quantify and describe. It is related to skin color and brightness—irrespective of tone, wrinkles, or texture. Skin with vitality appears young, healthy, energetic, and colorful. Skin with loss of vitality appears old, lifeless, tired, and pale.

Skin Roughness

Roughness relates to skin texture. In youth, skin is smooth, but with age, it becomes more rough and irregular.

Jodi, a twenty-five-year-old law student, was tired of her youthful-appearing freckled face. She would soon be entering the professional world and thought she could little afford the look of naïveté. She underwent several treatments with intense pulsed light (IPL), her freckles faded nicely, and she had no downtime.

Large Pores

Although some women are burdened with large pores in youth, many do not develop this problem until later in life. Large pores are visible and unattractive. They can be difficult to conceal with makeup. Small pores are considered more desirable.

Skin Discolorations

Discolorations are patches of skin that differ in color compared to the surrounding skin. Discoloration may be inherited (birthmarks and freckles), hormonal (melasma), sun-related (age spots), or multifactorial (rosacea). Some are brown or black, others are red. Some are superficial, others are deep. Their depth and color determine which treatment is most appropriate.

Birthmarks

Birthmarks vary in color and may range from cream colored to deep purple. The most common birthmarks are called café-au-lait spots because of their "coffee with milk" appearance. They may increase in size and number during childhood and puberty. These birthmarks respond well to laser treatment and may be effectively treated with one to three sessions. Red and purple birthmarks are more disfiguring and obvious. Most can be effectively treated with laser, but numerous treatments are required.

Freckles

Because freckles convey innocence and immaturity, many tire of this image as they age. As freckles increase in number and appearance with sun exposure, sunscreen and sun avoidance are helpful.

Melasma

Melasma is an area of dark blotchy skin that may develop on the faces or necks of women who are pregnant or using oral contraceptives. Melasma is distinctive: it has irregular borders and a "dirty" appearance. This condition may be precipitated or worsened by unprotected sun exposure. Sun avoidance and strong sunscreens may prevent melasma from worsening, but they probably will not improve it.

Treatment of melasma depends on its depth. Your plastic surgeon can determine if your melasma is superficial or deep by shining a black light, called a Wood's lamp, on your skin. Superficial melasma can be remedied through superficial chemical peels, IPL, medium chemical peels (Chapter 12), or daily application of bleaching agents. Deep melasma can be improved through Fraxel (Chapter 12).

Age Spots

Contrary to what their name implies, age spots are not due to age. They are due to ultraviolet light exposure. As the hands, face, and chest receive the greatest sun exposure, age spots are most prevalent in these areas. Age spots, not surprisingly, worsen during periods of unprotected sun exposure. Age spots can be treated with bleaching agents, chemical peels, laser, or IPL, depending on their depth.

Rosacea

Rosacea is a skin disorder in which the cheeks, nose, and chin become easily flushed in response to spicy foods, alcohol, or stress. After many years, the affected areas may become permanently flushed and develop small spider veins. Acne may also develop. Rosacea has been treated with prescription metronidazole gel (a daily skin-care product), laser, and IPL in various combinations.

Wrinkles

All wrinkles were not created equally, and all wrinkles are not treated equally. Treatment depends on the cause of the wrinkle. Each cause generates a specific type of wrinkle.

Crepe-Paper Wrinkles from Photoaged Skin

Crepe-paper wrinkles are fine wrinkles that occur on the lower eyelids or cheeks, where sun exposure is high and the skin is relatively thin and sensitive to its effects.

Dynamic Wrinkles from Facial Muscles

The most troublesome and abundant facial wrinkles are dynamic wrinkles, also called smile lines and frown lines. They are the result of facial expressions that we make hundreds of thousands of times over a lifetime. When we smile, laugh, frown, or brood, the skin of our faces is repeatedly moved. Each time the skin moves, it creases and eventually forms wrinkles.

Dynamic wrinkles may occur anywhere we have facial muscles, but they are worst in a few areas (Figure 11-1). The forehead has horizontal wrinkles (due to raising the eyebrows) and vertical wrinkles between the brows (due to scowling). Crow's feet develop around the eyes (due to smiling and squinting). Vertical wrinkles develop around the lips (due to pursing them).

Dynamic wrinkles are depressions or creases within the skin. Because they are lower than the skin on either side, light casts shadows into them. The deeper the wrinkle, the greater the shadow, and the more it is visible.

Skin-Fold Wrinkles from Drooping Cheeks

Skin-fold wrinkles may occur as your cheeks begin to sag. Skin folds, called nasolabial folds and marionette lines, can develop around your nose and mouth (Figure 11-2). As your skin folds develop, wrinkles accompany them.

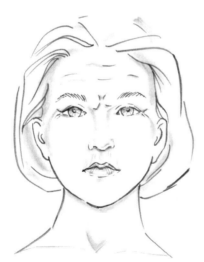

Figure 11-1: *Wrinkles due to facial expressions. Note the forehead horizontal wrinkles, scowl lines between the eyebrows, crow's feet, and vertical lip wrinkles.*

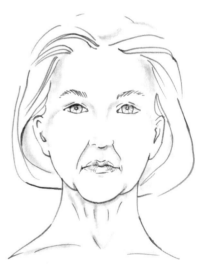

Figure 11-2: *Wrinkles due to skin folds. The skin fold between the nose and corner of the mouth is called a nasolabial fold or crease. The skin fold between the corner of the mouth and chin is called a marionette line. Both of these skin folds tend to be associated with deep wrinkles.*

Loss of Skin Tone

Poor skin tone may be due to genetics and worsens with age, sun exposure, and smoking. Loss of skin tone is evident by loose, droopy skin.

Overview of Skin Treatments

Skin care and superficial peels renew vitality by expediting skin turnover and bringing younger, healthier skin to the surface. Wrinkle fillers do not affect skin quality or tone, but camouflage wrinkles and creases by raising them to the height of the surrounding skin. Botox works on dynamic wrinkles by weakening the responsible muscles. Table 11-1 summarizes the simple solutions to damaged skin, which will be discussed in this chapter. For comparison, the table also shows more serious solutions, which are detailed in Chapter 12.

For skin-fold wrinkles, a facelift is usually the best treatment (see Chapter 2). It can tighten facial skin, improve heavy skin folds, and soften the associated wrinkles. Profound loss of skin tone is also best treated with a facelift. Deep chemical peels, laser, and dermabrasion (Chapter 12) can promote some skin tightening, but do not achieve that of a facelift.

Skin Care

Your skin is composed of damaged superficial cells and healthier deep cells. Every day, superficial cells die, shed, and are replaced by younger cells. This process becomes disorganized and slows down as you age. The older you are, the longer it may take to shed unhealthy cells, leaving you with a lifeless complexion.

Skin care and superficial chemical peels cause controlled injury to your damaged superficial cells, resulting in their uniform destruction and shedding. This allows the healthier deep cells to surface while they are still young and fresh. Skin turnover is organized and expedited, and it helps you reclaim younger skin.

The goal of skin care is to decrease roughness, brighten your complexion, minimize pore size, reduce blotches, and provide a healthier overall appearance. Some women also benefit through subtle improvement of fine wrinkles. You should not expect to see improvement in dynamic wrinkles, however. The changes seen with skin care occur gradually over six to twelve months.

Table 11-1 Summary of Simple and Serious Solutions for Aged and Sun-Damaged Skin

This table summarizes many of the treatment options that are described in Chapters 11 and 12.

	Fillers	Botox	Micro-derma-brasion	IPL (Intense Pulsed Light)	Radio-Frequency Treatments[1]	Skin Care	Superficial Peels[2]	Medium-Depth Treatments[3]	Deep Treatments[4]	Fraxel
Dull skin	0	0	+	+	0	++	+++	+++	0	+++
Rough skin	0	0	+++	+	0	++	+++	+++	+++	+++
Large pore size	0	0	+	+	++	++	+++	+++	+++	+++
Fine wrinkles	0	0	+	+	+	+	+	++	+++	+++
Dynamic wrinkles	+	+++	0	0	+	0	0	+	+++	+++
Discoloration —Brown	0	0	+	+++	0	++	++	++	+++	+++
Discoloration —Red	0	0	0	+++	0	+	0	0	+	+
Loose skin	0	0	0	0	+	0	0	0	++	+
Nasolabial folds	++	0	0	0	+	0	0	0	+	0
Acne scars	+	0	0	0	+	0	0	0	+	+

(continued)

Table 11-1 Summary of Simple and Serious Solutions for Aged and Sun-Damaged Skin (continued)

	Fillers	Botox	Microdermabrasion	IPL (Intense Pulsed Light)	Radio-Frequency Treatments[1]	Skin Care	Superficial Peels[2]	Medium-Depth Treatments[3]	Deep Treatments[4]	Fraxel
Total number of treatments recommended	Ongoing	Ongoing	Ongoing	2–5	1–2	Ongoing	Ongoing	1–2	1	3–5
Treatment interval	3–6 m	3–6 m	4–6 w	3–4 w	6 m	Daily	2–6 w	6 m	n/a	1–2 m
Skin preparation needed or advised?[5]	No	No	No	No	No	n/a	Yes	Yes	Yes, for most	Yes
Anesthesia[6]	T or L	None	None	None	T and L	None	None	T, L, O, or IV	G or IV	T and O
Cost per treatment	$300–$1,500	$200–$400 per area	$150	$100–$500	$1,500–$4,000	$30–$60/m	$70–$120	$1,000–$3,500	$3,000–$5,000	$1,000–$2,000
Recovery (days)	0–3	0	0	0	0–2	0	0	5–10	7–14	1

[1]Radio-frequency treatments include Thermage.

[2]Superficial treatments include MicroPeels, glycolic acid peels, lactic acid peels, salicylic acid peels, and microdermabrasion.

[3]Medium treatments include most TCA peels, resorcinol peels, Blue Peels, Jessner's Peels, erbium laser, and medium-depth dermabrasion.

[4]Deep treatments include phenol peels, deep TCA peels, carbon dioxide laser, and deep dermabrasion.

[5]Skin preparation involves stimulating and protecting the skin with topical creams. This is often accomplished through Retin-A, AHAs, and bleaching agents, which are included in most professional skin-care programs. It is recommended that patients be on these agents for at least four to six weeks prior to treatment.

[6]Anesthesia: T = topical, L = local, O = oral, IV = intravenous, G = general.

0 = no improvement   + = subtle or mild improvement   ++ = moderate improvement   +++ = marked improvement or resolution

Balanced Skin-Care Programs and Products

A balanced skin-care program is set up and monitored by a nurse or skin-care technician who will evaluate your skin and outline a program suited to your needs. In some states, a physician is required to evaluate you prior to your commencement in the skin-care program. Your program is geared toward four goals: exfoliation, stimulation, medication, and protection. These goals are achieved through daily or twice-daily home application of cleansers, alpha hydroxy acids, Retin-A, antioxidants (such as vitamin C cream and idebenone cream), bleaching agents, sunscreen, and moisturizers. The frequency of application and concentration of these agents can be increased as your skin becomes accustomed to them. If your skin reacts with redness or rash, your program will be tailored appropriately.

Mild Cleansers

You will begin skin care each day with a mild cleanser, which lifts dead superficial skin cells. This process of exfoliation facilitates penetration of stimulants such as alpha hydroxy acid and Retin-A.

Principles Behind Skin-Care Products

- *Exfoliation: Cleansers remove dead skin cells so that other agents can penetrate.*

- *Stimulation: AHAs, BHAs, and Retin-A enhance new skin growth and turnover.*

- *Medication: Bleaching agents treat or prevent discoloration for those at risk. Retin-A also belongs in this category.*

- *Protection: Moisturizers and sunscreen protect your skin from further damage.*

Alpha Hydroxy Acids (AHAs)

AHAs are naturally occurring acids that stimulate growth and turnover of skin cells. Glycolic acid derives from sugar cane, citric acid derives from citrus fruits, malic acid derives from apples, and lactic acid derives from milk. These acids may be used daily in very low concentration or may be used for superficial peels in higher concentrations (explained later in this chapter).

The most commonly used AHA is glycolic acid. It is available in concentrations of 4 to 15 percent for home use. Depending on your skin sensitivity, you may be started at a low or medium concentration until you demonstrate tolerance. The acids work by thickening the deep layers of your skin, resulting in improved skin texture, complexion, smoothness, and appearance. The effects of AHAs are enhanced by concurrent use of Retin-A.

Beta hydroxy acids (BHAs), such as salicylic acid, may also be incorporated into skin care. These acids may offer even greater improvement than AHAs for some people.

Retin-A

Retin-A is a brand name for tretinoin, a topical form of vitamin A. Retin-A stimulates circulation to your skin and facilitates skin-cell growth and turnover. It thickens the deep layers of your skin, leading to a brighter, healthier complexion with smoother texture. Retin-A helps reduce fine wrinkles, but does not affect dynamic wrinkles or skin-fold wrinkles. It can also reduce or eliminate a precancerous skin condition called actinic keratosis (AK).

One genuine disadvantage of Retin-A is that it may cause skin irritation even in low concentrations. You may develop a temporary rash or experience a transient burning sensation while using it. If this happens, you may be asked to temporarily decrease the amount of Retin-A you apply, decrease the frequency of application, delay application until at least twenty minutes after face washing, increase moisturizer use, or apply steroid cream. You are then slowly graduated to higher concentrations of Retin-A to achieve the maximum benefit. Another disadvantage of Retin-A is that it may worsen facial spider veins by stimulating blood flow. So if you have problematic spider veins, you may choose to have them treated with laser before you start Retin-A. Finally, Retin-A causes dry skin. Moisturizers alone may help you overcome this. If not, you may switch from Retin-A to Renova or retinol, which are similar to Retin-A but have less of a drying effect. Many doctors and skin-care specialists believe Retin-A is more effective and will ask you to continue Retin-A if possible. Despite the problems Retin-A may cause, its effect on skin, when used consistently, can be significant.

Bleaching Agents

Bleaching agents, such as hydroquinone, can be helpful in the prevention and treatment of blotchy, discolored skin. Bleaching agents do not actually bleach skin; rather, they suppress the activity of pigment-producing cells. If your skin is not blotchy or discolored, you do not need bleaching agents as part of your skin-care program. If you plan to pursue chemical peels or laser resurfacing, you may tempo-

Bad Press for Retin-A

When Retin-A was initially introduced in the 1970s, the media reported that it offered significant improvement in wrinkles. Most physicians who prescribed Retin-A were careful to explain that it would not affect dynamic wrinkles. Because of the overwhelming impact of the media, most consumers expected Retin-A to eliminate all wrinkles and were greatly disappointed when it did not. This led to widespread disappointment in the product. This is unfortunate because the other improvements seen with Retin-A are real.

rarily require bleaching agents for prevention of dark discoloration, which might otherwise ensue following such treatments.

Hydroquinone came under scrutiny in 2006 due to a study that showed an association between it and leukemia in rats. As a result, a ban was placed on 2 percent hydroquinone, which is the strength allowed for sale without a prescription. Interestingly, the study involved giving rats many times the amount of hydroquinone (based on weight) that humans receive. The prescription strength (4 percent) hydroquinone remains available.

Moisturizers

Moisturizers keep your skin healthy and soft while you shed your superficial, unhealthy skin layers. They also help you tolerate the drying effects of Retin-A.

Sunscreen

Sunscreen is essential to the success of a balanced skin-care program for two reasons. You should by now be aware of the damaging effects of the sun, and that should make you eager to protect yourself from further damage. Also, an effective skin-care program actually increases your skin's sensitivity to sun and makes you more likely to sustain a burn than if you were not using skin-care products. Sunscreen with a sun protection factor (SPF) of 15 or higher is recommended at all times.

Recovery

Skin care requires no recovery time. You may apply makeup immediately following application of your skin-care products.

Cost

The home products are affordable with an average monthly cost of $30 to $60.

Beware of Costly and Ineffective Products

Skin-care products available through department stores, beauty salons, and drugstores may claim they are effective and boast 20 percent glycolic acid or higher. Yet these products may offer little improvement when compared to skin-care products obtained through your plastic surgeon or dermatologist. The effect of glycolic acid and all AHAs depends on low pH (acidity). Products obtained through a physician have the appropriate pH for optimal results.

pH 1–2 Strong acid—the typical pH of effective skin-care products obtained from your plastic surgeon
pH 3–4 Medium acid
pH 5–6 Weak acid
pH 7 No acid (neutral)—the typical pH of skin-care products obtained outside of a doctor's office

A preparation of glycolic acid with a neutral pH is ineffective compared to your plastic surgeon's glycolic acid with an acidic pH, regardless of the concentration. Most products available in stores are safe; however, they also have less effect on your skin.

Physician-Supervised Skin-Care Programs

"Physician-supervised" means that a physician has ensured that the technician, nurse, or aesthetician has been properly trained to administer skin-care programs and perform safe and effective superficial peels. It does not mean that the physician will be present at the time of your skin-care evaluation or peel. Nor does it mean that you will necessarily meet the physician, unless you reside in a state that mandates it.

Physician-supervised skin-care programs are able to obtain and distribute the most highly effective skin-care products. The more effective a skin-care product, the greater is its potential to cause skin irritation and increased sensitivity to the sun. Thus these products must be administered by a trained medical professional. Your day spa or department store may insist that their products are effective, but be suspicious unless their programs are physician-supervised. Few are.

Duration of Results

Skin care maintains your skin vitality and smoothness as long as you use the products regularly. If you stop using them, expect your skin to return to baseline within a few months.

Satisfaction

Because physician-supervised skin-care programs are safe, effective, and affordable, satisfaction is immense. The few who are disappointed are those who fail to use the products consistently and those who expect too much.

Superficial Chemical Peels

Superficial peels are an important adjunct to any skin-care program. They achieve greater improvement in skin vitality, complexion, pore size, and fine wrinkles than skin care alone—and they do it sooner. Like other chemical peels, superficial peels apply a chemical irritant to the skin.

The agents most commonly used for superficial peels are glycolic acid, lactic acid, and salicylic acid. These are the same acids used in skin-care programs, but at a much higher potency. A number of skin-care corporations offer superficial peels, including BioMedic, MD Formulations, Skin-Medica, Gly Derm, and others. You should agree to the brand that your skin-care specialist recommends because she will be most familiar with it.

Microdermabrasion: Is It Worth It?

Microdermabrasion was introduced around the year 2000. Like many things in plastic surgery, there was an initial wave of excitement and hype followed by a wave of disappointment. Finally, the pendulum has centered, and most set their sights on realistic expectations. Microdermabrasion is a treatment performed by a technician or nurse using a microdermabrasion machine. The machine enables millions of tiny particles to impact your skin, causing superficial dead cells to flake off immediately. Its effects are very similar—if not identical—to dermaplaning. Recovery is immediate, and treatments are recommended every four to six weeks. Results are best when combined with skin care and superficial peels. The greatest disadvantage is cost, which averages $150 per treatment across the country. As microdermabrasion and dermaplaning each result in the removal of fifteen microns of skin thickness, and as dermaplaning is typically included in most superficial peels (which cost $70 to $100), many question whether microdermabrasion is worth the extra cost.

The peels are performed in a doctor's office by a trained skin-care technician or nurse and require about thirty minutes. First, dead skin cells are gently removed through a painless technique called dermaplaning (which is similar to shaving) or microdermabrasion. Then the peeling agent is applied. You may experience mild temporary burning and itching. Stimulants such as dry ice may then be applied, followed by moisturizing cream. Immediately following your peel, you can apply makeup and return to your usual activities.

Following each peel, your dead superficial skin cells shed either visibly or invisibly. You will see the biggest effect two weeks later.

To Flake or Not to Flake?

Superficial peels may or may not cause visible flaking. In general, peels performed with glycolic or lactic acid do not cause visible flaking. Dead skin cells fall away microscopically, so there is never any outward sign that you had a peel. These peels are initially performed every two weeks for three months, then every six to twelve weeks for maintenance. One of the most popular brand names for this type of superficial peel is MicroPeel by BioMedic.

Whereas lactic and glycolic peels offer greater improvement than skin-care products alone, they have less impact on discoloration than superficial peels that cause visible flaking. Superficial peels that cause visible flaking are most often accomplished with salicylic acid. Salicylic peels have a more immediate impact on discoloration than lactic or glycolic peels. Visible peeling lasts up to three days, which is why these are often called weekend peels. A popular brand name is MicroPeel Plus. To achieve optimal results, have this type of superficial peel repeated monthly for six months. Thereafter, peels every two or three months will maintain your result.

As with all peels, adherence to a physician-supervised skin-care program enhances your results and makes them more lasting.

Cost

The average cost of a superficial peel that causes invisible flaking (glycolic or lactic acid) is $70 to $100 per peel. The cost of a superficial peel that causes visible flaking (salicylic acid) is about $90 to $120.

Duration of Results

All superficial peels require maintenance. Following your first six peels, you must continue using skin-care products regularly at home and have maintenance peels every six to twelve weeks. If you cannot follow this regime, expect your skin to return to baseline within six months.

Satisfaction

Because superficial peels are safe, effective, and affordable, satisfaction is immense. The few who are disappointed either fail to sustain their results through maintenance peels or expect too much.

Intense Pulsed Light (IPL)

IPL is a treatment whereby a machine delivers high-intensity pulses of light to the skin. It is highly effective for nearly all skin

---

Retin-A and Superficial Peels

Whereas Retin-A and other skin-care products lay essential groundwork for peels of all kinds, Retin-A should be stopped five days prior to each peel—regardless of the type of peel. Doing this helps prevent a deeper peel than was intended.

It is important to ensure that you go to a qualified professional for any kind of chemical peel. A sixty-seven-year-old retired schoolteacher complained to her hair stylist about her wrinkles. Before her hair was dry, another woman appeared, touting the miracles of chemical peels. Following her hair appointment, she stayed for a peel. It burned intensely, but she assumed that the woman performing her peel was qualified. It took her three weeks to heal, and she was left with permanent scars on her neck. She has since undergone corrective surgery but has not regained a natural appearance.

Options for Wrinkle Fillers

Collagen

Bovine (cow) collagen (Zyplast, Zyderm)

Collagen from yourself (Isolagen, Autologen)

Collagen from cadavers (Dermalogen, Cosmoplast, Cosmoderm)

Synthetic Fillers

Hyaluronic acid (Hylaform, Restylane, Captique, Juvéderm, others)

Calcium hydroxyapatite (Radiesse)

Poly-L-lactic acid (Sculptra)

Fat

discolorations, regardless of color or depth. It also lends improvement to dull skin, fine wrinkles, large pores, and rough skin.

Treatment is painful, but afterward there is no discomfort and no recovery time. Two to five treatments are needed to treat most discolorations and can be performed every three to four weeks. Ironically, one of the greatest risks is discoloration, as this is the area in which IPL offers the greatest potential improvement. Risk of discoloration is greatest in those with darker skin, so IPL is best suited to lighter skin. Cost is $100 to $500 per treatment.

Wrinkle Fillers

Wrinkles are visible because they are lower or deeper than surrounding skin. Light casts shadows into them, making them visible. The deeper the wrinkle, the greater the shadow. The greater the shadow, the more visible the wrinkle. Hence, there is a big advantage in making wrinkles more shallow. Moreover, if a wrinkle can be brought to the same level as surrounding skin, its visibility diminishes, because the accompanying shadow vanishes. This can be accomplished by either lowering the surrounding skin or raising the wrinkle. Chemical peel, dermabrasion, and laser all attempt to lower the surrounding skin. Fillers attempt to raise the wrinkle.

Fillers are substances that can be injected into the base of the wrinkle, pushing the depressed wrinkle outward and making it less visible.

Collagen

Collagen is the protein matrix of the skin and is sometimes called the "meat" of the skin. It may be obtained from cow skin, cadaver skin, or your own skin. It is refined, sterilized, and processed so that it may be used safely. As a rule, implant materials such as collagen last longest if they are injected into skin, which is composed of collagen, rather than into the fat beneath the skin. This is why collagen is better suited to wrinkles than to hollows: wrinkles are a skin problem, whereas hollows are often due to deficient fat.

Bovine Collagen

Bovine collagen derives from cow skin and has been the mainstay of collagen therapy in the past. Bovine collagen injections have a number of drawbacks, such as short-lived duration (six to twelve weeks), allergic reactions, need for skin testing prior to use, and association with connective tissue disorders. For these reasons, bovine collagen has been largely replaced by other alternatives.

Collagen from Yourself

Autologen derives from your own skin, such as skin that was removed during a tummy tuck, facelift, or breast lift. A commercial laboratory extracts collagen and prepares it for reinjection. One month later, your collagen is sent back to your surgeon, who can inject it where it is needed or store it for you for up to five years. Autologen may last months or in some cases years. The average cost of preparing Autologen is about $1,200 to $2,500 for three injections.

Isolagen is cultured collagen-producing cells made from a small sample of your skin. First, your plastic surgeon removes a piece of skin the size of a pencil eraser from behind your ear and sends it to the Isolagen lab in New Jersey. Within a few weeks, the lab sends back your collagen-making cells. These cells are alive and must be injected the day they reach your surgeon. Thereafter, they begin producing collagen. The effect of Isolagen may last years, according to the manufacturer, but the length of duration of Isolagen may be variable. The cost of Isolagen is $500 to $1,000 for each injection.

Cadaver Collagen

Collagen obtained from deceased human donors includes brand names such as Dermalogen, Cosmoplast, and Cosmoderm. It is processed in liquid form for injection into lips or wrinkles and lasts three to four months. The cost of Cosmoplast and Cosmoderm is about $300 to $600 per injection, depending on the amount used.

Synthetic Fillers

Synthetic fillers are one of the fastest-growing areas in plastic surgery. Several new options have become available since the first edition of this book.

Hyaluronic Acid

Hyaluronic acid is a man-made filler. Brand names include Hylaform, Captique, Restylane, Juvéderm, and others. It can be injected into the nasolabial folds, marionette lines, or vertical lip lines to reduce the appearance of wrinkles. It may also be used for lip augmentation. Injections cost $400 to $1,000, depending on the type and amount of hyaluronic acid that is used. Results last three to six months.

Calcium Hydroxyapatite (Radiesse)

This is another man-made filler. It lasts up to two years, but has the consistency of toothpaste, making it difficult to inject smoothly into some tissues. It is most often used for the nasolabial folds. Injection into thinner tissues has an increased risk of lumpiness or extrusion. Cost is $600 to $1,200 for injection of the nasolabial folds.

Poly-L-Lactic Acid

This man-made filler is similar to the absorbable suture material called Vicryl. The brand name is Sculptra, and it works by inducing an inflammatory response. It is best for filling volume, such as nasolabial folds or hollow cheeks, rather than wrinkles. The cost is about $1,200 per visit. Injections are initially recommended every two months until three or four injections have been achieved. Thereafter, the results last two to five years.

Stem Cell Fat

Everyone has heard of embryonic stem cells, which can give rise to any human cell type. But much of the public is unaware that stem cells can also derive from adult bone marrow, brain, liver, skin, and fat. These cells are limited in what cell types they may become. Fat stem cells may be harvested via liposuction and coaxed into becoming fat, bone, or nerve cells. If cultured into fat, they may be reinjected into the donor in areas where fat is deficient, such as facial hollows. Researchers are optimistic that this will yield better and more reliable results than routine fat injections, but the cost is certain to be higher. Developments in stem-cell fat injections are sure to evolve as research progresses.

Fat Injection

Fat can be harvested through liposuction and reinjected. But it is not necessarily suited for filling wrinkles. The tissue into which fat is injected is important. Fat injections fare best when injected into fat. Because wrinkles are within the skin rather than in fat, fat injection for wrinkles is generally doomed to failure. Fat injected into skin will not last, and fat injected into fat will not improve wrinkles. In contrast, when fat is carefully harvested and injected into fat, it can produce a sustained improvement in fullness.

Botulinum Toxin

Dynamic wrinkles, such as crow's feet, frown lines, and forehead wrinkles, are due to repetitive facial expression. Weakening the responsible muscles via botulinum toxin injections can improve or eliminate these wrinkles. Botox is a brand name for botulinum toxin. With botulinum toxin, you begin to see improvement in your wrinkles within twenty-four hours and continue to see improvement for one to two weeks.

Areas most amenable to botulinum toxin are the forehead, frown lines between the eyebrows, crow's feet, upper lip, and neck. Some also benefit from injection in the marionette lines. The lower lip is not injected with botulinum toxin, as this might result in drooling. The cheeks are not injected either, as this would prevent the ability to smile. Results may last three to twelve months, and the average duration of effect is four to six months.

Questions to Ask Your Plastic Surgeon
What treatment do you recommend and why?
Will the treatment you recommend need to be repeated?
How many injections do you think I will need to accomplish my goal?
How long will it take to achieve my peak result, and how long will it last?

Cost

Your surgeon's cost per vial of botulinum toxin has increased each year from 2002 to 2007, at which time it was $505. Because the makers of botulinum toxin have no direct competitor at this time, the cost may continue to rise. One vial contains 100 units of botulinum toxin. About twelve to fifteen units are injected in each area (such as crow's feet, scowl line, etc.). You can expect to pay about $200 to $300 per area every four to six months.

Risks

No negative long-term effects have been observed. Very few short-term problems have arisen. Risk of allergic reaction is extremely small. If Botox migrates from your scowl lines to your upper eyelids, temporary upper eyelid droop may result. Injection of your forehead diminishes your ability to raise your eyebrows. This is not a problem for most, but those with low eyebrows may find that their brow positions worsen following injection.

Concluding Thoughts

Because of skin care's simplicity, safety, low cost, and advantage of home application, every woman should participate in a physician-supervised skin-care program. The improvement in skin appearance is reliable, and the cost is affordable—often lower than what you might pay for department store products.

Physician-supervised superficial peels have become immensely popular because of their simplicity, safety, effectiveness, and low cost. Here, too, the benefits are great, the risks negligible, and the cost affordable.

Of the multiple options for filling wrinkles, none have proved to be lasting. If you choose to have your wrinkles filled, you should anticipate the need for ongoing treatments.

Finally, botulinum toxin injection is a powerful treatment because of its dramatic effect and immediate recovery. It has become one of the most requested procedures in plastic surgery.

In short, if you have problems with skin texture, complexion, vitality, discoloration, and wrinkles, you need not commit yourself to an expensive procedure or lengthy recovery. Each of the simple solutions offers advantages, but their effects are less potent and shorter lived than those of the serious solutions discussed in the next chapter.

Tips and Traps

- *Enroll in a skin-care program through your plastic surgeon's office. It is simple, safe, effective, and economical.*

- *Skin-care specialists and plastic surgeons find most department store skin-care products to be little effective. Do not be misled by promises of effectiveness if the product is not recommended by your physician.*

- *Avoid unprotected sun exposure for at least three to six months following skin treatments. SPF 15–30 is usually adequate.*

- *Beware of laypeople who offer chemical peels.*

- *Decide what bothers you most about your skin, and seek a treatment that addresses your primary concern.*

12

Serious Solutions for Aged and Sun-Damaged Skin

Medium and Deep Chemical Peels,
Dermabrasion, Laser Resurfacing, and Fraxel

The field of nonsurgical facial rejuvenation has continued to evolve and is one of the fastest-changing areas in plastic surgery. With so many options available for rejuvenating aged or sun-damaged skin, it can be confusing to decide which is right for you. Yet this decision should be no more difficult than any other in plastic surgery. You simply need to identify which problems you wish to address, how much risk and recovery you are willing to tolerate, and how much you can afford to pay for treatment.

To help identify your skin problems, refer to the section "Identify Your Skin Problems" in Chapter 11. Whether your concerns are discolorations, wrinkles, rough skin, or large pores, a continuum of options is available, ranging from superficial to deep. As a general rule, the more superficial options (Chapter 11) impose less recovery time and lower cost but also yield less impressive results. The deeper remedies, covered in this chapter, impose greater risk, recovery time, and cost, but also offer greater rewards. Table 11-1 (on pages 129 to 130)

Glenda, a fifty-four-year-old socialite, has battled skin problems for as long as she can remember. During her twenties, she underwent multiple dermabrasion sessions—the only option at that time—for treatment of her acne scars. During her thirties, she received several medium chemical peels to brighten her complexion, smooth her skin, and soften some of her fine wrinkles. During her forties, she has pursued laser resurfacing for her increasingly problematic complexion and deeper wrinkles.

summarizes many of the simple and serious solutions described in these two chapters.

Similarities Among Chemical Peels, Dermabrasion, and Laser Resurfacing

Chemical peels, dermabrasion, and laser resurfacing should all be viewed as different hammers that hit the same (or similar) nails. Each may strike the nail lightly, with a medium firmness, or with a much stronger blow. This chapter focuses more attention on how hard the nail is hit (medium versus deep treatment) than on which hammer was used to hit it, although all aspects are considered.

Principles

Chemical peels, laser resurfacing, and dermabrasion are all guided by the same principles. Each treatment causes controlled injury to your skin's damaged superficial cells. Your skin then sheds those cells, allowing the healthier deep cells to surface while they are still young and fresh. Each of these treatments organizes and accelerates the process of skin turnover to give you brighter, healthier, fresher, and smoother skin. (Skin care and superficial peels are also guided by these principles, although their effects are less profound.)

Each of these treatment modalities may be performed to a variety of depths. For example, chemical peels may be superficial, medium, or deep. The same is true of laser resurfacing and dermabrasion. This chapter focuses on only medium and deep treatments.

Multiple Treatments

All of the treatments in this chapter, with the exception of deep peels, may be required more than once to achieve optimal results. Dermabrasion, medium chemical peels, and laser resurfacing may require a total of one to four treatments at six-month intervals to achieve your desired result.

Differences Among Chemical Peels, Dermabrasion, and Laser Resurfacing

The main difference among these options is the way that each achieves controlled injury, or removal, of the top skin layer. Chemical peels involve applying a chemical that penetrates the skin and causes a chemical burn, which results in dead cells that peel and flake away for several days. Dermabrasion uses a high-powered rotor that essentially sands skin off the face, leaving an open wound that heals within one to two weeks. Laser resurfacing causes a controlled burn to the skin with or without immediate vaporization of the superficial layers.

Complications and Telltale Signs

Before going into detail on medium and deep treatments, an understanding of the complications and telltale signs is helpful. Chemical peels, dermabrasion, and laser resurfacing may all discolor skin, increase sensitivity to the sun, scar the skin, or trigger an outbreak of cold sores. With most of these, the risk is greater with deep treatments compared to medium treatments.

Dark Discoloration

Dark discoloration, or hyperpigmentation, appears as dark, blotchy, irregular patches of skin in the treated area. It may also occur at the border between treated and untreated areas, thus drawing attention to the area of treatment. It may develop within several weeks of your treatment and may last weeks or months. It is usually not permanent. Hyperpigmentation may be both prevented and treated by topical bleaching agents (see "Skin Care" in Chapter 11), an important part of preparing your skin for any medium or deep treatment.

Women with olive or dark skin are at highest risk for dark discoloration. Because of this, deep treatments are not recommended for these women. As most medium treatments are less likely to cause discoloration, many may be safely performed on women with olive or dark skin. One exception is erbium laser resurfacing, which has a high risk of discoloration and demarcation in women with medium or dark skin. Birth control pills, antidepressants, and tetracycline may further predispose skin to dark discoloration.

Because chemical peel, laser resurfacing, and dermabrasion may sensitize your skin to the sun, even minor sun exposure may cause severe burn or dark discoloration. The already high risk is even higher if sunlight strikes unprotected skin that is still red from treatment.

Sunscreen with sun protection factor (SPF) 15 or higher is recommended. Its importance cannot be overstated. If you are unwilling or unable to avoid the sun or wear sunblock, you should not have these treatments.

Light Discoloration

Light discoloration, or hypopigmentation, appears as blotchy, irregular patches of skin that are lighter than the surrounding skin. It may develop within several weeks of your treatment and may last only temporarily. Risk of developing hypopigmentation is highest in those with light skin and in those receiving deep treatments.

Lines of Demarcation

As some medium treatments, especially erbium laser resurfacing, and all deep treatments cause a change in skin color, there is often a visible line distinguishing the treated versus untreated skin. Most surgeons strategically plan to have that line fall just below the lower border of the jawbone, because shadows naturally fall there, making a change in skin color less obvious. Nevertheless, if the change in color is dramatic (as it often is with phenol peels) or if the treatment results in permanent loss of freckles (as is the case with erbium laser resurfacing and all deep treatments), this line of demarcation can be very obvious. Further, having a facelift can shift the line of demarcation higher, making it more obvious. Finally, areas with permanent pallor (especially following carbon dioxide laser or phenol peel) never tan. So if you tan the rest of your body and neck, this line of demarcation becomes even more obvious. If demarcation is a concern, you are safer with medium peels than the other options.

Scarring

The deeper the treatment, the greater is its effectiveness. Yet if performed too deeply, any procedure may cause permanent scarring. Your surgeon will try to balance depth and safety, giving you the greatest improvement while trying to avoid scarring (see Figure 12-1).

If you have had radiation treatments to your face, you have a higher risk for scarring. Your surgeon can perform a spot test with the laser or chemical peel to determine your skin's response in a tiny area. If healing is poor, it may leave a small scar, which will likely go unnoticed. If healing is uncomplicated, you may then have your entire face treated with reasonable assurance that scarring will not occur.

If you take Accutane, you must discontinue this oral acne medication and defer chemical peels, laser resurfacing, and dermabrasion for at least one year. Accutane markedly slows healing and predisposes to scarring.

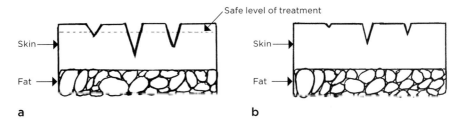

Figure 12-1: *Cross section of skin. (a) Before treatment: wrinkles and acne scars are lower than the surrounding skin. The dotted line shows the safe level of treatment. If treatment is carried deeper, permanent scarring may result. (b) After treatment: wrinkles and scars are shallower following treatment with dermabrasion, deep chemical peel, or laser. Because all of these wrinkles are deeper than the line of safety, one treatment will not eradicate them without causing scars. Therefore, multiple treatments are necessary. After each treatment, the deep layer of skin thickens and the wrinkles become shallower.*

Patterned Look

The so-called patterned look can occur following carbon dioxide laser and is due to the shape of the laser tip, which is usually a square or rectangle. When these squares are perfectly aligned at the time of treatment, the treated areas are seamless. However, if they are not perfectly aligned, as they seldom are, it can appear as though there are squares or rectangles across the face. This is clearly an unfavorable and unnatural outcome, and resolution can be difficult.

Cold Sore Outbreak

These skin treatments may trigger a cold sore outbreak with resultant scarring. Taking antiviral medication prior to and following your treatment reduces your risk. Defer your skin treatment until any active sores have healed.

Milia

Milia are skin eruptions that appear as tiny whiteheads. When they occur, they may do so throughout the treated area and appear quite obvious and unattractive. Because they are raised, they are not easily concealed with makeup. They may last weeks or months. Whereas it is common for milia to occur temporarily, it is uncommon for them to persist beyond several weeks.

Depth of Treatment

The greatest determinant of depth of treatment is not the hammer that is used, but how hard it hits.

Medium Treatments

Medium-depth treatments tend to give marked improvement for fine wrinkles, some dark discolorations, pregnancy masking, age spots, large pores, and rough skin. They make dull, lifeless skin appear more fresh and vibrant. They give very little improvement for dynamic wrinkles, and they offer no improvement for loose skin. They offer relatively little improvement in acne scarring. Recovery typically involves five to seven days of peeling or weeping skin, followed by several weeks of skin that appears sunburned but can be concealed with makeup. A medium-depth treatment can be achieved with trichloroacetic acid (TCA) peels, resorcinol peels, Blue Peels, Jessner's Peels, medium dermabrasion, erbium laser, and others.

Preparation

Preparing your skin prior to a medium or deep treatment (with the exception of phenol peels) results in faster recovery, lower risk of discoloration, and a better result. Apply Retin-A, glycolic acid, and bleaching agents daily for four to six weeks. Retin-A stimulates your skin to regenerate and heal more quickly. Alpha hydroxy acids, such as glycolic acid, enhance the effects of Retin-A. Women with dark skin are at increased risk for developing blotchy skin after a medium treatment. Bleaching agents used before and after the treatment minimize this problem. If you are on a skin-care program, you are probably already prepared for a medium treatment. Some practitioners may perform medium treatments in patients who do not prepare their skin. If so, the results may not be as dramatic, recovery may be longer, and risk of discoloration is greater. An exception to this rule is phenol peels, which seem to be little affected by such preparation.

What Determines the Depth?

The type of treatment alone does not determine the depth of a peel. Its strength and the technique of application also matter. For example, glycolic acid used in low concentration may produce a superficial peel, but used in high concentration it may yield a medium peel. (Note that although glycolic acid can be used as a medium peel, it is almost exclusively used as a superficial peel.) Dermabrasion can be performed superficially (see "Microdermabrasion: Is It Worth It?" in Chapter 11), or it can be performed to a medium or deep level.

Sue, a forty-nine-year-old manicurist, had been using skin-care products and getting superficial peels for three years. While pleased with her results, she wanted a more dramatic effect. She had a five-day weekend approaching in which she could recover from a medium peel. A TCA peel provided her with the improvement she sought and allowed her to return to work with makeup in six days.

What to Expect: Medium Treatments

- **Examples:** *TCA peel, rosorcinol peel, Jessner's Peel, Blue Peel, erbium laser resurfacing, and medium dermabrasion.*

- **Anesthesia:** *Topical or oral sedation.*

- **Practitioner:** *Most medium-depth treatments can be performed safely by nurses who have been properly trained and supervised.*

- **Location of procedure:** *Office.*

- **Length of procedure:** *Thirty minutes to two hours.*

- **Length of stay:** *Outpatient (home same day).*

- **Discomfort:** *During the procedure, discomfort can be mild, moderate, or (rarely) severe, depending on how you were prepared and your pain threshold. Afterward, discomfort is minimal to none. Anticipate up to two days of prescription pain medication.*

- **Swelling:** *Improves in three to seven days.*

- **Dressing:** *After erbium laser resurfacing or medium dermabrasion, the treated areas weep, ooze, and hurt when exposed to air. To facilitate healing and minimize discomfort, your treated skin may be covered with a masklike dressing that spontaneously lifts off within a few days. Alternatively, ointment may be applied. Most patients prefer the masklike dressing because it is less messy and more comfortable. After a medium peel, you will have no open wounds, and you will apply ointment regularly until the dead skin sloughs off (usually five to ten days).*

- **Healing:** *Your skin will heal in five to ten days and will then appear sunburned. Redness will improve over one to four weeks, depending on the depth of your treatment.*

- **Makeup:** *May be worn after your skin heals, usually five to ten days.*

- **Presentable in public:** *You will be presentable once you can wear makeup.*

- **Work:** *You may feel capable of returning within a day, but your appearance will be the limiting factor.*

- **Exercise:** *May be resumed in one week.*

- **Sun protection:** *SPF 15 or higher for three to six months.*

- **Resume skin care:** *You should resume skin-care products after your skin has healed.*

- **Final result:** *Seen after redness fades.*

- **Duration of results:** *Medium chemical peels will last six months to two years. If you use skin-care products regularly, you will extend the duration of improvement. Most women who choose medium treatments as the mainstay of their facial rejuvenation have a repeat treatment every six months to two years.*

Cost

Expect to pay about $1,000 to $2,500 for a medium peel of the full face and neck. Erbium laser resurfacing and medium dermabrasion may cost up to $1,000 more per treatment.

Deep Treatments

Deep treatments are capable of profound improvement in all wrinkles and dark discolorations. They reduce acne scarring. They also promote some skin tightening so that a facelift might be postponed in some women. A final benefit is that, in contrast to medium treatments, usually only one deep treatment is necessary to obtain the desired result (with the exception of acne scarring, which usually requires multiple treatments).

Despite these impressive benefits, deep treatments have fallen out of favor because they cause two unnatural and irreversible side effects. First, they cause profound pallor such that the skin appears bleached, colorless, and ghostly. This is why deep peels are not recommended for women with Mediterranean or African-American skin. But even in Caucasians the result can appear unnatural, as a line of demarcation is certain to occur. Second, it causes the skin to feel waxy or rubbery. Women who have undergone deep treatments often regret it for these reasons.

In an effort to avoid the unfavorable color and texture changes that commonly follow a deep treatment, your surgeon can perform a more conservative procedure that is not quite as deep. The trade-off is that you will not gain the benefits of a deep treatment, and you will still be at risk for pale, waxy skin, albeit a lower likelihood.

Deep treatments can be accomplished with phenol chemical peels, deep dermabrasion, or carbon dioxide laser resurfacing, among others. Recovery is about twice that of a medium-depth treatment.

Louise, a sixty-nine-year-old with marked wrinkles around her mouth and very light skin, wanted to improve her wrinkles in a single treatment. Because she had light skin, she was a good candidate for a deep peel. The peel was performed around her mouth only. She had dramatic improvement in her wrinkles, and she looked natural because of her inherently pale complexion.

Lexy, a sixty-three-year-old grandmother with a pale complexion, wears turtlenecks year-round. She had a phenol chemical peel years ago, resulting in removal of all of her freckles. Because the peel stopped at her jawline, the freckles of her neck and chest remained. This sharp contrast was eye-catching, clearly unnatural, and made her extremely self-conscious. Unfortunately, the results of her deep peel were permanent. Her facial freckles could not be restored. Performing a deep peel on her neck would be medically ill-advised because the neck does not heal consistently following a phenol peel. It would also offer little improvement because it would only move the line of demarcation farther down. Her freckle-free neck would then sharply contrast with her freckled chest and back. This is why deep treatments are not typically recommended for heavily freckled women.

What to Expect: Deep Treatments

- **Anesthesia:** *General or heavy sedation.*

- **Practitioner:** *Physician.*

- **Location of operation:** *Office or hospital.*

- **Length of procedure:** *Thirty minutes to two hours.*

- **Length of stay:** *Outpatient (home same day).*

- **Discomfort after the procedure:** *Mild to severe. Anticipate up to five days of prescription pain medication.*

- **Swelling:** *Moderate to severe after phenol peel and carbon dioxide laser resurfacing and may temporarily interfere with opening the eyes. It will improve over seven to ten days. Swelling is less following dermabrasion.*

- **Dressings:** *Two methods of dressing are used: open or closed. If the open method is used, your treated skin will be covered with ointment and you will be instructed to wash your face and apply ointment beginning the day following your peel. If the closed method is used, your skin will be covered with tape or a flexible adherent mask immediately following the peel. You will return to your plastic surgeon's office within a few days to have the mask removed. You will then begin to wash and to apply ointment twice daily. Many patients prefer the closed method because it is less messy and less painful.*

- **The healing process:** *Your face will be swollen, red, oozing, and crusted. If you had a phenol peel, your face will become stiff and dark, and then your skin cells will dry and begin to flake. You will be advised to avoid picking at your flaking skin and to limit your facial expressions to prevent premature peeling. If you had carbon dioxide laser resurfacing or deep dermabrasion, your skin will heal within seven to ten days. Regardless of the treatment, you will have healthy, smooth, bright red skin about seven to ten days after the procedure. This sunburned appearance may take two to three months to improve. Thereafter, your skin is likely to appear extremely pale.*

- **Makeup:** *May be worn about four days after your skin has finished peeling and flaking, approximately ten to fourteen days after the procedure.*

- **Presentable in public:** *You will be presentable in ten to fourteen days with makeup.*

- **Work:** *You may feel capable of returning within three days, but your appearance will be the limiting factor.*

- **Exercise:** *May be resumed as soon as your skin has finished peeling, approximately seven to ten days.*

- **Sun protection:** *SPF 15 or higher should be worn indefinitely.*

- **Final result:** *Seen after your redness fades, approximately two to three months.*

Cost

The fee for a full-face phenol peel, deep dermabrasion, or carbon dioxide laser resurfacing is about $3,000 to $5,000. Treating a portion of the face costs less but increases the risk of obvious demarcation.

Satisfaction

Women with pale skin who have profound sun damage gain dramatic improvement with deep treatments and may be pleased with their results. Because their change in appearance is overwhelming and because any bleaching of their skin is less obvious against their pale complexion, these women are satisfied, provided they can tolerate the waxy texture. Women with less sun damage and those with medium or dark complexions are likely to be highly dissatisfied with the results of a phenol peel, due to permanent pallor and demarcation.

Colleen, a forty-five-year-old lawyer, helped her best friend recover from carbon dioxide laser resurfacing. She wanted similar results but could not afford two weeks to recover. She chose erbium laser resurfacing with the understanding that her wrinkle reduction would be less impressive. Following one treatment, she had reasonable improvement in her wrinkles and was back to work in six days.

Fraxel

Fraxel laser deserves special attention, because it achieves the favorable results of a deep treatment with the risks of a medium treatment. Thus it does not fall neatly into either category.

Technology

Fraxel is a laser that, instead of treating all of the skin, only treats 20 percent with each treatment. As a result, recovery is substantially faster and easier. To understand how Fraxel laser works, think about digital photographs and how they are made up of millions of pixels. Fraxel treats 20 percent of the so-called pixels that make up the patient's skin. When a treatment is performed, only one in five pixels are affected in the treated area. With four out of five so-called pixels of the face being unaffected, recovery time is greatly diminished.

Benefits

Because of the depth of treatment, Fraxel can ultimately achieve the benefits of a deep treatment. It results in marked improvement in fine lines

Fraxel Can Treat Lines of Demarcation

As noted, when Fraxel is applied, lines of dermarcation can be avoided. Additionally, Fraxel can be used to soften lines of demarcation that have been caused by previous erbium laser resurfacing or deep treatments.

and dynamic wrinkles, reduction in pore size, improvement in skin texture, resolution of most brown discolorations, improvement in acne scarring, and a modest degree of skin tightening. Because only 20 percent of the skin is treated at any given time, the face, neck, and chest can all be treated safely. Demarcation can be avoided by changing the line of treatment each time the patient is treated.

Treatment and Recovery

Fraxel treatment can be safely performed by a trained nurse under topical anesthesia with or without oral sedation. With oral sedation and topical anesthetics, the treatment is quite tolerable, but without these aids, Fraxel treatment is extremely uncomfortable. Full-face treatment requires thirty to forty-five minutes. Immediately following the treatment there is no pain, and the skin is red for about one day. There is no open wound, and makeup can be applied immediately. Following resolution of redness the day after the procedure, skin turns gray and dry. This lasts for about two weeks and can be camouflaged with very heavy makeup. Most are able to return to work the day following the treatment.

Number of Treatments and Duration of Results

Because Fraxel only addresses 20 percent of the so-called pixels of the skin at any given time, five treatments are recommended for the full effect, but gradual improvement is seen after each treatment. Following the third treatment, some see such marked improvement that they see no need to pursue treatments number four and five. Those who do pursue the last two treatments are usually well rewarded with even greater improvement. Treatments can be performed as frequently as once every month or can be performed several months apart.

Cost

Fraxel costs about $1,000 to $2,000 per treatment. As three to five treatments are recommended, the total cost can range from $3,000 to $10,000. Considering that most can undergo this treatment without time away from work, and considering that multiple medium-depth treatments can cost the same or more, many have found Fraxel to offer such substantial advantages that it is replacing many alternative medium and deep treatments.

Concluding Thoughts

The solutions to the problem of aged and sun-damaged skin presented in this chapter are for women who seek dramatic change. Until recently, women seeking such improvement had to choose between medium treatments, with limited results and lower risks, and deep treatments, with profound improvement and higher risks. Recently, Fraxel has become available and has offered a combination that was not previously available.

Questions to Ask Your Plastic Surgeon

What treatment do you recommend and why?

How many treatments will I need?

What recovery should I anticipate?

Am I at risk for skin-color changes following treatment?

Will the treatment you recommend need to be repeated?

How long will my results last?

How can I best prepare my skin for the treatment you recommend?

Tips and Traps

- *Avoid unprotected sun exposure for at least three to six months following any skin treatment. SPF 15–30 is usually adequate once you are back in the sun.*

- *Ask to be treated with antiviral medication prior to a medium or deep peel, dermabrasion, or laser resurfacing. This reduces your risk of cold sore outbreak and scarring after treatment.*

- *If you seek a deep treatment, expect your skin to become permanently pale in the area treated.*

- *Anticipate some improvement with each treatment, but do not expect one procedure to cure all skin problems. The exception to this rule may be a deep peel.*

13

Touching Up This and That

Spider Veins, Permanent Makeup, Unwanted Hair or Tattoos, and Thin Lips

Whether you are a plastic surgery veteran who has undergone major procedures or a novice who is looking to try plastic surgery for the first time, you are likely to find something of interest in this chapter. It presents a potpourri of problems that don't quite fit neatly into other chapters, yet still merit attention.

Many of these are minor problems that can be improved through simple treatments. These procedures have come to be known as "lunch-hour treatments," because they are relatively quick and painless, and they impose little or no recovery time. Spider veins of the legs and face are amenable to injections or laser therapy. Decorative tattoos can be removed, and permanent makeup can be placed. Lunch-hour treatments can temporarily halt the growth of unwanted hair or augment thin lips. All of these things can be accomplished through office procedures that are generally safe, effective, and affordable.

Yet these treatments are not necessarily innocuous. Many of these remedies do pose potentially serious consequences. Some treatments provide only temporary improvement, even though advertisements may state otherwise. Others may provide no improvement. Unfortunately, in the arena of

Lisa, a forty-two-year-old freelance artist, had a number of concerns as she prepared herself for her annual trip with her husband to Key West. She was embarrassed about spider veins around her knees and hair around her belly button. She also did not want to be bothered with daily eye-makeup application. In a short time and at a reasonable cost, she had spider veins treated, abdominal hair removed, and eyeliner tattoos placed.

minor office procedures, false claims prevail. As a consumer, you must edu-cate yourself so that you are not misled.

Lasers are the treatment of choice for many of these minor problems, so this chapter begins with a short explanation of lasers.

Explanation of Lasers

The word *laser* is an acronym for *l*ight *a*mplification by *s*timulated *e*mission of *r*adiation. Laser technology was developed decades ago but continues to be improved and refined. In laser therapy, a beam of light is amplified and its wavelength is adjusted to target particular colors or substances.

Lasers are important treatment options for many minor skin problems. In the realm of plastic surgery, laser therapy treats spider veins, tattoos, and unwanted hair. It is also used for skin discoloration and wrinkles (see Chapter 12).

Lasers do not vanquish all skin problems, and lasers are not appropriate for every procedure. They play a role in some cosmetic treatments, but their use must be kept in perspective. Lasers are a tool, not a panacea.

Different Lasers for Different Problems

There are as many different lasers as there are skin problems. Each laser has strengths, weaknesses, and targeted areas of effectiveness. For example, some lasers are effective for treating shades of brown and red—and there-fore are used for the removal of age spots, brown birthmarks, and red tat-toos. Other lasers are effective for vascular problems such as spider veins, red or purple birthmarks, and exuberant scars. Other lasers target blue, black, yellow, and green pigments and are used in an attempt to remove decorative tattoos.

Three lasers—the carbon dioxide laser, the erbium laser, and Fraxel—are used to treat wrinkles and are discussed in Chapter 12. The lasers discussed in this chapter are markedly different, particularly in terms of discomfort and recovery. The lasers in this chapter are often used without anesthetics, enable quicker recovery, are more affordable, and can be per-formed by a nurse, technician, or physician.

Laser Treatments

Laser treatments for spider veins, tattoos, and unwanted hair are performed in the office and require no special preparation. Treatments are associated with some discomfort. Some liken it to the feeling of being splattered with hot bacon grease. The discomfort is well tolerated when small areas are treated, but if large areas are treated, such as in hair removal, discomfort may interfere with the procedure. Treatment of small areas usually does not involve sedatives, pain medications, or injections of a local anesthetic. Treatment times vary depending on the size of the area treated. A small tattoo can be treated in five minutes. Hair removal from both legs and groins may require two hours. Dressings are often unnecessary except for tattoo removal.

Recovery

Recovery is rapid. Bruising might occur following some laser treatments and disappears in three to ten days. Some lasers may cause temporary dryness, crusting, blistering, and roughness of the skin, which also improve in a few days. You usually can resume normal activities immediately following laser treatment, but you may prefer to keep the treated areas covered with clothing until appearance is back to normal. Your skin may temporarily become darker or lighter than the surrounding skin. If your skin is olive, brown, or black, you will have a higher risk for dark discoloration. If your skin is pale, you will have a risk for light discoloration. These dark or light areas are blotchy, irregular, and unsightly, but usually disappear within a few months. Unprotected sun exposure may trigger dark, blotchy skin, so you are advised to wear sunscreen with sun protection factor (SPF) 30 or higher for several months following laser treatment.

Scars

Permanent scarring may occur if lasers are applied too intensely or too deeply. This is rare with the lasers discussed in this chapter. One of the great advantages of laser surgery is that lasers usually leave no scars.

Number of Treatments

The number of treatments necessary depends on your problem, its severity, your response to treatment, and your goal. Some problems can be effectively treated with one or two treatments. Others require a dozen treatments. Some problems, such as unwanted hair, are only temporarily improved by laser and may require routine maintenance treatments.

Cost

For tattoos, spider veins, hair removal, and other minor skin problems, laser treatment in the United States costs $200 to $1,000 per session with a typical fee of $400. Prices vary depending on the type of laser used and the size of the area being treated.

Spider Veins on the Legs

Spider veins, or telangiectasias, are small, visible vessels that develop within the skin. They may be blue, red, or purple and can vary in size. Spider veins have no known medical consequences. Those who seek removal of spider veins do so for purely cosmetic reasons. Lower-extremity spider veins develop when deep leg veins are subjected to increased stress, such as during pregnancy or after prolonged standing (Figure 13-1). They are also more common in women with varicose veins, those who take oral contraceptive pills, and those whose mothers had spider veins.

Varicose Veins

Varicose veins are distended veins beneath the skin, whereas spider veins are new, small veins that develop within the skin. Varicose veins may appear as bluish bumps on the skin. Those with unsightly varicose veins and associated aching pain often seek treatment that involves surgical removal or injection of the faulty veins. General and vascular surgeons manage varicose veins; plastic surgeons usually do not.

If you have both spider veins and varicose veins, your varicose veins must be treated first. If your spider veins are treated first, you will be at increased risk for rapid recurrence of spider veins and matting (see "Complications"). If your varicose veins are treated first, these problems will be minimized. Also, the successful treatment of varicose veins may reduce your spider veins before they are treated.

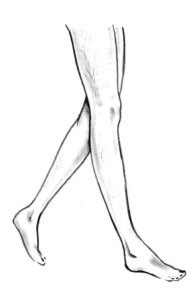

Figure 13-1: *Spider veins.*

Sclerotherapy for Treatment of Spider Veins of the Legs

Sclerotherapy involves injecting a liquid chemical through a tiny needle directly into your spider veins, causing them to contract and collapse. The chemical may be highly concentrated salt water, a biological detergent, or a natural chemical compound. Because this technique relies upon fitting a tiny needle into a tiny vein, it is best suited to medium and large spider veins, although some clinicians are able to successfully treat small spider veins.

The procedure is performed in the office by a physician or a nurse and is relatively painless. Even those who fear needles tolerate this type of injection well because the needles are extremely small. As spider veins are often interconnected, like branches of a tree, a single injection at the base may cause an entire family of spider veins to collapse. Depending on the number of spider veins, the procedure may require up to one hour. Afterward, you will wear Ace bandages or compression hose for three to ten days. For best results, you should avoid exercise, hot baths, and alcohol for five days, because they cause blood vessel dilation, which may compromise the effectiveness of your treatment.

Anticipate 50 to 90 percent improvement in spider veins following each sclerotherapy session. Some veins may fail to respond due to small vein size, lack of compression following injection, or features of the vein that you cannot control. You may need multiple sessions to achieve your desired results.

Laser Treatment of Spider Veins of the Legs

During laser treatment of spider veins, the laser is applied to the skin over your spider veins. Laser energy causes your spider veins to coagulate and shrink. Laser therapy is most often used for small and medium spider veins. Large spider veins are best treated with sclerotherapy.

Immediately following treatment, spider veins will appear darker and more visible. Over a few weeks, they will fade. Avoid unprotected sun for six weeks to decrease your risk of skin discoloration. Ace wraps and support hose are not necessary. You may exercise immediately. Laser treatment usually leaves no scars, but it can cause permanent light discoloration, or hypopigmentation. If so, it will appear strikingly unnatural, not unlike the branches of a tree—except the branches will look more like a string of pearls than a branch. These branches remain pale and do not tan. As such, they will become even more obvious when the surrounding skin darkens with tan.

An average of three treatments is required at three-month intervals. After the first treatment, you will see a 70 to 80 percent improvement in the appearance of your spider veins, but all of them will still be visible. Each subsequent treatment results in an additional 70 to 80 percent improvement. Compared to sclerotherapy, laser treatment offers greater improvement in small spider veins and less improvement in large ones. Many plastic surgeons believe that although lasers continue to improve, sclerotherapy remains the most effective way of treating most spider veins of the legs.

Renee, a forty-two-year-old salesperson, was in the top one hundred of all salespeople in her corporation. As a result, she won a trip to Hawaii with the other top performers. She did not want her colleagues to see her spider veins while she was on the beach. After injection of the medium and large spider veins, she underwent three laser treatments. By the time she left for the trip, there was no evidence of spider veins or their treatments.

Combination Therapy for Spider Veins of the Legs

If you have small, medium, and large spider veins, you may benefit from both sclerotherapy and laser therapy. You may wish to start with sclerotherapy because sometimes all veins are improved after injecting the larger ones. This may reduce the number of veins that need to be treated by laser, lowering your overall cost. Many plastic surgeons use the laser for only those spider veins that are refractory to injection.

Complications

When performed or supervised by a qualified plastic surgeon, your procedure and recovery are likely to be uneventful. Yet even in ideal circumstances, complications may occur.

Matting

The sudden appearance of patches of new, tiny spider veins, known as matting, may occur anywhere on the treated extremity. Matting appears somewhat like a red bruise. Matting occurs in 10 to 20 percent of patients following sclerotherapy, occurs in 5 to 15 percent following laser, and is most common in women who have spider veins treated in the presence of varicose veins. Obese women and those who take hormones or oral contraceptive pills are also at increased risk. Matting may improve on its own, but it may take one year to do so. Persistent matting can be treated with either laser or sclerotherapy.

Discoloration

Following either sclerotherapy or laser, treated spider veins commonly appear brown due to breakdown of blood within the veins. This dark discoloration disappears in 80 percent of women within six weeks, in 95 percent within twelve weeks, and in the remainder within six months. In rare cases of persistence, a different laser may be used to treat such dark discoloration.

Those with dark skin have a higher risk for discoloration. The lighter your skin, the less likely you are to have dark discoloration, and the more likely you are to have light discoloration. Light discoloration (as previously described) occurs in 10 to 20 percent of women who have spider veins treated with laser.

Skin Death

During sclerotherapy, if the chemical is injected into skin or fat, rather than into the vein itself, it may cause a small area of skin death. This results in a small open wound. If this occurs, the wound may require two months to heal and leaves a scar. Skin death is not a risk following laser therapy.

Swelling

Swelling may occur anywhere, but it is more common if spider veins around your ankles are injected. Swelling occurs in fewer than 5 percent of those treated, can be prevented by wearing compression hose, and improves within two weeks. Swelling is uncommon following laser therapy.

Cost

Sclerotherapy costs about $300 per session. Laser treatment costs about $400 per visit. Expect to pay more if your spider veins are extensive or if the treatments are performed by a physician rather than a nurse.

Duration of Results

Once your treated spider veins are no longer visible, they usually do not return. However, you should anticipate the development of new spider veins over time, just as you would if your spider veins had not been treated. Spider vein therapy treats current spider veins but does not prevent new ones.

Spider Veins on the Face

Spider veins may occur anywhere but are particularly annoying when they occur on the face. Facial spider veins tend to be red, whereas leg spider veins can be red, purple, or blue. Sclerotherapy of facial spider veins has been ineffective and unreliable. Laser therapy of facial spider veins is the treatment of choice. The good news is that the newer lasers for facial spider veins do not cause purplish discoloration like the older lasers did in the 1990s.

Placement of Permanent Makeup

Cosmetic tattooing, or micropigmentation, can mimic eyeliner, eyebrow pencil, lip liner, or full lip color. When placed by a trained medical professional, these makeup tattoos can appear natural and attractive. The greatest advantage of permanent makeup is not needing to bother with daily application. Also, by the end of the day, permanent makeup does not fade. The greatest disadvantage is that it is permanent. So, unless you are certain that it is what you wish, you should not have it.

Placement of permanent makeup takes one to two hours. Many find this procedure uncomfortable and choose to have the area numbed prior to tattooing.

The cost of permanent makeup varies depending on the extent, the training of the person performing it, and the quality of the result. The cost for a single area, such as the lips, eyes, or eyebrows, ranges from $400 to $1,200.

Beware Nonprofessional Permanent Makeup

Permanent makeup is widely available and not closely regulated. Your greatest risk is having an untrained individual perform this procedure. If contaminated needles are used, infections can be transmitted or the ink may not be of medical-grade quality and may cause irritation.

Permanent makeup of cheek blush is commonly offered by nonprofessionals and often looks distinctly unnatural. Natural cheek color changes from season to season, day to day, and moment to moment. A tattoo does not change and therefore appears unnatural. If you later regret the decision to have blush tattoos, removal may be difficult,

Linda, a forty-year-old pharmacist, requested permanent lip color of "bubble-gum pink." After she selected the shade, the pigment was placed. She was immediately pleased, but returned a few days later to complain about the color, which her husband apparently did not like. Unfortunately, the pigment might outlast their marriage.

Candace had lower eyelid liner placed at a beauty parlor. Her tattoo had been injected into fat rather than skin. Because fat cannot retain pigment as skin does, blue ink spread throughout her lower eyelid, giving her the appearance of a blue smudge.

Vanessa, a forty-five-year-old stay-at-home mom, received permanent lip liner at a spa, but it was placed too thick and too high. It gave her the appearance of a fat lip. When she returned to the spa to complain, the aesthetician said she could fix the problem by tattooing over it in white. Because the white tattoo did not match her skin, it looked like a milk mustache. Frustrated, Vanessa sought help, only to discover that white tattoos are among the most difficult to remove with laser and have a risk of turning black in the process.

as flesh-colored tattoos may turn black in response to attempted laser removal.

If your eyebrow tattoo is placed too high, you may have a permanent look of surprise, and eyeliner placement has little room for error. If a cosmetic tattoo is botched, removal (with laser) may damage the hair follicles and result in loss of eyelashes or eyebrows. Placement of permanent makeup demands precision. When it is performed in your plastic surgeon's office, you have the greatest chance for a satisfactory outcome.

Removal of Decorative Tattoos

Many choose to have decorative tattoos in youth but live to regret this decision as they discover that removal is often much more difficult than placement.

Options for tattoo removal include surgical excision, dermabrasion, and laser. Surgical excision is best employed for small tattoos on loose skin, but it always leaves a scar. Dermabrasion involves sanding the skin with a rotating wire brush and may leave a scar or a pale area. Even after several treatments, the tattoo may still be visible.

Laser has largely supplanted surgical excision and dermabrasion for the removal of tattoos. Lasers target tattoo ink and rapidly heat it. Heat causes ink to expand and break up into smaller particles. The body then is able to absorb the small ink fragments and carry them away. Each treatment is somewhat painful, although pain can be reduced with topical anesthetic.

Multiple Treatments

Each laser targets a different family of colors. Following each laser session is partial clearing of one or more families of colors. To completely remove a family of colors, two to ten sessions may be required. Because most tattoos are composed of multiple color families, several different lasers may be required. If three different lasers are required to remove one tattoo, and each laser must be used five times, a total of fifteen laser sessions is necessary. Some tattoos require many more laser treatments for complete removal.

Many other factors determine the number of treatments necessary. Tattoos obtained in a tattoo parlor are difficult to remove, because professional tattoos are typically deep, dark, and made with complex ink. Homemade tattoos are variable in their difficulty of removal, based on the type of ink used and the depth they were placed at. New tattoos are difficult to remove because they have a higher concentration of ink than old ones.

The total number of treatments necessary to remove a tattoo cannot be known for sure at the outset. The common range is between six and twelve. Treatments may be performed every one or two months or may be spaced over several years. The tattoo begins to fade one week after each treatment and continues to fade for several months.

Some women choose to over-tattoo to hide an undesirable tattoo. This is especially common when the original tattoo contains the name of a former boyfriend. If you have done this, expect to need even more laser treatments.

Judy, a forty-three-year-old insurance claims examiner, was embarrassed by the tattoo on her forearm. It served as a reminder of her impulsive high-school days. She wore long sleeves to conceal her tattoo, even in the summer. She finally decided to seek removal. She was fortunate that in six treatments it was removed with no scars.

Samantha, a twenty-nine-year-old hairdresser, had a tattoo of a heart with her first husband's name on her buttock. It was composed of multiple colors and required a total of fourteen treatments for removal. According to her second husband, it was well worth the cost.

Complications

Permanent scarring occurs in fewer than 3 percent of those treated. Permanent bleaching, fading, or hypopigmentation of the treated area may occur and is much more common than scarring.

Turquoise Tattoos

Turquoise tattoos, as well as most tattoos with some shade of green, are particularly difficult to remove with laser. Although some lasers target green, they are much less effective than lasers that target other colors. Turquoise in particular is very difficult to remove or even improve.

Removal of Red, White, and Flesh-Colored Tattoos

Laser removal of red, white, and flesh-colored inks is notoriously difficult. These ink particles may contain iron, which turns black after treatment. It may then be impossible to remove this black pigment. If you have red, white, or flesh colors in your tattoo, your surgeon should test the response by performing laser treatment on a small area before treating the entire tattoo. If it does not turn black, laser treatment of the entire tattoo should be safe.

Jessica, a thirty-six-year-old investment adviser, had pubic hair that extended to her groins and thighs. Because she spent her summers in a bathing suit, she made many attempts at hair removal. Waxing and electrolysis were painful. Shaving caused ingrown hairs. Laser hair removal was like a miracle treatment. Each session took about thirty minutes, and hair did not return for three months. After four treatments, she found that her hair took over two years to return and was so thin that it was barely visible.

Cost

The typical cost is $200 to $800 per session, with the typical fee of $400. If your tattoo is large, expect to pay more. As five to twenty sessions may be required, the total fee may range from $1,000 to $16,000. This is yet another reason to choose tattoos carefully and think twice before having them applied.

Unwanted Hair

Women have long tried to rid themselves of unwanted hair of the face, legs, underarms, abdomen, and groin. Laser hair removal remains the most popular choice, as waxing, plucking, and electrolysis are painful and must be performed regularly. Laser causes controlled damage to hair follicles, causing them to go into shock temporarily. While in shock, the follicles do not generate hair.

Laser hair removal relies on the principle that the laser targets hair follicles. It works best on dark hair in light-skinned women. Results for women with light hair and tan, olive, or black skin have been disappointing. As laser technology improves, ideally it will have something to offer all women.

Duration

Hair eventually returns, but it will not do so for over two months in 80 percent of women. Some have enjoyed one- or two-year periods without hair growth, but many require regular treatments at three- to four-month intervals. When hair returns, it is usually thinner and lighter. Arrested hair growth following six treatments is now being seen more commonly, as laser technology continues to improve.

What to Expect

Treatments are performed in your doctor's office by a nurse or a trained technician and last from fifteen to ninety minutes depending on the size of the area treated. You may return to work immediately after treatment. Unlike waxing, you may shave immediately prior to your laser hair removal. Anticipate that your treated skin may turn sunburned red, and this will persist for several days. Some areas may scab and blister temporarily.

Recovery

As with all laser therapies, light and dark discoloration may occur, but it is usually temporary. Wearing sunscreen with an SPF of 15 or higher helps protect you from dark discoloration. If you like to tan, note that quarterly or biannual treatments prohibit tanning year-round.

Cost

Cost ranges from $150 to $1,000 per session depending on the size of the area, with a typical fee of $500. If you have extensive hair growth on your back, abdomen, and thighs, expect to pay more.

Thin Lips

Full lips are a sign of youth and sensuality, whereas thin lips can reveal advanced age or detract from an otherwise youthful appearance. Although all women's lips thin as they age, some young women have thin lips despite their age. Thus women of all ages seek lip augmentation. Augmentation may be performed for one or both lips. Many women choose to have both lips augmented to preserve harmony.

Lip Augmentation

Lip augmentation has a long history. In the 1960s and 1970s, liquid silicone injections were used, but they were abandoned when they were shown to

---

Is Laser Hair Removal Permanent?

In the first edition, I reported that laser hair removal lasted three months in most people. At that time, many unethical profiteers promoted laser hair removal as permanent, because to advertise that something is permanent, it only needs to last three months. Yes—three months. Interestingly, since that time, laser technology has evolved and there are people whose laser hair removal is lasting for years. Whether it is truly permanent, however, remains to be seen.

Elizabeth, a sixty-seven-year-old retired schoolteacher, had recovered from a facelift, eyelid surgery, and a forehead lift. She was pleased with her results but thought her thin lips revealed that she was actually older than she appeared. Lip augmentation gave her full youthful lips and restored harmony to her face.

distort and disfigure lips. In the 1970s and 1980s, bovine collagen and fat injections were used, but these were later cast off in favor of implants in the form of sheets, which were used largely in the 1990s. Most recently, many surgeons have returned to injectable fillers (see Figure 13-2).

Sheet Implant Options for Lip Augmentation

Some materials lend themselves to sheet form in that they are broad and flat. One example is AlloDerm, a manufactured sheet of freeze-dried collagen derived from human cadavers. Another example is fascia, a dense, white connective tissue that envelops your muscles and can be harvested through an incision hidden above your ear. Another example is Gore-Tex, the same popular material used to make raincoats. The advantage of sheet implants is that they may be rolled into a log shape and then placed into the lips through a tiny incision in the corner of the mouth. The result can be impressive and smooth. Sheet implants, however, have several disadvantages. AlloDerm and fascia shrink and become completely resorbed within a year or so. Gore-Tex never shrinks, but it makes the lips feel stiff and phony. It can also extrude. Because placement of sheet implants involves incisions, there can be moderate swelling and occasional bruising. Cost of lip augmentation with any of these options is about $500 to $1,200 per lip. Although sheet implants remain an excellent option for some women, their disadvantages make them less ideal than some of the newer options.

Injectable Fillers for Lip Augmentation

The newest options for injectable augmentation for lips have mostly evolved since 2000. They include many synthetic fillers (e.g., Hylaform, Restylane, and Captique) as well as liquid forms of collagen that tend to outlast bovine

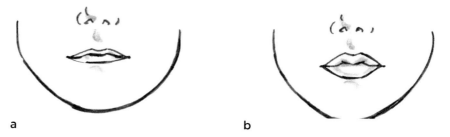

a   b

Figure 13-2: *Lip augmentation. (a) Thin lips before augmentation. (b) Full lips following augmentation. Scars are not shown, because typically they are not visible.*

collagen (e.g., Dermalogen, Cosmoplast, and Cosmoderm). These are explained in Chapter 11, as they are also used as wrinkle fillers.

Trends in lip augmentation have changed over the past forty years. And until a single, lasting, affordable, smooth, and natural option becomes available, you should expect this area of plastic surgery to continue to evolve.

Lip Lift

As with so many body parts, the lips tend to sag with age. This is particularly true of the upper lip, which elongates with time, sometimes precluding any show of the upper teeth. A long upper lip can be the remaining giveaway of your true age, even after you have addressed loose skin, wrinkles, and other skin issues. Long lips also look flat and thin, thereby compounding the problem.

A lip lift is an operation that addresses the issues of an elongated lip. By removing excess skin of the upper lip, the lip is lifted, upper teeth again become visible, and the vermillion (pink part of the lip) appears thicker and less flat. Because the scar falls along the natural crease between the nostrils and the lip, the scar usually becomes imperceptible. This procedure can

Beware Liquid Silicone Injections

Liquid silicone (which differs from silicone gel contained in breast implants) was injected into the faces and breasts of numerous women during the 1960s and 1970s. The initial results were aesthetic, soft, and natural. However, within weeks, months, or years, the injected areas became hard, lumpy, red, and painful. Some women appeared unnatural, unsightly, and even diseased. Because silicone disseminated throughout the injected area, its removal was not a simple procedure, and attempts at removal often compounded the cosmetic problem induced by the silicone.

Despite the unfavorable history of liquid silicone injections, some companies are again manufacturing fillers that include liquid silicone. They claim that the small size of each silicone particle reduces the likelihood of untoward results and that silicone offers the advantage of sustained results. As it will take years to substantiate these assertions—if even true—you may wisely choose to decline injection of synthetic fillers with claims of permanence.

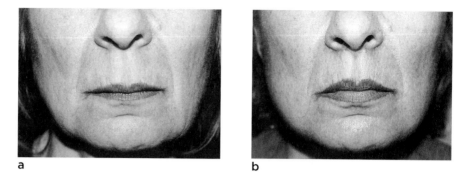

Lip lift. (a) A sixty-year-old woman before surgery. (b) Six weeks after a lip lift, her upper lip is shorter and the vermillion (pink part) appears more full even though it received no fillers.

Creases Around the Mouth

Creases around the mouth, or nasolabial folds, are formed by sagging skin. Plastic surgeons use the same options available for lip augmentation to treat these creases. The same principles and methods apply.

Questions to Ask Your Plastic Surgeon

Can laser solve my problem?
Will the effects be temporary or permanent?
How many treatments will I need?
What materials do you recommend for lip augmentation?
How long will my lip augmentation last?

be performed under local anesthesia with little or no time off work—provided you don't mind others seeing your fresh suture line. Otherwise, plan on a week off work. Cost ranges from $1,200 to $2,500, and the results typically last over ten years.

Concluding Thoughts

The currently available treatments for many miscellaneous problems can be relatively safe, effective, convenient, and affordable. They may impose little recovery time, but they are not without risk. Be certain that you are fully informed before having any procedure, no matter how innocuous it may seem.

Tips and Traps

- *Laser treatments are not a panacea.*

- *Varicose veins should be treated before spider veins.*

- *Injections can be effective for small, medium, and large spider veins; laser is most effective for small or medium spider veins.*

- *A supervised technician may safely perform laser spider vein treatment, laser hair removal, and laser tattoo removal. A physician must perform laser treatment for wrinkles (see Chapter 12).*

- *Beware of laypeople who offer cosmetic tattooing of your face.*

- *Laser hair removal offers many benefits, but its permanence has not been proven.*

- *Understand that the options available for lip augmentation continue to evolve.*

Afterword

You now are aware of the many new, exciting things plastic surgery can offer. You also appreciate that whereas many things have changed since the first edition of this book, many have remained the same. Hopefully, you have developed a balanced view of each.

Amidst this plethora of new and evolving technologies, and despite all of the information in this book, you also realize that this book has not yet answered the most important question: will cosmetic surgery be worth it? As with the first edition, this question cannot be answered by me—nor by anyone other than the person contemplating it.

In spite of all the recent advances, plastic surgery still poses risks, costs, recovery, and time away from work or play, while not providing any guarantees of satisfaction. Of the millions of women who have had cosmetic surgery, about 95 percent were very satisfied, with two-thirds of them having additional cosmetic surgery. Although only 5 percent were neutral or dissatisfied, at least some of those were devastated. So the question really is this: how can you get yourself out of the 5 percent and into the 95 percent?

You can minimize the risk of dissatisfaction by identifying and consulting with a qualified plastic surgeon. Visualize your expectations and carefully discuss them with your surgeon. You may try to safeguard yourself from disappointment, but be forewarned that there is no foolproof way. Emotions sway the intellect and alter the perception of reality.

You can reduce your risk of complications by complying with your surgeon's instructions. But you can never eliminate risk, and the more you understand and accept potential complications, the better you will deal with them if they arise.

The popularity of cosmetic surgery speaks for itself. Yet in the end, the decision is yours alone. This book and your plastic surgeon can provide you only with information and expertise. The rest is up to you.

Appendix

Summary Table for All Procedures

	Greatest Advantages	Greatest Disadvantages	Recovery[1]	Cost[2]
Facelift	*Improves heavy cheeks, jowls, and loose skin of the face and neck; removes neck fat*	*Does not improve skin quality, does not affect forehead or eyelids*	*10–14 days*	*$9,000*
Radio-frequency treatment (Thermage)	*Nonsurgical tightening of skin; improves wrinkles*	*Some have no improvement*	*1 day*	*$1,500–$4,000*
Forehead lift	*Improves forehead wrinkles, scowl lines, and droopy eyebrows*	*Does not tighten loose eyelid skin*	*7–14 days*	*$4,400*
Eyelid surgery	*Improves eyelid bagginess and puffiness*	*Does not improve crow's feet or loose skin due to droopy brows*	*3–14 days*	*$4,100*
Nose surgery	*Can change nasal appearance in numerous ways*	*Up to 20% of patients seek revision surgery*	*1–2 weeks*	*$5,400*
Chin or cheek implant	*Provides stronger facial contour and profile*	*All synthetic implants pose potential risks*	*1–2 weeks*	*$3,400 (chin) $4,600 (cheeks)*
Lip augmentation	*Can create full lips*	*Depending on the material used, the results may be temporary*	*3–14 days*	*$500–$1,200 per lip*
Breast augmentation	*Can enlarge breasts to desired size*	*All synthetic implants pose potential risks*	*3–10 days*	*$6,000 (saline) $7,500 (silicone)*
Breast lift	*Can raise breasts to a more youthful position*	*Scars can be extensive*	*3–7 days*	*$6,100*

(continued)

	Greatest Advantages	Greatest Disadvantages	Recovery[1]	Cost[2]
Nipple reduction	Reduces hypertrophic nipples	None	1 day	$1,500
Tummy tuck	Can restore a flat, tight abdomen	Surgery is much more extensive than the name implies	1–2 weeks	$6,700
Inner thigh lift	Will tighten loose inner thigh skin; scars are usually hidden in the groin crease	Moderately large operation	1–2 weeks	$6,100
Outer thigh and buttock lift (buttock lift)	Will lift droopy outer thighs and buttocks; most often done along with tummy tuck	Recovery and scars are extensive	1–3 weeks	$7,000
Lower body lift (belt lipectomy)	Combines tummy tuck and outer thigh/buttock lift	Recovery and scars are extensive	2–3 weeks	$11,200
Total body lift	Combines tummy tuck, inner thigh lift, and outer thigh/buttock lift	Surgery, recovery, and scars are extensive	2–6 weeks	$15,000
Arm lift	Tightens loose hanging skin of upper arms	Permanent scar from armpit to elbow	5–10 days	$5,100
Liposuction	Will reduce localized areas of fat deposit; will not improve cellulite	Will not tighten loose hanging skin	5–10 days	Variable, see Chapter 10
Mesotherapy	Nonsurgical shrinkage of fat or cellulite	Improvement is subtle; multiple sessions required	0–3 days	$400 per treatment
Skin care	Improves skin color, tone, texture, and complexion	Final results not seen until after 6–12 months of regular use; will not affect dynamic wrinkles	Immediate	$30–$60 per month
Superficial peel	Improvement in skin color, tone, texture, and complexion within several weeks	Multiple peels and maintenance peels required; will not affect dynamic wrinkles, skin may flake	Immediate or a few days of flaking	$70–120 per peel
Medium peel	Dramatic improvement in skin color, tone, texture, and complexion within a week; improves fine wrinkles	5 days of obvious flaking afterward; several peels may be necessary; minimal effect on dynamic wrinkles	4–7 days	$2,500 for full face
Deep peel	Overwhelming and lasting effect on wrinkles	Unnaturally pale complexion and waxy skin are permanent	10–14 days	$4,000 for full face
Erbium laser	Improves dynamic wrinkles, fine wrinkles, and acne scars	Not as effective as carbon dioxide laser	4–7 days	$3,000 for full face

	Greatest Advantages	Greatest Disadvantages	Recovery[1]	Cost[2]
Carbon dioxide laser	Improves dynamic wrinkles, fine wrinkles, and acne scars; may be more effective than erbium	Lengthy recovery; waxy pale skin results if treatment is deep	10–14 days	$4,500 for full face
Dermabrasion	Improves acne scars and lip wrinkles	Risk of pale discoloration; need for multiple treatments	7–10 days	$4,000 for full face
Fraxel	Improves skin color, texture, vitality, discoloration, and wrinkles—without imposing pale or waxy skin	3–5 treatments are recommended	1 day	$1,500 per treatment
Wrinkle fillers	Provides temporary improvement of wrinkles	Requires multiple treatments	Immediate	$300–$1,500 each visit
Botox injection	Dramatic improvement in dynamic wrinkles	Must be repeated every 3–6 months	Immediate	$300 per area
Laser for spider veins	Most effective for treatment of small to medium spider veins	Causes temporary brown discoloration, usually three sessions are required	Immediate	$400 per treatment
Injection of spider veins (sclerotherapy)	Most effective for medium or large spider veins	Requires up to 6 sessions; may not clear all spider veins	Immediate	$300 per treatment
Cosmetic lip liner or eyeliner tattoo	Obviates the need for daily makeup in these areas	If not performed by a skilled professional, it may yield disastrous results	Immediate	$800
Laser removal of decorative tattoos	Results in gradual disappearance of tattoo without scars	Requires multiple treatments	Immediate	$400 per treatment
Laser hair removal	Arrests hair growth for 2–4 months; when hair returns, it is lighter and thinner	Is not permanent; requires quarterly treatments	Immediate	$500 per treatment
Lip lift	Higher, more youthful upper lip	Does not affect wrinkles	1–7 days	$1,200–$2,500
IPL: intense pulsed light	Improves brown or red skin discoloration at low cost	Minimal affect on other skin problems; 4–6 treatments are recommended	Immediate	$100–$500 per treatment
Endermologie	May improve cellulite and tighten skin	Benefits rely upon concurrent diet and exercise as well as regular treatments	Immediate	$65 per treatment

[1]"Recovery" is the time required before one can resume sedentary work and be comfortable in public either with makeup or with the treated part covered.

[2]"Cost" is the average cost across the United States in 2008 and includes surgeon's fee, operating room fee, anesthesia fee, and implant fee, where relevant. (Add 2 percent per year to arrive at the average cost after the year 2008.) The cost of each procedure in or around New York is about 50 percent higher than the rest of the country. If you are having more than one procedure, reduce the total by 10 percent. When multiple treatments are customary, the cost listed is per treatment.

Glossary

Abdominoplasty: *Same as* Tummy tuck.

Adrenaline: *Same as* Epinephrine.

Aesthetic surgery: *Same as* Cosmetic surgery.

AHA: *See* Alpha hydroxy acids.

AlloDerm: Freeze-dried collagen that is obtained from deceased human donors and prepared in sheet form for soft-tissue augmentation.

Alpha hydroxy acids (AHAs): Naturally occurring fruit acids that stimulate growth and turnover of skin cells, improve skin texture, reduce fine wrinkles, and restore skin vitality. The AHAs include glycolic acid, citric acid, malic acid, and lactic acid.

American Board of Plastic Surgery (ABPS): The only board recognized by the American Board of Medical Specialties for certifying plastic surgeons in the United States.

American Society of Plastic Surgeons (ASPS): The predominant organization in plastic surgery, which inducts only surgeons who are certified by the ABPS. 800-635-0635, plasticsurgery.org.

Anatomic breast implant: An obsolete term for breast implants that are teardrop shaped rather than round.

Anesthesia: *See* General anesthesia, Local anesthesia, or Sedation anesthesia.

Anesthesiologist: Medical doctor who specializes in making surgery safe and comfortable via medications.

Anesthesiologist's fee: Usually depends on the length of the procedure. (If your surgeon administers your sedation or if only local anesthesia is used, there should be no anesthesiologist's fee.)

Anesthetist: A nurse trained in the administration of anesthesia.

Areola: Pigmented area around the breast nipple.

Arm lift: Removal of loose skin of the upper arms.

Attached earlobe: Undesirable appearance of the earlobe following a facelift.

Augmentation mammoplasty: *Same as* Breast augmentation.

Autologen: Collagen from your own skin, harvested during a previous operation and processed into liquid form for injection.

Autologous fat graft: Fat obtained through liposuction for injection into another part of the body.

Belt lipectomy: Abdominoplasty combined with outer thigh and buttock lift.

Beta hydroxy acids (BHAs): Chemicals with slightly more potency than alpha hydroxy acids; an example is salicylic acid. Often used for superficial peels.

BHA: *See* Beta hydroxy acids.

Bleaching agents: Improve or prevent dark discoloration by suppressing the activity of pigment-producing cells.

Blepharoplasty: *Same as* Eyelid surgery.

Body contouring: Any procedure that reshapes the body, such as liposuction, a tummy tuck, or a thigh lift.

Botox: Medical-grade botulinum toxin. Weakens the muscles responsible for dynamic wrinkles, causing the wrinkles to temporarily improve or disappear.

Botulinum toxin: *Same as* Botox.

Bovine collagen: A protein matrix extracted from cow skin, then purified, sterilized, and processed into liquid form for injection into wrinkles.

Brachioplasty: *See* Arm lift.

Breast augmentation: The placement of implants into women with normal breasts that are smaller than desired. One of the three most common cosmetic procedures performed in the United States.

Breast droop: Defined by plastic surgeons based on the position of the nipple compared to the breast crease. Mild droop exists when the nipple is at the level of the crease, moderate droop exists when the nipple is below the crease, and advanced droop exists when the nipple is on the lowest part of the breast, pointing downward.

Breast lift: An operation to raise the nipple by tightening the skin envelope around it.

Breast ptosis (pronounced *toe-sis*): *See* Breast droop.

Brow lift: *Same as* Forehead lift.

Buttock lift: *Same as* Outer thigh and buttock lift.

Buttock/outer thigh lift: *Same as* Outer thigh and buttock lift.

Button chin: Unnaturally small or round chin, which may result if a chin implant is too small or narrow.

Cadaver bone: Human bone, harvested from donors shortly after death.

Calcium hydroxyapatite: Synthetic liquid soft-tissue filler, most commonly injected into the nasolabial folds. Similar to toothpaste in consistency.

Cannula: *Same as* Liposuction rod.

Canthopexy: Surgical procedure to tighten a loose lower eyelid.

Capsular contracture: Abnormally tight scar that may form around a breast implant. Mild contractures cause the breast to feel slightly firm and the implant edges to be felt through the skin. Moderate contractures cause the breast to feel firm and the implant to be both felt and visually perceived through the skin. Severe contractures cause the breast to feel hard, distorted, and painful.

Captique: *See* Hyaluronic acid.

Cauterization: Use of low-level electrical current on tiny blood vessels during surgery to stop them from bleeding.

Cellulite: A common but unattractive dimpling and puckering of the skin, due to a combination of superficial fat, fibrous tissue, and gravity.

Cheek augmentation: An operation to increase the cheeks' projection via placement of an implant.

Cheek lift: A limited version of the subperiosteal facelift. Effective in rejuvenating the cheek area. Also called mid-facelift.

Chin augmentation: An operation to increase the chin's projection, usually via placement of an implant. Also called mentoplasty.

Citric acid: An alpha hydroxy acid (AHA) derived from oranges and grapefruits.

Cohesive gel silicone breast implants: This type of silicone gel is cohesive in nature, such that it tends to bind together rather than spread out.

Collagen: The protein matrix of the skin. Sometimes called the meat of the skin. May be obtained from cow skin, cadaver skin, or your own skin—refined, sterilized, and processed for safe use.

Computer imaging: A technology that enables surgeons to take your photograph and manipulate it to show you how you might look following your proposed procedure.

Connective tissue diseases (CTDs): Autoimmune diseases—the body's own defense system identifies normal body tissue as foreign and attacks it. Joints become stiff, skin develops rashes, muscles ache, and the body tires easily. Examples of CTDs include rheumatoid arthritis, lupus, scleroderma, fibromyalgia, and chronic fatigue syndrome.

Cornea: Outer layer of the pupil.

Corneal abrasion: Inadvertent scratch to the cornea, which is temporarily painful. Treated by patching the eye closed for one to three days.

Corrugators: Muscles that together with the procerus muscles are responsible for vertical frown lines between the eyebrows.

Cosmetic plastic surgery: *Same as* Cosmetic surgery.

Cosmetic surgery: Surgery that focuses solely on improving appearance. A subspecialty of plastic surgery.

Cosmetic tattooing: Permanent tattooing that mimics eyeliner, eyebrow pencil, or lip liner.

Cosmoderm: Collagen obtained from cadavers.

Cosmoplast: Collagen obtained from cadavers.

Cost: *Same as* Fees.

Crepe-paper wrinkles: Fine wrinkles that occur on the cheeks, where sun exposure is high and the skin is relatively thin.

Crow's feet: Wrinkles that radiate from the corners of the eyes. Especially prominent while smiling or squinting.

Dark circles: Dark areas of the lower eyelids that give a tired appearance. May be caused by shadows or discolored skin.

Dark discoloration: Dark, blotchy, irregular patches of skin, typically on the face or neck. May develop following laser treatment, chemical peel, or pregnancy.

Deep chemical peel: Procedure whereby a chemical, usually phenol, is applied to the skin, causing a controlled injury. The most effective chemical peel in treating wrinkles, which are markedly improved and in many cases eliminated. Leaves the skin permanently pale and waxy.

Deep peel: *Same as* Deep chemical peel.

Deep vein thrombosis (DVT): Blood clot, usually within a thigh vein, which may form during or after surgery. Can travel through your bloodstream and lodge in your lungs. Can create catastrophic breathing problems and debilitating leg problems.

Deflation: Complication of saline implants in which the implant leaks and flattens. The body then absorbs the saline.

Dermabrasion: Removal of superficial skin by a process similar to sanding. Allows healthier skin to surface and results in smoother texture and tighter skin.

Dermalogen: Collagen from human cadaver skin that has been sterilized, purified, and processed into liquid form for injection.

Dermaplaning: An office procedure performed by a skin-care technician in which the top layer of dead skin cells is shaved. Typically included as part of a superficial peel.

Discoloration: *See* Dark discoloration, Light discoloration, or Melasma.

Dog ears: Areas of puckered skin. May occur when there is more skin on one side of an incision than on the other. Occurs most commonly when skin is removed as part of a procedure such as a tummy tuck.

Droopy upper eyelids: Eyelids that appear to hang at "half-mast." The lower edge of the upper eyelid blocks more than the very top of the iris. Also called eyelid ptosis.

Dry eye syndrome: Complication of eyelid surgery in which the eyes feel dry and gritty, and as though sand is in them. Eyes actually are watery, and vision may be blurred.

Dynamic wrinkles: The result of repetitive facial expressions. Smiling, laughing, frowning, or brooding causes the skin to be moved in the same way over and over again. Each time the skin moves, it creases, eventually forming wrinkles.

Early relapse: Premature return of sagging parts after surgery, well before expected. May occur after a facelift, a forehead lift, a breast lift, or a body lift.

Ectropion: *Same as* Lower eyelid retraction.

Endermologie: A nonsurgical procedure that theoretically stimulates the breakdown of fat and cellulite.

Endoscope: Long, thin metal rod with a fiber-optic camera at the tip.

Endoscopic surgery: Uses an endoscope, which is slipped under the skin. Has been applied to forehead lifts, breast augmentation, tummy tucks, and facelifts. Allows smaller incisions and hence smaller scars.

Epidermis: Outermost layer of skin.

Epinephrine: Hormone used with local anesthetic to constrict blood vessels and reduce bleeding. Also called adrenaline.

Excise: To surgically remove something, such as a mole or excess skin.

Excision: The act of excising.

Exfoliation: Removal of dead superficial skin cells. Facilitates penetration of stimulants such as alpha hydroxy acid and Retin-A.

External ultrasound-assisted liposuction (EUAL): Delivery of ultrasonic energy to skin overlying the fat before performing liposuction.

Extrusion: Erosion of skin or mucosa overlying an implant, which may then become exposed and will likely need to be removed. Extrusion may occur following placement of any implant.

Eyelid ptosis (pronounced *toe-sis*): *Same as* Droopy upper eyelids.

Eyelid surgery: May involve the removal of excess upper eyelid skin, upper eyelid fat, lower eyelid skin, and lower eyelid fat.

Facelift: Operation to remove excess face and neck skin, while lifting and tightening the remaining skin and tissues.

Facialplasty: *Same as* Facelift.

Facility fee: Cost charged by the surgery center, hospital, or doctor's office where surgery is to be performed.

Fascia: Dense, white connective tissue that envelops your muscles. In some areas of the body, fascia is unnecessary and can be harvested for cosmetic use. In other areas, such as the abdomen, fascia is an important structural element that helps determine body shape.

Fat embolus: Fat globules that migrate into the bloodstream and clump into a larger mass of fat. Can interfere with the exchange of oxygen and carbon dioxide if it travels into the lungs. Severe and potentially fatal respiratory problems may result.

Fees: Cosmetic surgery involves fees for the surgeon, anesthesiologist, facility or hospital, and implant. Not all fees apply in every case.

Forehead lift: An operation to raise brow position, reduce lateral hoods, and soften horizontal forehead wrinkles and scowl lines.

Foreheadplasty: *Same as* Forehead lift.

Fraxel: A type of laser that treats the skin in pixels.

Frontalis muscle: The forehead muscle that raises the eyebrows and causes horizontal forehead wrinkles.

Frown lines: *See* Dynamic wrinkles.

General anesthesia: Induces a deep sleep and temporarily paralyzes the body. Spontaneous breathing stops, so the anesthesiologist places a tube (connected to a respirator) into the windpipe.

Genioplasty: Augmenting the chin by surgically breaking a portion of the chinbone, moving it forward, and securing it with screws or wires.

Glycolic acid: The alpha hydroxy acid (AHA) most commonly used in cosmetic surgery. Derived from sugar cane.

Gore-Tex: A cross between cloth and rubber that is used for implants. Technical name is expanded polytetrafluoroethylene (ePTFE).

Graft: Living tissue such as fat, cartilage, skin, or bone that is moved from one part of the body to another. Must receive nourishment from the surrounding tissues.

Gummy bear breast implants: *See* Cohesive gel silicone breast implants.

Hematoma: Accumulation of blood within the surgical site after the skin incision has been closed. May require immediate surgery.

Hospital fee: What the hospital will charge if you stay overnight following your procedure.

Hyaluronic acid: A synthetic filler used for wrinkles.

Hydroquinone: A bleaching agent.

Hydroxyapatite: A porous ceramic material used for chin and cheek implants. Resembles sea coral.

Hylaform: *See* Hyaluronic acid.

Hyperpigmentation: *See* Dark discoloration.

Hypertrophic nipples: Enlarged and floppy nipples. Note that this is irrespective of areola and breast size or droopiness.

Hypopigmentation: *See* Light discoloration.

Implant deflation: *Same as* Deflation.

Implant extrusion: *Same as* Extrusion.

Implant fee: The cost of medical materials such as breast implants, facial implants, and collagen.

Inframammary crease: The skin crease beneath the breast.

Inner girdle: Fascia of the abdomen.

Inner thigh lift: Removes excess skin from the inner thighs, tightening and lifting the remaining skin.

Intense pulsed light (IPL): A nonsurgical, nonlaser light treatment of the face that is directed at improving discolorations.

IPL: *See* Intense pulsed light.

Iris: The colored ring around the pupil of the eye.

Isolagen: Collagen from your own skin, cloned in a laboratory and processed into liquid form for injection.

Lactic acid: An alpha hydroxy acid (AHA) derived from milk.

Lasabrasion: *Same as* Laser resurfacing.

Laser: A tool that emits an intense, focused beam of light. Used to treat wrinkles, scars, birthmarks, spider veins, skin discolorations, age spots, and tattoos.

Laser desurfacing: *Same as* Laser resurfacing.

Laser peeling: *Same as* Laser resurfacing.

Laser resurfacing: Treatment of skin with carbon dioxide laser or erbium laser, which vaporizes the top layers of skin. Deeper, healthier cells replace the outer damaged cells and allow reorganization, resulting in reduced wrinkles and improved skin tone.

Laser vaporization: *Same as* Laser resurfacing.

Lateral hoods: Folds of skin between the eyebrow and the eyelid near the outside corner of the eye. Named for the hooded look they give the eyes.

Lateral thigh and buttock lift: *Same as* Outer thigh and buttock lift.

Lidocaine: A local anesthetic, similar to Novocaine.

Light chemical peel: *Same as* Superficial chemical peel.

Light discoloration: Blotchy, irregular patches of skin that are lighter than nearby skin. May develop within several weeks of laser treatment or dermabrasion.

Lipoplasty: *Same as* Liposuction.

Liposculpture: *Same as* Liposuction.

Liposuction: Removal of fat deposits by way of suctioning.

Liposuction cannula: *Same as* Liposuction rod.

Liposuction garment: Similar to a girdle. Essential for good results following liposuction. Provides firm pressure and support to suctioned areas. Facilitates skin retraction and optimizes final body contour.

Liposuction rod: Long, thin metal rod used to suction fat during liposuction.

Liquid silicone: A substance that was injected into breasts and lips for augmentation. No longer used because it caused the surrounding tissue to become distorted, hard, and unnatural.

Local anesthesia: Injection of local anesthetic agents only. No sedation, paralysis, or deep sleep. (When doctors refer to performing a procedure "under local," this is what they mean.)

Local anesthetic: Medication such as lidocaine that is injected into an area of the body to cause temporary numbness there. Similar to Novocaine. Some wear off within a few hours, others last for half a day. Used in both local anesthesia and sedation anesthesia.

Love handles: Fat deposits above the hip bones. Also called hips, flanks, and iliac crests by plastic surgeons.

Lower body lift: *Same as* Belt lipectomy.

Lower eyelid retraction: A complication of eyelid surgery. The lower lid is pulled downward, due either to a loose lower eyelid or removal of too much skin.

Malar implants: Cheek implants.

Malic acid: An alpha hydroxy acid (AHA) derived from apples.

Mammogram: Breast x-ray.

Mammography: *See* Mammogram.

Marionette lines: Vertical creases from the corners of the mouth to the jowls.

Mastectomy: Surgical removal of a breast, usually for cancer.

Mastopexy: *Same as* Breast lift.

Matting: The sudden appearance of new spider veins. May occur anywhere on an extremity recently treated with sclerotherapy or laser for spider veins.

Medial thigh lift: *Same as* Inner thigh lift.

Medium chemical peel: A controlled injury to the skin from applying a chemical, usually TCA, to treat wrinkles and discoloration. More effective than superficial peels, but less effective than deep peels.

Medium peel: *Same as* Medium chemical peel.

Melasma: A type of hyperpigmentation with a "dirty" appearance and irregular borders. An area of dark, blotchy skin that may develop on the face or neck during pregnancy or while using oral contraceptives.

Membranes: *Same as* Mucosa.

Mentoplasty: *Same as* Chin augmentation.

Mesotherapy: A treatment whereby deep fat or cellulite (superficial fat) is injected with a solution aimed at fat breakdown.

Microdermabrasion: Procedure whereby a machine is used to lightly "sand" the skin of the face. Involves no downtime.

Micropigmentation: *Same as* Cosmetic tattooing.

Mid-facelift: *Same as* Cheek lift.

Milia: Skin eruptions that appear as tiny whiteheads. May occur along suture lines following eyelid surgery or throughout areas treated with deep chemical peels or laser. May either improve on their own or require further treatment.

mL: Abbreviation for *milliliter*, which is a metric measure for fluid volume. One mL is equal to one cc. One pint is roughly equal to 500 mL. One ounce is equal to 30 mL.

Mucosa: The lining on the inside of the nose or mouth. (Some doctors refer to mucosa as "the membranes.")

Nasal dorsum: The roof or backbone of the nose. Also called the dorsum of the nose.

Nasal septum: *Same as* Septum.

Nasolabial fold: The skin fold extending from the side of each nostril around the corner of the mouth, down toward the chin. Present with aging and formed by sagging cheeks. Usually improved by a facelift.

Nipple reduction: Operation directed at improving hypertrophic nipples.

Nose job: *Same as* Rhinoplasty.

Operating room fee: *Same as* Facility fee.

Outer thigh and buttock lift: Removes excess skin in the buttock and outer thigh region, resulting in tightening and lifting of the remaining skin.

Outpatient surgery: Allows the patient to return home the same day. Also known as day surgery or ambulatory surgery.

Panniculectomy: An operation to remove skin and fat from the lower abdomen, without tightening the fascia. Typically performed on previously obese people with back pain or hygiene problems related to extremely droopy abdominal skin.

Parrot beak: A nasal deformity in which fullness above the tip of the nose causes the tip to lose its distinction from the dorsum of the nose. Also known as polly beak.

Pectoralis muscle: The muscle between the ribs and the breast.

Phenol peel: *See* Deep chemical peel.

Photoaging: Accelerated skin aging that results from the cumulative effects of unprotected exposure to ultraviolet radiation from the sun and tanning beds.

Pixie ear: *Same as* Attached earlobe.

Plastic surgery: A broad surgical specialty that includes both reconstructive surgery and cosmetic surgery.

Platysma: A broad, thin neck muscle that may become prominent with aging.

Platysmal bands: Cords of the platysma muscle that form with aging, extending from the jaw to the collarbone. May create a "turkey-gobbler" appearance if severe.

Platysmaplasty: An operation to tighten the two platysma muscles by sewing them together in front of the neck, creating one continuous muscle instead of a pair of prominent bands.

Polyethylene: A plastic material used for facial implants. Resembles sea coral.

Poly-L-lactic acid: A synthetic filler similar to absorbable suture material.

Preoperative testing: The required x-rays, EKG, and blood tests a few days prior to surgery. May be performed at a hospital or surgery facility.

Price: *See* Fees.

Procerus muscles: Muscles that together with the corrugators make the vertical frown lines between the eyebrows.

Proplast: A plastic implant material similar to chewing gum. Formerly popular for facial augmentation. Withdrawn from the market after causing many complications.

Prosthetic material: Any material implanted into the body that is not derived from the body. May be synthetically made, such as plastic polymer, or naturally occuring, such as cadaver bone.

Ptosis: The medical term for *droop*. Pronounced *toe-sis*. (Brow ptosis refers to droopy eyebrows, and breast ptosis refers to droopy breasts.)

Pug nose: An upturned nose that is unattractive and unnatural.

Radiesse: A synthetic filler made of calcium hydroxyapatite.

Radio-frequency facelift: Nonsurgical facelift using radio-frequency energy to stimulate skin tightening.

Reconstructive surgery: The treatment of patients due to accidents, cancer, burns, birth defects, or other problems.

Rectus muscles: Abdominal muscles, also called abs.

Restylane: *See* Hyaluronic acid.

Retin-A: A prescription topical cream that stimulates circulation to the skin, facilitates skin cell growth and turnover, thickens the deep layers of skin, and leads to a brighter, healthier complexion with smoother texture. Also called retinoic acid or tretinoin. Derived from vitamin A.

Revision surgery: Repeat surgery on the same part of the body, either to further improve the result or to correct a deformity.

Rhinoplasty: Cosmetic nasal surgery. The word derives from the Greek terms *rhino* meaning "nose" and *plasty* meaning "to shape or reform."

Rhytidectomy: *Same as* Facelift.

Rippling: A visible phenomenon that may follow breast augmentation. Small waves of liquid within the implant are transmitted to the skin of the breast, causing it to wrinkle or ripple.

Rosacea: A skin disorder in which the cheeks, nose, and chin become easily flushed in response to spicy foods, alcohol, or stress. Acne and spider veins may also develop.

Saddlebags: The fat deposits of the outer thighs. Also called trochanters.

Saline: Water with dissolved salt in the same concentration as it exists in the human body.

Saline breast implants: Breast implants filled with saline. The shell is made of a durable, pliable plastic material called solid silicone.

Sclera: The white part of the eyeball.

Scleral show: Unnatural-looking result of lower eyelid retraction, which exposes the sclera below the pupil. May cause dry eye syndrome.

Sclerotherapy: Injecting a liquid chemical through a tiny needle directly into spider veins, causing them to contract and collapse.

Scowl lines: Furrows and vertical wrinkles between the eyebrows that give an angry appearance.

Sculptra: A synthetic filler made of poly-L-lactic acid.

Sedation anesthesia: Uses intravenous medication to induce drowsiness and relaxation. Also called twilight anesthesia or monitored anesthesia care (MAC).

Septoplasty: Surgical modification of the septum of the nose with the goal to straighten it and improve breathing.

Septum: The wall inside the nose that separates the right and left nasal passages.

Seroma: A collection of clear fluid that weeps into the surgical site, under the skin, following surgery. A surgeon can remove most seromas with a needle in the office.

Silastic: A solid plastic that may be white or clear, and pliable or stiff. May be used for facial augmentation.

Silicone gel: Liquid silicone that is used in silicone gel breast implants.

Silicone gel breast implants: Breast implants filled with liquid silicone gel.

Sinusitis: Sinus infection. Usually due to internal nasal swelling if it occurs following rhinoplasty. Symptoms include foul nasal drainage, facial pain, headaches, and fevers. (If you have any of these symptoms, contact your plastic surgeon immediately.)

Skin care: A home-based program designed to decrease roughness, brighten complexion, minimize pore size, reduce blotches, and provide a healthier overall appearance.

Skin death: A complication of surgery that may occur where the skin is under tension or its blood supply is poor. May follow infection or hematoma. Most common in smokers.

Skin-fold wrinkles: Wrinkles that develop around the nose and mouth as the cheeks sag with age. May be treated by facelift.

SMAS: Stands for *subcutaneous musculoaponeurotic substance* or *superficial musculoaponeurotic system*. The layer of fibrous tissue under the facial skin, lifted and tightened during some types of facelift.

Smile lines: *See* Dynamic wrinkles.

SPF: *See* Sun protection factor.

Spider veins: Tiny blood vessels that form within the skin, typically on the legs and face.

Steroids: Hormones given to patients orally or intravenously to reduce swelling and give a psychological lift following surgery.

Stretch mark: A tear in the deep layer of skin, resulting in a thinned, streaky appearance.

Subglandular: Describes where a breast implant can be placed—under the breast, which is a type of gland.

Submental fat: Fat under the chin.

Submuscular: Describes where a breast implant can be placed—under the pectoralis muscle.

Subpectoral: *See* Submuscular.

Subperiosteal facelift: The deepest possible facelift, in which all tissues are separated from the underlying bone and moved higher.

Suction lipectomy: *Same as* Liposuction.

Sun protection factor (SPF): The degree of a sun block's strength; the higher a product's number, the better it protects skin from harmful ultraviolet light.

Superficial chemical peel: A very controlled, mild injury to the skin from applying a chemical such as salicylic acid or glycolic acid to improve skin texture, vitality, pore size, and fine wrinkles.

Superficial peel: *Same as* Superficial chemical peel.

Surgeon's fee: The amount you pay your surgeon to perform a procedure. (The average surgeon's fee listed in each chapter derives from a poll of plastic surgeons across the country. Cosmetic fees are similar throughout most of the country with the exception of the New York area, where they consistently are about 50 percent higher.)

Symmastia: The merging of the breasts into an indistinct mass. Occurs when the skin between them loses its attachment to the breastbone during surgery.

TCA (trichloroacetic acid): The chemical most commonly used for medium peels.

Telangiectasias: *Same as* Spider veins.

Telltale sign: A physical clue to the fact that someone had cosmetic surgery. Looks unnatural; can only be due to previous cosmetic surgery.

Thermage: *See* Radio-frequency facelift.

Thigh lift: *See* Inner thigh lift or Outer thigh and buttock lift.

Total body lift: Includes a tummy tuck, an inner thigh lift, and an outer thigh and buttock lift.

Traditional liposuction: The original method of liposuction. Suctions out fat deposits through a thin tube after stiffening the fat layer via tumescent fluid.

Transaxillary breast augmentation: Placement of breast implants through an incision in the underarm.

Transconjunctival incision: An incision on the inside of the lower eyelid; sometimes used to remove fat from the eyelids when skin removal is not necessary.

Transumbilical breast augmentation: Placement of breast implants through an incision in the belly button.

Tumescent fluid: A mixture of saline, lidocaine, and adrenaline that is infused into fat prior to liposuction, making the fat stiff and therefore easier to suction.

Tummy tuck: Surgery that removes excess abdominal skin and fat and tightens underlying fascia.

Twilight anesthesia: *Same as* Sedation anesthesia.

Ultrasonic liposuction: Combines the application of high-frequency sound waves with gentle suctioning.

Upper arm lift: *See* Arm lift.

Varicose veins: Large distended veins beneath the skin. May appear as bluish bumps on the skin.

Witch's chin: Droopy chin skin after chin surgery has disrupted the attachments between thin skin and bone.

Wrinkle filler: A substance, such as collagen or synthetic filler, that is injected into the skin under each wrinkle. Pushes the depressed wrinkles outward and makes them less visible.

Wrinkle laser: *See* Laser resurfacing

Wrinkles: Linear depressions in the skin. Classified according to their cause as either crepe-paper, dynamic, or skin-fold wrinkles.

Zyderm: Collagen obtained from cow skin.

Zyplast: Collagen obtained from cow skin.

Bibliography

American Society of Plastic and Reconstructive Surgeons. *Plastic Surgery Procedural Statistics.* Arlington Heights, IL, 1999.

Nash, Joyce D. *What Your Doctor Can't Tell You About Cosmetic Surgery.* Oakland, CA: New Harbinger Publications, 1995.

U.S. House Committee on Small Business. Subcommittee on Regulation, Business Opportunities, and Energy. *Unqualified Doctors Performing Cosmetic Surgery: Policies and Enforcement Activities of the Federal Trade Commission—Part I.* 101st Congress, first session, 4 April 1989.

U.S. House Committee on Small Business. Subcommittee on Regulation, Business Opportunities, and Energy. *Unqualified Doctors Performing Cosmetic Surgery: Policies and Enforcement Activities of the Federal Trade Commission—Part II.* 101st Congress, second session, 31 May 1989.

U.S. House Committee on Small Business. Subcommittee on Regulation, Business Opportunities, and Energy. *Cosmetic Surgery Procedures: Standards, Quality, and Certification of Nonhospital Operating Rooms—Part III.* 101st Congress, third session, 28 June 1989.

Index